Hike Your Own Hike

Hike Your Own Hike

A Pacific Crest Trail Adventure

Amy Pike

Hike Your Own Hike

Copyright © 2025 by Amy Pike

All Rights Reserved. No part of this publication may be reproduced, stored in a retrieval system, or transmitted in any form or by any means—electronic, mechanical, photocopy, recording, or any other—except for brief quotations in printed reviews, without the prior permission of the author.

This is a true story of the author's lived experience. She has recreated events, locales, and people to the best of her abilities from her memories of them. Some names and identifying details may have been changed to protect privacy. The views expressed in this story are solely those of the author.

First paperback edition September 2025

Published by Amy Pike

ISBN: 979-8-218-77595-7 (paperback)

Library of Congress Control Number: 2025918397

Book design by Cameron Crites
Front cover image by Amy Pike

For Madison and Hailey

PROLOGUE

From the moment I first started talking about wanting to thru-hike the Pacific Crest Trail, "You're crazy!" is all I kept hearing. And for good reason. I get it. It's 2,654 miles long for one thing—stretching from Mexico up the entire length of the US all the way to Canada. Not to mention that choosing to step away from the world of modern conveniences in order to roam through the wilderness in a state of perpetual homelessness for four to five months is a bit, well, extreme.

The real kicker for me, though, was what they *always* asked next. "So, who are you doing it with?" At which point, upon discovering that I planned to go solo, they would *gasp*, horrified, stare at me disapprovingly, and try talking me out of it. Their main argument being, "That's far too dangerous for a woman to be off doing alone." Aside from me then reassuring them (over my shoulder while walking away) that I knew what I was doing, the conversation, in most cases, was over.

Not that I did—know what I was doing, that is. Truth be told, I hadn't even ever been backpacking. I had been going through a divorce, though, after almost 19 years of marriage, and in a sea of unknowns during that time, as far-fetched as it was, I had clung to the dream of one day doing the PCT like a lifeboat. Whether I had it in me to actually do the whole thing, I hadn't a clue. All I knew for certain was that I at least had to try.

For the next five years then, following my divorce, I did everything in my power to make it happen. From saving up enough money to cover my bills during the months I'd be gone, to working out and gradually increasing the lengths of my training hikes. I spent countless hours researching ultralight gear as well as how and where to resupply. I took classes on how to navigate, avalanche awareness, and wilderness first aid. All the while, piece by piece, acquiring the gear and supplies I would need.

Until the day finally arrived for all my planning to be put to the test, and I set out, alone, in an attempt to thru-hike the Pacific Crest Trail. The following is how that journey unfolded.

"As you embark upon this exciting next chapter in your book of life, may the wind be at your back and the weight of the world be lifted from your shoulders.

Be well, be safe, be free."

–your proud dad
(Written in a "Good luck" card given to me a week prior to starting the trail)

PART ONE

Going Solo

"Belonging so fully to yourself
that you're willing to stand alone is a
wilderness—an untamed, unpredictable place
as dangerous as it is breathtaking,
a place as sought after as it is feared.
The wilderness can often feel unholy
because we can't control it, or what people think
about our choice of whether to venture
into that vastness or not.
But it turns out to be the place of true belonging,
and it's the bravest and most sacred place
you will ever stand."

–Brené Brown

Day 1: April 26, 2021

LIFE IS FULL OF ORDINARY DAYS, where uneventfulness is the norm, and the steady rhythm of repetition breeds comfort. This was not one of those days. This day found me scrunched up in the back seat of a VW Bug. My barely broken in pack was perched upright in the seat next to me, stuffed full of all the various items I would need to survive over the next several months, plus a bottle of lemon-lime Gatorade and one week's worth of food. With my youngest daughter, Hailey, in the front seat driving, and my oldest, Madie (short for Madison), sitting next to her navigating, the sky's predawn hues began to emerge from the darkness as we made our way from the divey motel where we'd shared a room the night before, to the US-Mexico border where the two of them would soon be dropping me off.

I sat motionless, studying their faces, listening intently to the sound of their voices, trying to soak up as much as I could, as if by some kind of magic I could store up this feeling of being with them so I could later tap into it.

My train of thought, suddenly interrupted by various bits of motherly advice any decent mom would be sharing at this point, I felt a desperate urge to start spewing towards the front seat, "Don't forget to keep a snack and some spare cash in the glove box in case of an emergency, and be extra aware of your surroundings when you're out by yourself, and for god's sake, if you sell something to some random stranger on Facebook Marketplace DO NOT tell them where you live—meet them in a public place with lots of people around." It was no use, though. The words, all of them, stuck in my throat as one particularly horrifying thought came to mind: *What I'm about to do is THE most selfish thing I've ever done in my life. What kind of mom walks away from her kids for five months?*

Granted, at 23 and 20-years-old now, I'd long since finished my job of raising them. I'd never gone more than a week in her life without seeing Hailey before, though, and two weeks tops without seeing Madie. The thought of now spending several months apart from them was too extreme to fathom. A nauseating mix of nervousness, excitement, and panic churned my stomach. *I'm gonna be sick.* I looked out the window as the road beneath us whizzed by and took a few slow deep breaths in an effort to calm myself down.

Twenty minutes later, now deep in the desert, we arrived at a seemingly uninhabited dot on the map known as Campo, California. Although hidden by clouds, the sun had finally risen as we parked as close as we could to the monument marking the southern terminus of the Pacific Crest Trail (aka the PCT)—a set of stone pillars which, up until now, I'd seen only in photographs. After wrestling my pack out of the back seat of the car, the three of us walked over to the monument and took a few pictures. Between the intimidating nature of the freshly constructed border wall, the sketchy looking guy I'd seen ducking into the bushes a quarter of a mile or so back, and the fact that my girls now had a grueling 16-hour drive back home to Idaho, I said a hurried good-bye and ordered them back to the car.

As they drove away I stood there, as still and as silent as the pillars beside me, watching as they made their way back up the same dirt road we'd all just driven down together. A puffy little cloud of dust trailed behind them, shrinking ever smaller as the minutes passed. Warm, wet tears streamed down my face as a sobering awareness of how alone I now was—and would be for the next several months—sunk heavy in the pit of my stomach like a rock in a pool of water. *I know I said I wanted to do this, but it feels wrong that I'm not in that car with them.* I buckled the waist belt on my pack and cinched the straps as snugly as I could, as if the sensation of being held might help lessen the uneasiness I was feeling.

With their car now nearly out of sight, I wiped my eyes with the backs of my hands and took my first real look around. In front of me, off in the distance, lay a beautifully sculpted mountain range. Behind me, stretching out as far as I could see, both to my left and to my right, stood the border wall—as unnatural and obnoxious looking as it was uninviting. Ready now to get started, I scanned the open patch of dry desert dirt and shrubbery I was standing in for some sort of clue as to which way to go. *Hmm, no trail signs. That's weird.* All I could make out were several fairly worn foot paths, each one leading a different direction. *Well shit. If I can't even tell where to take my first steps, how the hell am I gonna make it to Canada?!*

Just then a piece of advice I'd read from someone who'd previously done the trail came to mind, something along the lines of, "When in doubt, head up and north." I pulled my phone out of the side pocket of my hiking pants, opened the compass app, pointed it north, and started walking.

Within a few minutes I came upon my first official PCT trail sign. Certain now that I was on the right path, my mind drifted back to my girls. *What a shitty good-bye. I should have hugged them longer. Said something meaningful. I'm a horrible mom!* I got about a quarter of a mile before I could no longer resist the urge to call them. Grateful they answered and that I was still within range for cell service, I apologized for rushing them off, thanked them both for believing in me and for sharing the start of this journey with me, and reminded them to look after each other. Then one more set of, "I love yous" and "Goodbyes."

Feeling a bit better as I ventured on from that point, a happy sort of disbelief began to set in. *I'm really doing this. After so many years of dreaming and planning. After landing a permit last year and then not being able to use it because stupid Covid shut everything down. Here I am, and this is finally happening!*

Reaching a bright green sign with a PCT logo and a big "Mile 1" written on it, I again dug my phone out, arranged myself accordingly, flashed my signature selfie smile, and took a few pictures. And then I kept taking pictures, as every few minutes I seemed to happen upon some other new-to-me flower or variety of cacti. Struck by how different the landscape was compared to back home in Idaho, everything, from the Manzanita bushes and terracotta colored dirt to the rolling hills covered in dark green shrubbery, seemed equally deserving of a spot on my camera roll.

After the first several miles the sky grew dark and it started to rain. I took out my brand new, ultralight (at least according to the price tag) rain jacket as well as the waterproof cover designed to fit around the outside of my pack, and slipped them both on. Unlike the wide open, fairly flat stretch of land I'd been walking through so far, the trail now began to veer off into a more mountainous section. It was thick with trees, providing somewhat of a canopy from the storm, and a heavy mist settled in around me as I continued upward into my first set of hills.

Throughout the rest of the day I came across no more than a handful of other hikers. One while rushing past me in an attempt to catch up with a girl he'd just met, and by the size of the smile on his face, fancied. Along with two women stopped for a lunch break. And a couple, around the same age as my girls, who I found myself in the same place at the same time with, as all three of us lost the trail for a minute. My normally friendly self, though, so deeply immersed in a stubborn sort of *I'm doing this thing solo for a reason* frame of mind, wanted nothing to do with any of them. Not that I was rude, I just kept my distance—content enough to be alone with my thoughts.

This seemed fitting, given the fact that being alone with my thoughts is what had gotten me hooked on hiking in the first place—several years back now, when, attempting to push myself out of my comfort zone, I started going for walks off in the mountains near where I lived. As these outings grew longer and the trails I chose became more remote, I began to notice that the more time I spent alone in nature, the more therapeutic it was, especially in regards to helping me process things. And not just everyday things like workplace drama and parenting fails, but heavier, more complicated thought knots[1] as well, which, as anyone who's ever attempted untangling one of these can attest to, is no easy feat. Assuming you're willing, not only to admit to some pretty major flaws in your thinking, but to examine them, you also need a sizable enough chunk of time to unpack them. Not to mention the amount of courage required to then stay present with whatever it is you do end up unraveling long enough to sort through some of the "hows" and "whys" and "what nows" surrounding them.

Having found in nature a space I felt safe enough to be able to do this in, where my mind was free to wander as well as focus in ways and on things it normally couldn't, the more I tapped into it, the more progress I made. The only problem was, because I could only ever get so far before it was time to head home again, I was never able to do much more than scratch the surface of any of my older, more menacing thought knots. Although frustrating at the time, this only fueled my desire to do the PCT as, if there was ever going to be an opportunity for me to walk far enough for long enough to finally have a shot at tackling them, that would be it.

My plan for the day had been to walk an even 20 miles, which would get me to Lake Morena, and then camp there for the night. Uncertain, though, as to how far I'd come as I was reaching that point, I mistakenly passed it—going so far, in fact, that by the time I figured out what I'd done it made more sense to push on than double back. Not that I didn't

---

[1] Mental clusterfucks of trauma-triggered rationalizations, worst-case-scenario assumptions, and ultra negative, non-reality based beliefs; usually developed over the course of many years; often leading to unhealthy, irrational decision making; potentially havoc wreaking.

have a general, big picture sense of where I was, but being brand new to Guthooks,[2] and not yet having figured out how to get the little white dot that pops up on the screen showing you your own real time location to work, other than a few of the more distinguishable landmarks earlier in the day, I couldn't tell precisely where I was on the map.

Trudging on with my eyes peeled for a big enough flat spot to set up my tent, it was another couple of miles before I finally found one. The rain, which had been relentless for the better part of the day, let up just as I did. Exhausted, and with my clothes so soaked they were sticking to me, I pitched my tent in what felt like slow motion. Then I climbed inside, blew up my air mattress, laid out my sleeping bag, and peeled off my wet clothes. I draped my raincoat and ballcap on top of my pack and hung up my bra (which was more damp from sweat than rain by the smell of it) by one of its hooks on the mesh lining of my tent. I then spread my hiking pants, tank top, and underwear out next to my sleeping bag, and set my socks on top of my shoes where I'd left them just outside the tent under the rain flap. Patting myself dry, as best I could with my "washcloth" bandana,[3] I put on a fresh pair of underwear and the only other set of clothes I had with me—a black capri length pair of yoga pants, a light grey, ribbed, cotton undershirt, and a thin, green and white, long-sleeve flannel. Staring, half-disbelievingly for several seconds at how pruney my feet looked from being stuck in wet shoes all day, I slid on the pair of flip flops I'd thankfully thrown into my pack on a last minute whim, and climbed out of the tent.

I found a rock large enough to sit on, screwed my tiny portable fuel canister onto my stove, and boiled some water while I watched the sun set. Then I made a packet of ramen noodles and let it cool down for a few minutes before eating it. Aside from an occasional bird calling out as it flew past overhead, the silence was so intense it felt unsettling, like

---

[2] A navigational app detailing routes, campsites, water sources, etc., all of which users have the capacity to leave comments for each other about; has since been renamed FarOut.

[3] As a long time fan of a good cotton bandana, I had a few of them with me. One to use as a hair tie, one as a washcloth, and one as a pee rag; each a different color so as to avoid any mix ups.

something was missing. After I'd eaten, I rinsed out my pot, brushed my teeth, and found an out of the way spot to pee before climbing back into my tent for the night. As I zipped my tent flap closed I paused to admire the moon peeking out from behind the clouds, then plugged my phone into my little portable solar charger, and crawled into my sleeping bag.

My eyes, being the only part left of me willing to move at this point, traced the stitching along the inside ceiling of my tent as I lay on my back trying to decide which part of my body was the most sore. The bottoms of my feet? My shoulders from carrying a fully loaded pack so far for the first time? My calves? My quads? The front of my hips from where my waist straps had already rubbed me raw? Unable to decide, I dug a couple of ibuprofen out of the little Ziploc baggie style first aid kit I'd put together, hoping to at least take the edge off. As I lay back down, unable to sleep, with my body now still, my mind kicked into overdrive.

Within minutes—my little experiment from the car failing miserably—I was missing my girls so bad I felt achy. They'd been checking in with me periodically throughout the day. Last I'd heard, though, they'd just hit a stormy patch and it was already getting dark and they still had several hours to go. The longer I laid there not sleeping the further I fell down a rabbit hole of worry. *What the hell am I doing out here? If my girls don't make it home safe I will never forgive myself. What made me think I could do this goddamn stupid thing anyway?!*

Through a blur of tears, I scrolled through picture after picture of the two of them on my phone, until the weight of how powerless and alone I was feeling grew so heavy it was hard to breathe. Having reached the limit of my ability to cope with this on my own, I knew the best thing to do would be to reach out for help. This also just so happened to be one of the hardest things for me to do, as I'd long ago adopted a thought knot based on needing help being a sign of weakness and weakness being a luxury I, as a single mom, couldn't afford. *You also can't afford to be losing your shit out here right now, either.* Swallowing my pride, I found the one person in my list of contacts whose enthusiasm for the PCT rivaled mine—my friend, Don—and dialed his number. Having met through a running club I'd joined in an attempt to reintegrate myself back into the social scene after my divorce, his track record for always being there for me when I needed a friend was impressively spotless. As soon as he answered I launched into a full blown account of the downward turn I'd just taken. After listening patiently, he did his best to reassure me that my girls were fine, that, "No news is good news." Then he asked me a bit about what my first day had been like, and how the trip getting down here had been. Then we both were quiet for a minute, and when he spoke again his tone had shifted from lighthearted to serious.

"You're stronger and more capable than you realize, Amy," he said. "And I'm certain that if you want this—and if you don't that's okay, too. There is no shame in having tried and coming home. But if you do…if you really do want this, you're one of the few people who have it in you to make it happen." Flattered, although a bit taken aback by his level of confidence in me, his words did the trick—deflating my anxiety like a pin jabbing into a balloon. Not that I had nearly as much faith in myself at the moment, but my head was now back in the game.

It was well past midnight by the time a message from the girls came through saying they'd made it home safe, at which point the sweet relief of finally knowing they were okay gave way to sleep. It was anything but restful, though. I kept waking up every 30-40 minutes, either to some noise outside my tent or a cramp in one of my legs, and even with my air mattress it was hard to get comfortable again each time I tried to fall back asleep. At the first sign of daylight I gave up trying.

With my head pounding and my eyelids puffy from all my crying the night before, I undressed and used a couple of wet wipes to clean myself. Then I slipped on my only other, still clean, pair of socks, a fresh pair of underwear, and the rest of my now mostly dry, although already not smelling great, hiking clothes. Peeking my head out as I unzipped my tent flap, I could tell it had rained again during the night, and by the looks of it, I had another stormy day ahead.

Realizing my shoes were still damp as soon as I put them on, my socks were soaked through by the time I finished tying my laces. Grimacing as I went to stand up, my disgust at how gross my feet felt quickly turned to shock at how stiff my legs were—suddenly hyper aware of each and every muscle (a few I had no idea even existed) required to get myself up off the ground. I returned to the same rock where I'd eaten my dinner and boiled enough water for a cup of instant coffee and a packet of oatmeal. As I ate, I ran my fingers through my hair, or at least tried to, in an attempt to untangle it. Immediately regretting my decision not to carry the extra weight of a hairbrush, I gave up, sweeping it, tangles and all, into one big messy side braid, then topped it off with my ball cap. Then I slipped my rain jacket on, shook the moisture from my tent, packed up, and started walking.

It drizzled off and on all morning, making my lunch break all that much sweeter, as not only did the water source I chose to stop at (a small campground with a couple of spigots) have a picnic table to sit down at, but the sun broke out from behind the clouds just as I got there. Between the warmth of its rays and a light breeze, I figured I might as well try drying my tent out while I could. I hung it, along with my ground cover, over some tree branches. Then I filtered enough water to refill my water bottles and, boiling a bit of it, ate another packet of ramen.

Once everything was dry I shoved it all back in my pack and continued on. Again keeping to myself on the rare occasion I came across anyone, I logged another 20 miles by the end of the day. I pitched my tent and blew up my air mattress, stretched a little as my shoulders and legs were now in a nonstop state of achiness, and ate a protein bar for dinner as I was too tired to bother boiling water.

By midafternoon on my third day I came across "5-0" spelled out with little gray pebbles in the dirt alongside the trail. Stopping short as soon as I saw it, a huge childlike grin stretched slowly across my face. *The 50 mile marker!* A small accomplishment considering the full length of this journey, but it felt wonderful, nonetheless, as not only did it mean I was still on the right track, but that here I was, actually doing this. Kneeling down I picked up one of the pebbles, studying it as I rolled it around between the tips of my fingers for several seconds, and then set it back down. Still smiling, I stood back up and took a selfie with the 50 in the background over my shoulder.

As I walked on from there I thought about how most of what I'd read as I'd been researching the trail had warned against logging big miles in the first week—the main reason being that it increases your risk of injury. There was no doubt 50 miles within my first two and a half days fell well within the "big miles" range but, so far, aside from an expected amount of soreness, I felt good. Not that I wasn't constantly conscious of the fact that suffering an overuse injury at this point could very well be the end of this for me. Only managing to have saved up a certain amount of money to cover the bills back home while I was out here, though, meant my timeframe was limited. With 50 miles down and 2,600 still to go, as long as I was feeling okay, I had zero interest in taking it slow.

My solar charger, on the other hand, was by no means keeping up. With these past two days of nearly constant cloud cover preventing it from being able to recharge, and having used up however much juice had been left last night, it was officially dead. And with the batteries in my devices running dangerously low now as well, not only did this mean no more picture taking for the time being, I was also in jeopardy of not being able to access Guthooks. Even worse, though, was that all too soon my inReach[4] would be of no use to me either. Not that every hiker on the trail even carried one, but ever since scaring the shit out of myself the one and only time I'd been out alone in the wilderness before without mine, it was a non-negotiable piece of gear for me.

Granted, that had been almost two years ago now, but it had shaken me up badly enough I could still remember it vividly. It was my very first solo trip and only my second time backpacking. The first time I'd been with a group—all women, in fact, who I not only gleaned a wealth of

---

[4] A compact GPS and satellite communicator with the capacity to send SOS signals to emergency response teams.

11

knowledge about surviving in the wilderness from during that weekend, but whose attitudes and approaches to life had been downright empowering. So empowering, it turns out, I felt confident enough to head out on my next trip alone—deep into the backcountry of Idaho's Sawtooth Mountains, no less, where, after continuing on through a snowy patch with no tracks to follow long enough to start doubting I was even still on the trail, I stopped to have a look at the map. As I stepped to one side to swing my pack off, my foot broke through the surface, crashing straight down through, not only snow, but what felt like a pile of jagged sticks. Stopping short just shy of my knee while the rest of my body fell forward, I landed hard on my forearms with my other leg bent awkwardly behind me and my pack, one strap still looped around one of my arms, on the ground lying beside me. Too stunned to move in those first few post-accident, out-of-body-ish seconds while your brain's still trying to register the extent of your injuries, the only thing I knew for sure was that I'd heard a loud *Crack!* on my way to the ground. *Oh my god! What if that was one of my bones breaking? What if I can't walk out of here? I don't have service—my phone is useless out here. And if I'm not even near the trail— That means no one's ever gonna find me!*

Suddenly aware that my face had grown hot and my breathing too fast and too shallow, I lowered my forehead so it was resting in the snow, closed my eyes, and counted to three while I slowly inhaled. *You can't figure this out unless you stay out of panic mode.* And then exhaled. *One, two, three. You just gotta stay rational.* Lifting my head, I focused on my hands in the snow on the ground right in front of me. They looked small and surprisingly frail. The deep plum colored polish I'd chosen while doing my nails with Hailey, back when I'd been home, all safe and cozy, on the living room floor, was chipping slightly, exposing a layer of dirt caked under each nail.

Breathing normally again, I felt a new sensation—pain. In the lower part of my leg still buried below the surface. I tried lifting it out. It wouldn't budge. *What the hell? If I can't even get my foot out–* Wanting no part in another round of panicking, I took a couple more deep breaths. Then, sliding my arm out of the strap still wrapped around it, I rolled over and sat up. Brushing some of the snow away from the hole I'd just made, my foot appeared to be wedged in a shrub. *WTF?!* I had no clue the snow I'd been walking on had been so deep. Still not sure the cracking sound I heard hadn't come from one of my bones, this new possibility that it might instead have been from one of these branches, was a welcome idea. After trying a few more times to pull my leg free, I finally just loosened my laces and slid my foot out of my shoe, prompting myself to take another deep breath at the sight of a two-three inch tear in the front of my pant leg. I leaned back on my hands with my leg stretched out in front of me and wiggled my toes. *Well, that's a good sign.* Gently, I then eased my pant leg up over my knee, which was already in the process of bruising and swelling. The rest of my leg, clear down to my sock, was covered in scratches—the deepest and bloodiest being right in line with the rip in my pants. *Okay, gross!, and ouch!, but nothing too serious.* I then put both hands behind my knee to help lift my foot off the ground and tried circling my foot, slowly, once in either direction. *Definitely some pain there on the outside of my ankle— but, I can move it. Which means it isn't broken. Which means— I can walk out of here. Which means I don't have to die yet!* Grateful that my fall hadn't been a death sentence after all, and humbled by how easily a minor accident could potentially turn tragic out here, I promised myself, then and there, "Never again!" would I ever be caught alone in the wilderness without some sort of GPS device.

True to my word, having settled on a Garmin inReach Mini after a fair bit of research, I had gone so far as to upgrade to the full coverage service plan[5] for the PCT. This meant, even when I didn't have cell service, I'd still be able to send and receive messages—to and from my girls in particular. In addition, of course, to the SOS feature all of the plans included, allowing access to emergency responders who could then pass your exact coordinates on to the nearest search and rescue crews if need be. Even if I never ended up needing it, at least now I would have the peace of mind of knowing that calling for help was an option. As long as I could keep the damn thing charged, that is.

---

[5] These devices only work once you activate them by subscribing to a monthly service plan.

Day 4: April 29, 2021

I woke the next morning to a bad smell in my tent. Realizing that it was me, after three days of hiking, sweating, and sleeping without showering, I was mortified. I pinned the outer flap of my tent back to let some fresh air circulate through the mesh "door" while I got dressed. Not that it helped much, and not that I ever would have simply gone about my business smelling this foul back in the "real world" but, for one thing, there wasn't anything I could do about it and, for another, I had something far more pressing to contend with. Namely, a nearly 20 mile stretch coming up with no access to water. A challenging enough feat in the best of circumstances, but the fact that I was now in the middle of a desert meant, not only would I be dealing with temperatures close to 100 degrees Fahrenheit, I'd also be at the mercy of the sun's rays for hours on end. Carrying enough water to keep myself properly hydrated in those conditions for that great of a distance was going to be tricky, not to mention, heavy. With one liter, for instance, weighing in at 2.2 pounds, and my plan being to load up with as much as I could hold, which was 4.5 liters, that meant adding an extra 10 pounds to my already nearly 30 pound pack, at least until I started drinking some of it.

To make matters worse, the final water source before you could even begin this grueling 20 mile dry stretch was a full mile off trail. Which, there and back, was really two. Irritated by the fact that I had to do any extra miles beyond the 2,654 I'd signed up for, I turned off in a bit of a huff onto the forest service road leading down to it.

Thankfully, as promised, one hot and dusty mile later, there was plenty of what I came for—refreshingly cold, even, flowing steadily out of the ground through a set of pipes, along with two giant shade trees with a dozen or so other hikers sprawled beneath them, most of whom I'd met in passing at least once or twice. As I stood waiting my turn to get water, one of them started trying to make small talk with me. Possessing neither the energy nor the desire to converse with her, I took the irritation I was feeling as my cue to find a spot off on my own.

Sitting as far away from the others as I could get without leaving the shade, I filtered my water while snacking on trail mix. Despite my best efforts not to eavesdrop on anyone, I couldn't help noticing that, unlike myself, everyone seemed to have trail names[6] already. Growing more and more jealous the longer I listened as I'd gotten it in my head that until I had one myself, I wasn't officially a thru-hiker, once I filtered enough water, I packed up to head out. Drenching my hair tie bandana in the water as I left, I draped it around the back of my neck to help keep me cool and made my way back up the dirt road. The sun now felt hotter after lounging in the shade for a bit, and my pack, noticeably heavier, loaded with water.

By the time I got back to the trail my bandana was dry and the back of my shirt soaked with sweat. From there I made my way over and around a seemingly endless number of sand covered rolling hills, stopping now and then for either a few sips of water, a bite to eat, or to apply another layer of sunscreen—not that it wasn't just sweating right off each time, but with my shoulders in particular starting to burn, I figured it was best to keep trying.

Several hours later, after seeing no one since the last water source, I came across the first woman, other than myself, that I'd seen out here alone so far. Impressed, as I knew first hand what it took for her to be out here on her own, I introduced myself. It was evident right away that she was frazzled. For one thing, she'd already set up camp for the night which, given how far away we still were from the next water source, was deeply odd considering how early it was. The more we talked the more evident it became she was dehydrated and running low on water. She also happened to be a nurse, though, and therefore fully aware of just how much of a concern heat exhaustion could be. Reluctant to leave without doing what I could to try and help, I gave her a few electrolyte tablets and some of my water. Not that I had any to spare. I just figured since I'd be getting to the next water source, most likely, well before she would,

---

[6] A nickname you "earn" while doing a trail; usually given to you by fellow hikers and having to do with a specific experience or personal preference for something; once you have one it then becomes the only name you're known by along the rest of the trail.

she might need it more. I would just need to re-ration out what I had left now. She was grateful and far more calm after that. I gave her my phone number, asked her to message me when she got cell service again to let me know she was alright, and got going.

Still at it as the sun dipped below the horizon, the temperature dropped slightly as well, which, with it being as hot and dry as it had been, felt like a godsend. Although, what I really wanted was just to be done. To stop walking. To take off my pack. To lay down, close my eyes, and just sleep. The strain of pushing myself so far beyond my limits for so many days in a row now had finally begun to catch up with me, and not only was I feeling it in my body, with my achy feet and my neck all stiff and my legs like dead weight, it was evident in my pace as well. Over the past couple of miles I'd been slowing way down, to the point where I was now moving at less than half of the rate that I had been this morning. Of course, I only knew this thanks to the fact that every 5-10 minutes I kept checking to see how much farther I'd gone, partly as a way of trying to distract myself from thinking about how thirsty I was with only a few sips of water left. It was backfiring on me, though, as every time I checked, thinking I'd come so far, I'd really only covered a fraction of that distance. Becoming more and more frustrated each time at my body's inability to move any faster, I finally just forced myself to stop checking.

As the dimming light of dusk began to expire, I gave up what little hope I had left of being done before dark. Exhausted and on the verge of tears, I stopped to dig out my headlamp. Noticing a body-sized flat spot on the ground off to the side of the trail, everything in me wanted to just lay down and sleep there. *What's the worst that could happen?* I stood staring at it, imagining my pack on the ground as a pillow for my head. *An animal could come and get you.* My puffy jacket spread out over the top of me like a blanket. *True.* My shoes off, lying beside me. *You need to get to the water, though.* Warm tears trickled down my cheeks and now that I was standing still my calf muscles were beginning to cramp. *I know—you're spent. But you have to keep going.* Knowing there was no way around it, I let out a long, despondent sigh, tightened the straps on my pack, and started walking again.

Thirty to forty minutes later I heard the faint sound of voices and saw tiny lights bobbing up ahead in the darkness. *Headlamps. Which means hikers. Which means I finally made it!* Allowing myself, now that I was done, one more look at my mileage, I'd done over 26 miles. My biggest day yet. Plus, the length of a marathon. I couldn't help feeling proud of myself.

My elation was short-lived. Not that I also wasn't happy to see a fairly large stash of water jugs on the ground for those of us passing through, but this "campsite" was an underpass. As in, a patch of loose dirt and gravel between huge cement pillars with a busy state highway running over the top of it. On so many levels, the very idea of spending the night here felt both wrong and dangerous. *My family would kill me if they knew this is where I was sleeping tonight.*

Introducing myself to the small group of hikers whose headlamps I'd seen from a distance, I felt an overwhelming sense of relief—*at least I won't be here alone*. Not that I normally had any qualms about being alone, but in this particular situation the old saying about there being safety in numbers had a comforting ring to it.

And then my heart sank. Having been too exhausted to have made any sense out of the fact that they all had their packs on as I'd been walking up to them, it wasn't until one of them actually told me they were heading out that it hit me they were leaving. Lost for words, I stared back at him, dumbfounded. Adjusting his pack, he went on to explain that their plan for this section was to rest during the heat of the day and hike during the night when the temperatures were lower. It was then I noticed an odd man out—sitting off by himself in the dark, and from the sounds of his murmuring, quite drunk. He clearly wasn't going anywhere. *Great! My first night ever sleeping under an overpass and I get the added bonus of being left alone with some random drunk guy.*

"What about him?" I asked, nodding in the drunk man's direction.

Following my gaze to see who I was looking at, "He's a thru-hiker," he said, in a tone as if to suggest I had nothing to fear from one of our own.

"Yeah, but—?" I questioned him, unconvinced.

He shrugged his shoulders and gave me a look as if to say, "I'm sorry, but I'm guessing you'll be fine." Then he and his fellow hikers were off. Legitimately scared now for the first time since starting the trail, I hurriedly went about the task of setting my tent up. As I did, the man sitting in the dark began calling out a woman's name, loudly, over and over. After about the fifth time, I stopped what I was doing and, shining my headlamp in his direction, yelled back, "I don't know who you think you're talking to, but that's not my name." He laughed at this, heartily, then mumbled back something to the effect that it wasn't me he was talking to. Unsure whether to be relieved or alarmed by this, I tried my best not to act like he was freaking me the fuck out and got back to pitching my tent—my only hope at this point was to convince him I was too tough to mess with. I then heard him make a phone call. A slurry string of something about where he was and "Can yuh plee juhs cham geh me?" Then some long pauses and what sounded like pleading on his end. Then one more round of that same hearty laughter, and then silence.

With my tent finally up, I climbed inside, and zipping it shut as if it were an actual door, felt a little bit safer. I laid out my sleeping bag but didn't bother with my air mattress. For one thing, I didn't have the energy to blow it up. More importantly, though, it was noisy, and I figured the quieter I could be, the more likely you-know-who might be to forget I was there. Biting into a protein bar, it suddenly hit me—*I forgot to get water!* In my rush to get my tent up I'd completely forgotten how thirsty I was. There was no way in hell I was going back out there right now, though. I choked down as much of the bar as I could. Then laid down, still fully dressed, on top of my sleeping bag, clutching my bear mace with both hands on top of my stomach. Practically screaming at me to stretch them, I could feel my legs and shoulders tightening, and my poor feet were throbbing. More concerned with being quiet, I remained still, though. Wide-eyed and listening intently for any kind of movement outside my tent, I counted the cars as I heard them passing by until, eventually, I dozed off.

Day 5: April 30, 2021

A little after 4:00 in the morning I woke up. Grateful to have been spared thus far from harm, I laid motionless for a few minutes, listening. Hearing nothing other than an occasional semi-truck pass by, I peeked out from my tent. Taking a good look around by the light of my headlamp, the man from the night before was nowhere to be seen. Relieved, I ventured out to pee, filled up one of my water bottles, drank the whole thing, and then went back to sleep.

An hour or so later, I was up for the day. I made coffee, ate another protein bar, filled my water bottles, and packed up. Then, crossing over to a small parking/turn around area on the far side of the underpass, no more than 50 feet from where I'd been sleeping, I set my pack down and braided my hair as I decided what to do next. A 30 minute hitch from here would land me in Julian—a popular spot among thru-hikers looking to resupply, enjoy a meal in a restaurant, and/or rent a room for the night. Not that my initial plan involved stopping there. As long as I was fine carrying enough food, the idea of getting all the way there and back seemed like a huge waste of time. Time better spent hiking. Unfortunately, though, at this point, I couldn't go any further without charging my devices first. The only problem was, the one thing I'd promised my family I would not do alone out here was hitchhike. Seeing no other option than to wait for some other hiker(s) to catch up and then try hitching with them, I lathered a coat of sunscreen onto my face, neck, and shoulders, and then found a seat on a concrete road construction barrier. Within the first 20 minutes, two separate cars pulled up, each dropping off hikers on their way back from town. Each time the driver offered to give me a ride back to town by myself, and each time I politely declined. *A promise is a promise.*

Another 20-30 minutes after that, I spotted two people walking towards me along the shoulder of one of the side roads. Greeting them as soon as they got close enough, I learned they were married, she was thru-hiking, and that her husband, whose trail name was Boomerang, was following along as best he could in their RV, assisting her. As soon as they discovered I had no desire to head into town, but simply needed my batteries charged, Boomerang offered to help. As his wife continued on to the trailhead, I grabbed my pack and walked back up the sideroad with him to where their RV was parked. He plugged in my devices, offered me a chair in the shade, a big slice of fruit pie, and a fresh cup of coffee, and then sat down and talked with me. Over the course of the next hour we covered pretty much everything—places we'd been, people we'd known, jobs we'd had, the allure of the trail. He was easy to talk to and I found myself, for the first time in days, really, grateful for some company. Touched by his generosity and happy to have been spared the fate of breaking a promise, once my batteries were pretty well charged, I thanked him and got back to the trailhead.

I had another long, dry stretch ahead of me—although today's 14 mile water carry sounded far less intimidating than yesterday's 20. Right away the trail began steadily climbing, up and around one mountainous hillside after another, each one the same—dirt, rocks, shrubs, and—rattlesnakes! Seeing at least four within the first couple of hours (which was already three more than I'd previously ever seen in my life), it was the same routine each time. It would start with me unassumingly rounding a corner to find a giant, scaly, full blown snake body, all creepy and still, stretched out across the whole trail, apparently sunning itself. Startled, I would instinctively back up, wait a few minutes for my heart rate to drop back down to normal, and then talk myself into moving forward. Nearing the snake, I would then explain to it my situation of there being no other way around, plead with it to spare my life and do me the kindness of being on its way. The snake, unfazed, would then do nothing, of course, leaving me to storm off, in the only direction I still could—right back to where I'd just come from. A few minutes later, utterly incensed by this point at the injustice of being held hostage on the wrong side of the trail, I would then boldly return. No more talking this time, though. Instead, I would resort to kicking up a bit of dirt or tossing a pebble or two, not right at the snake, just in its general direction. At which point, fearing I had just crossed a line and that now it was after me, I would then take off running—again in the "wrong" direction. Then I'd spend a few minutes pacing nervously, chattering on to myself about how much time I was wasting and what unreasonable creatures these damn things were. Then, finally, out of sheer desperation, I'd head back for one more go at it, at which point, by some miracle it was always either on the move, or had disappeared completely.

Aside from that, another thing starting to get to me was the heat. With temperatures rivaling yesterday's, it was once again almost 100 degrees. The sun, too, was relentless, and with no cloud cover, no shade trees, not so much as a breeze even, there was no chance of escaping it. Feeling as if I was being baked alive inside of an oven, my poor shoulders were so burnt now they were hot to the touch. Even rationing my water became a test of my willpower as every time I took a sip I had to fight the urge to guzzle it. Envious now for the first time of all the hikers out here carrying sun umbrellas, I was beginning to understand the appeal of night hiking this section.

With the threat of heat exhaustion at the forefront of my mind, mostly because I couldn't stop wondering how the woman I'd given water to yesterday was doing, I started checking in with myself periodically to make sure I was okay. *Am I drinking enough? Does my head hurt? Am I nauseous? Dizzy? Pale and clammy? Do I feel weak?* After a few rounds of this, I could no longer tell if I was actually starting to feel sick for real or if my imagination was getting the best of me. After several hours of seeing no one, I felt a wave of relief as I spotted a couple of sun umbrellas set up along the side of the trail a little ways ahead of me. Knowing I wasn't completely alone, especially if I really was in jeopardy of keeling over from the heat, was comforting. As I got closer, though, I realized what I thought had been the tops of two sun umbrellas had really just been the sun reflecting off a couple of lightly colored boulders. There was no one there. *Well, shit, I'm hallucinating! Is this how it's all gonna end for me? I'm gonna die, all alone out here in the middle of the desert from stupid fucking heat stroke? I haven't even made it 100 miles yet. I'll never get to finish the trail.* Afraid to go any further without first getting a grip on myself, I looked around for a spot to rest. Not finding one, as the trail at this point was more of a narrow strip carved out along the side of a mountain, with a steep decline to my left and shooting straight up to my right, I simply sat down right where I was. With my back reclining into the mountain and my legs stretched out in front of me across the trail, I poured a bit of water on one of my bandanas and wrapped it loosely around my neck. One at a time, I pulled my shoes off. Dark red stains covered the toes and heels of both of my socks. I stared at them for a minute, confused. As soon as it registered those stains were dried blood, I felt nauseous. Equal parts curious and scared to find out just what state my feet were in, I carefully peeled off my socks. Of course, I knew there had been blisters forming. The pain over the past few days of my skin being rubbed raw had been constant. I hadn't gotten a good look at them, though. Waking up before dawn and not going to bed until late, I'd been getting dressed and undressed in the dark. Now sockless, I again sat staring, half fascinated, half disgusted by the gnarly mix of puss and blood oozing out from under so many loose flaps of skin—between and beneath almost every one of my toes and all across the backs of both of my heels. *What a mess. I am literally falling apart out here.* At the same time, oddly enough, I was also a little proud of myself. Albeit gruesome, possessing the ability to have pushed myself hard enough to have gotten them to reach this point felt kind of badass.

What I needed was a sinkful of soapy water, some rubbing alcohol, a whole bunch of clean bandages, and a few days off from hiking to let them heal. What I had was a travel size container of hand sanitizer, a tiny tube of antiseptic ointment, five band-aids, and no time. After doctoring them up as best I could, I eased my socks back onto my feet so I wouldn't have to look at them any longer. Far too engrossed in this new development to be paying attention to anything else, I hadn't even noticed another hiker approaching. As he was practically standing in front of me by the time I saw him, my first thought was to sit up, tuck the strands of hair that had fallen loose from my braid back in place, and brush as much dirt off of me as I could. It was clearly too late, though, for pretending I had my shit together—he'd already seen me. *Fuck it. Worst case, he'll peg me as someone who doesn't belong out here.*

And maybe I don't.

With no choice but to stop once he reached me, as my legs were blocking the trail, he said hello and then took a drag of a cigarette. *Who the hell smokes out here? I thought hikers were supposed to be healthy.*

"Hey," I said back, staring up at him, hoping to god I wasn't hallucinating him, too. Searching his face for any visible signs of judgment, I was surprised not to see any. "I'm Amy," I offered, still staring up at him. He seemed 10 feet tall from where I was on the ground, and handsome, with broad shoulders and a bit of a beard growing in—dark brown with a smattering of grey. He looked close to my age. He wore a bright orange bandana on top of his head and had tattoos on the inside of each forearm. Although drenched in sweat he seemed calm and collected, like he was enjoying himself even. *How is he making this look so easy?!*

"Tim," he nodded back.

I repositioned my legs to give him room to pass by. Before he had a chance to, though, I heard myself asking, "Can I tell you something?"

"Sure," he replied. Jumping at the opportunity to give someone some sort of clue as to what had happened should I meet my demise out here, I confessed to him my whole sun umbrella hallucination ordeal. Listening patiently while he finished his cigarette, he then pulled a hard pack of Marlboro's out of his pocket and slid the butt into it. Immediately embarrassed for basically just admitting to a complete stranger that I was scared and struggling out here, I again searched his face, this time for a sign of whether he thought I was crazy.

"I'm okay, though," I said, laughing nervously, trying to convince myself at this point more so than him. "I'm okay." *Yeah, sure you are.* Once he finally managed to pass by me I sat watching him until he rounded the next corner out of sight. Then I slipped my shoes back on, reassessed how much water I had left, and got started walking again.

I spent the next mile or so scolding myself for how quickly I'd apparently lost my ability to behave normally around other people, wondering if perhaps this was a naturally occurring side effect of spending so much time alone. Slowing my pace in an effort to avoid any further heat-induced hallucination scares, it took me the rest of the day to reach the next water cache.

The first thing I did once I got there was drink enough to give myself a full-on stomach ache. Then I set up my tent, climbed inside, and laid down. The entire area was crowded with hikers. More so than any other spot I'd seen yet. And while I was grateful to have them around me after spending such a long, unsettling day alone, the seclusion of being tucked away in my own tent was a nice buffer.

Day 6: May 1, 2021

Determined not to have a repeat of the day before, I decided to try night hiking. Waking to my alarm, which I'd set for 3:30 in the morning, I stretched my legs to the tune of crickets chirping, ate a protein bar, and packed up. By the light of the moon I made my way to the trailhead. A small group of 8-10 other hikers was already there, strapping on headlamps and signing their names in a log book that was on a stand near the trail marker. After a somewhat sleepy round of introductions they invited me to join them. This being my first time night hiking, and having no idea what to expect, I happily accepted.

With the faster paced people towards the front, we made our way, single file, through the darkness. It was comfortably cool at this hour, and the stars were out in full force, shining with an intensity you simply don't see in populated areas. As I walked on, though, making small talk with the guy in front of me while doing my best to keep up, I couldn't help wondering what kinds of views I was perhaps missing out on. Once the sun rose I broke off from the group—hanging back to rest for a bit and eat something.

A few hours later I reached the 100 mile marker. After striking up a conversation with a couple who was there taking selfies, I walked with them for a bit. The more we chatted the more I liked them. So much so, I was bummed to find out they weren't thru-hiking the whole trail, but rather just out for a long weekend. Both being seasoned backpackers by comparison to me, Flamingo (on account of his dark blue hiking shorts covered in bright pink flamingos) reminded me a lot of my brother, Eddie, and Sarah—god bless her!—showed me how to turn my GPS setting on Guthooks on so I could finally see my real time location, along with exactly where I was now in relation to everything else on the map. A mile or so later we reached the next water source, which, surprisingly enough, was an actual trough. Filtering as little as I thought I could get by with, as I really didn't like the looks of it, I then set out on my own again, leaving Sarah and Flamingo to chat with the handful of others who were already there.

Midway through the morning, I reached Eagle Rock—a giant rock structure in the shape of an eagle with its wings spread wide, so massive and impressively realistic looking it's an actual tourist attraction. It was swarming with day hikers,[7] all of whom, having walked no further than a few miles from where they'd parked to get here, smelled luxuriously of laundry detergent, scented soaps, deodorant, and perfume. I, on the other hand, having last showered nearly a week ago, smelled more like a hard boiled Easter egg someone hid (a little too well) behind the couch a few months ago. I sat off to the side for a few minutes, people watching, until the sight of one too many moms with their kids in tow had me missing my girls so bad that I took off again.

With the little trail town[8] of Warner Springs just ahead I spent the next several miles daydreaming about various things I was looking forward to doing and, in particular, eating, once I got there. Having had my fill of trail mix and ramen, I was craving, of all things, a green apple and fresh bread. I also had a care package waiting there for me—the first of several a few different people had volunteered to send as a way of supporting me.

---

[7] People on hikes short enough to be completed in a single day; distinguishable from thru-hikers by how much smaller and lighter their packs are, how much cleaner their clothes are, and how much better they smell.

[8] Communities near long-distance trails that welcome, support, and offer services to thru-hikers.

I picked my package up first from the post office as soon as I got there and then joined a small group of hikers who were sitting on the ground next to some electrical outlets behind the town's only gas station. Introducing myself, as I didn't recognize anyone, I then plugged my devices in next to theirs. What I was quickly discovering to be the standard set of thru-hiker questions then followed. "Where are you from? Are you by yourself? What day did you start? Are you going all the way to Canada? Where did you camp last night? How many miles are you doing today? What's your trail name, and how did you get it?" Not that I minded. It was a nice switch from the usual set of job, status, and relationship questions you'd get back in the "real world."

Using my little Swiss Army pocket knife to cut through the tape, I then tore into my care package like a five-year-old on Christmas morning. It was full of candy and dehydrated meals, lip balm, a charming little necklace with an outline of a mountain range, and a handwritten card cheering me on—all from my friend, Craig, who, despite never actually having met in person, I'd become sort of pen pals with during Covid via a mutual friend. I put on the necklace, ate some of the candy, and reread the card. Then I went into the gas station and bought a beer and a hot dog and, although I'd never seen one before in my life, a green apple flavored Gatorade. *No fucking way—craving satisfied!*

Once my devices finished charging, I wandered over to the community center where they had a big covered patio with several picnic tables where hikers were welcome to hang out. Among a large group of others, Sarah and Flamingo were there. My happiness at seeing them again, though, quickly turned to panic as I heard behind me the sound of a familiar voice. It was the drunk guy from the night I'd spent scared shitless under the overpass. His laugh was unmistakably recognizable. Turning around so I could see his face, as it'd been too dark that night to actually see him, he, yet again, called out that same woman's name. "Abby!" Tail wagging, a happy little short haired dog came running up to him. Reaching down, he gave it a bite of something. *Oh my god— It was a dog, not a woman he was talking to!* Although it was an innocent enough mistake on my part, I felt ashamed of myself for having thought he was crazy and embarrassed by the fact I'd been so scared of him. I could see now that he was harmless—although, with scraggly long hair, a beard nearly down to his chest, tattered clothing, and a tooth or two missing when he smiled he looked a bit more like a homeless person than a thru-hiker.

After camping out in a grassy field there that night, the next morning I took my first ever "bucket shower." The gist of which, as the name suggests, is that you pour a bucket of water on yourself, lather up with soap, and then rinse yourself off. The community center, in the true spirit of accommodating hikers, had set up two makeshift shower stalls out of plywood and a great big industrial sized sink outside on a wooden deck. They even had a stash of little travel size soaps and shampoos we could use. After filling up one of the big five gallon buckets with warm water from the sink, I hauled it, sloshing, into one of the stalls with me and undressed. Once I finished washing I used what was left in the bucket to rinse off and then, having no towel, spent the next few minutes awkwardly trying to coax my dry clothes back on over my wet skin. Obviously there was nothing fancy about it, but after marinating in a mixture of my own sweat, sunscreen, and dirt for a week straight, it felt fabulous. Before putting my socks and shoes back on I wrapped the blisters on my toes with little strips of KT tape another hiker had given me. Then, after rearranging my pack to make room for the contents of my care package, I took off, back to the trail.

Later that afternoon I stopped and laid out my sleeping pad along a quiet little stream. This being the end of my first full week, I'd decided to celebrate with a picnic and a nap. As my body rested, my mind drifted back over the various events of my first 100 miles, and then forward, to the enormity of how far I still had to go.

In lieu of a somewhat leisurely day, I covered 14 miles by the time I stopped for the night.

And then, the next day, another 17.

Day 9: May 4, 2021

Once again I set an alarm for 3:30 am, partly so I could get a few hours of night hiking in before having to deal with the sun, as my shoulders, now peeling, were in pretty bad shape, and partly because I was anxious to get into the next resupply town as soon as possible, as my devices were all just about dead again. Other than one solid charge after being plugged into an electrical outlet, my solar charger had completely stopped working—utterly unable to recharge itself by the sun.

Unlike last time when I'd been with a group, as I made my way in the darkness alone now it felt scary. Every time I heard something scampering past or rustling in the bushes I found myself frozen with fear, heart racing, skin tingling, and my mind scrambling to fill in the blanks of what it was I could not see. *Was it a fox? A coyote? A chipmunk? A bird?* Even worse, though, were the bright yellow eyes I'd occasionally catch peering at me through the darkness. *Is whatever that is stalking me? What if it's a mountain lion?!* It didn't help that I was deep in a valley where, even with the moon being nearly full, it was too low in the sky to help much. Plus, my headlamp was beginning to fade. I hadn't even thought to check those batteries, although I seemed to recall they weren't rechargeable. Wanting to save what little juice they had left in case of some kind of emergency, I switched to using the flashlight setting on my phone for a few minutes until I thought better of that, as well. I couldn't chance wasting what little phone battery I had left. After standing still for a few minutes as my eyes adjusted to the now complete darkness I slowly kept going, clicking my headlamp on briefly every couple of minutes to make sure I was still on the trail. Stumbling occasionally over a rock or branch I couldn't see, once I made my way to the edge of the valley floor, I began traversing back and forth along a ridge of switchbacks as I climbed my way out.

Already tired by the time the sun finally rose, my pace for the entire rest of the day was far slower than usual. Calling it quits after a long 19 miles, I was soon sound asleep in my tent again.

The day after, though, I barely managed 12, thanks mostly to my blisters. They'd been getting worse instead of better, and now, having spread from my heels and toes to the balls of my feet, as well, the pain was so bad it was hard to think about anything else. In a desperate attempt to manufacture some sort of relief I'd begun a new routine of stopping every few miles for an hour or so to take my shoes and socks off to air them out. Although it did seem to be helping, it was also slowing me down.

This day also had me facing, yet again, the tragic necessity of having to walk a whole extra mile off the trail to get water. An impressive old shade tree with several fallen logs set up as benches to sit on beneath it was my consolation prize for getting there. Taking full advantage of the shade, I parked myself under the tree, allowed my feet to air out, and made a meal of instant mashed potatoes with a packet of tuna fish mixed in. Another hiker, showing up a few minutes after me, sat and joined me, as well. Chatting as we ate, I was relieved to discover my ability to interact normally had been restored. There were no awkward, near death, hallucination confessions this time. His name was Robert. He struck me as someone artsy—he spoke softly and purposefully and seemed both kind and intelligent. He was thru-hiking, too, and had started a week or so before me. After not seeing anyone for the past few days, I found myself, as I had with Boomerang, once again grateful for the company.

My plan for the day had been to do more like 20 miles, but the thought of putting my shoes back on after I stopped around 12 miles to air my feet out again was unbearable. The pain had grown so bad it felt as if my feet were on fire. I set my tent up, ate an early dinner, and then sat in the dirt with my back against a tree while I used the nail file on my little Swiss Army knife to dig the dirt out from under my fingernails. *God, I miss soap and water!*

With nothing more to do once my nails were as clean as I could get them I slid my knife back into my pocket and rested my head back on the tree I was leaning against. A pair of birds, each on opposite sides of the forest, took turns calling out back and forth to each other as a couple of chipmunks chased each other frantically up and down the side of a pine tree for several minutes before scrambling off. The air was still, with no breeze whatsoever, and comfortably warm now that the hottest part of the day had passed. Soothed by the simplicity of all that surrounded me, aside from an occasional ant crawling around on the back of my neck, which I promptly flicked off, I felt completely content. Noticing the ground was littered with pinecones the size of my head, I thought back to family camping trips when I was a kid. How we'd drive right up to the campsite with our coolers and folding chairs in well frequented places with outhouses and sometimes even showers. We'd pitch our tents, and then my two older brothers and I would go off exploring. If there was water, we'd swim. We'd build a fire and roast hot dogs and marshmallows on sticks we'd made a competition out of seeing who could whittle the pointiest tip on with our pocket knives. My favorite part, though, was always lining pinecones up on top of a downed log so we could take turns shooting them with my dad's .22 or, better yet, his pistol. As a 10-year-old I remember thinking I was the shit, being able to do that. *And look at you now. Some 30 years later and you're braving the wilderness, alone. You're still the shit, Girl.*

Eventually I crawled into my tent. With it being as warm as it was I hadn't bothered to put the rain cover on. I lay there staring through the mesh "ceiling" of my tent at the tree tops above me, marveling at how quickly the same silence I'd found so unsettling initially had become such a welcome part of being out here, until I drifted off to sleep.

Day 11: May 6, 2021

I woke at dawn and, tiptoeing around gingerly in my bare socks, packed up. With less than 20 miles until the next resupply town I was anxious to get moving. Putting my shoes back on my blistered, as well as now slightly swollen, feet, on the other hand, I was not looking forward to. I sat down on a log and loosened my laces to open my shoes up as wide as they'd go and then, biting down on my bottom lip as a way of dispersing the pain, slid them on. The pain was excruciating. Tasting blood as I then laced them up, it was all I could do to remind myself to breathe so I wouldn't pass out. After several deep breaths I swung my pack on and, with the back of my hand pressed to my mouth to stop my lip from bleeding, got going. Somewhere around a mile later the pain evolved into numbness, and my only worry at that point was whether the pain would return if I stopped for a break. Scared to find out, although knowing full well that 20 miles in one straight shot was beyond me, I decided to just do what I could for the time being to keep going.

At the first sign of other people it was evident I was clearly on edge, though. Hearing their voices before I saw them, as they were coming up the trail from behind me, whereas I normally wouldn't have minded, I found myself irritated. I was jealous of their pace for one thing as they were gaining on me quickly and I was practically hobbling. The trail was narrow and on a bit of a ledge as they reached me. I stepped to the side so they could pass me. A girl around Madie's age with long blond braids, bright blue eyes, and a T-shirt covered in dust and smudges of dirt brushed past me first. She was naturally pretty and the same height as me.

"Hi," she said, tentatively, looking at me like a stray dog who might be friendly but could just as easily be vicious.

"Hey," I nodded, faking a smile. Then a guy wearing a ball cap, a pair of trendy looking sunglasses, and a fanny pack in addition to his backpack waved and nodded to me as he followed behind her. Roughly the same age as her by the looks of it, he was nearly a foot taller, and had the build of a man who knew his way around a gym. Then lastly, a guy who looked to be about 30, with a scruffy face, a boyish smile, and an impressive amount of tattoos on his arms brought up the rear.

"How's that tank top working out for ya?" he asked, sliding his sunglasses down his nose with one hand, eyeing my sunscorched shoulders as he passed by. *Asshole. What are you, the fashion police?* Truth be told, he wasn't the first to have commented on what I was wearing out here. Some other guy had made fun of my flannel shirt at one of the water sources. Granted, neither that nor the tank top now in question were traditional, moisture wicking, hiking garments, it wasn't my fault I didn't get the memo that long-sleeve sun hoodies were all the rage this season (over half of the people out here were wearing them). Not that I would have splurged on one anyway. Knowing I had nothing nice to say, I simply scowled at him, daring him with my eyes to say anything else to me. He did not. Backing away towards the others once it was evident I wouldn't be answering, he then turned around with a small wave and a, "See ya," and they were gone.

Soon after that I found myself entering a stretch previously ravaged by wildfire. With a shitload of fallen trees left in its wake, one after another, blocking the trail, I had to keep stopping to take my pack off either to climb over or shimmy under them. After an hour or so it began to feel more like an obstacle course than a hiking path, which under normal circumstances would have been more fun than discouraging, but all I could think about was how much extra time it was costing me.

By early afternoon I came upon the granddaddy of all the obstacles as of yet—a massive boulder. It was so big, in fact, and blocking the trail to such an extent that not only did Guthooks have it labeled as a "dangerous rock slide," they'd even mapped out an alternative route for those opting to bypass it. That detour meant adding extra miles, though, which I, of course, wanted no part of. Plus, after reading through several of the comments on Guthooks from those who'd already traversed it on how best to do so, although I was still nervous, I thought I could manage it.

That, of course, was last night, though, from the comfort of my tent, all warm and safe inside my sleeping bag. Standing before it now it was intimidating to say the least. Not only was it blocking the trail, it was hanging several feet out over the edge of the side of the mountain which was far too steep to scramble beneath, around to the other side. Scared shitless or not, though, I was too far past the turnoff for the detour to turn back now. No way was I going to waste that much time backtracking. *You can do this.* Feeling nauseous as I stood there staring at it, I took a few slow deep breaths while mentally picturing myself hoisting my body up and over it. *You got this.* Heart racing, I wiped my sweaty palms down along the sides of my pants, reached my arms out as I stepped up to it, gripped onto the rock with each hand, and began climbing it. Before I knew it I was halfway over it. Pausing briefly to adjust my footing as I figured out how best to maneuver my next move, I made the mistake of looking down, over the edge. Gripped by fear at the sight of how steep of a drop-off it was from this angle, my body froze as my thoughts ran wild. *What if I slip?...and fall all the way down there? How long would it take for someone to find my body? I don't wanna die like this! My family would never forgive me for having taken such a risk. Plus, then I'd never get to finish the trail.*

Half a minute later, fueled by pure adrenaline and a desire to live, there I was, safe and sound, standing on the other side of it, beaming like a teenager who just scored their first kiss. *I did it!* With the boulder as a backdrop I took a few selfies to document my accomplishment.

As the miles wore on from there, my thoughts wandered back to other times over the years since my divorce when I'd pushed myself to do something hard. Something that, going into it, I, as well as everyone else, wasn't even sure I was capable of. Like hiking alone in the wilderness, for starters, and dating again for the first time in 20 years, and learning how to build a website, and replacing a part on my car, and buying my own gun for the first time, and teaching myself how to refurbish furniture so I could sell it at consignment shops to help pay the bills. And perhaps the biggest of them all was somehow rising to the challenge of facing each day as a newly single mom while simultaneously mourning the loss of life as I had known it.

I thought about how the more of these kinds of things I did, the more I learned to trust myself. The more ownership I started taking in regards to where I was in my life, and the more I actively started pursuing things rather than passively allowing them to happen to me. Granted, it was more "one step forward, two steps back" in the beginning, but sticking with it led to progress that proved incredibly empowering. And with a newfound sense of inner strength, after a lifetime of allowing my fears to dictate my choices, my hopes and aspirations were finally guiding me—

in all kinds of new and exciting directions. Like being out here on the PCT. The prospect of starting over in my 40s had scared the hell out of me, but the end result, thus far, was that I was far more adventurous and confident now than any younger version of myself had been.

Which is where my thoughts shifted next—to my younger self and how different she'd been. To the overwhelming sense of helplessness with which she had approached life—constantly at the mercy of others' whims and incapable of eliciting any real or lasting change for herself. A mindset that, unfortunately, had resulted in an ongoing pattern of self-destructive behaviors such as binge drinking, eating disorders, and toxic relationships. Trying to untangle the thought knot as to how this way of thinking had come about, I called to mind various traumas I'd experienced. The shame and mistrust and anxiety that had followed each of them, and then festered. The next string I pulled from this knot was how, being the youngest as well as the only girl in my family growing up, I'd had a sort of free pass in many cases as far as things being done and/or decided for me. A double-edged sword, as such perks not only had the capacity to elicit feelings of inferiority, but a fair amount of doubt, as well, regarding my ability to handle things on my own.

Hearing a noise, I scanned the trail ahead of me to find a man heading towards me from the opposite direction. As we neared each other I noticed him looking quizzically past me along the trail where I'd just come from. Stopping short within a few feet of each other, "Are you alone out here?" he asked bluntly. *What the fuck?! Why is he asking that? And how should I answer? If I say yes, and he's a creep or a killer, he's gonna think I'm an easy target. If I say no, then I'm lying, plus he can see there's no one with me. I could say someone's behind me, though. By the time he found out the truth, I'd be far enough ahead to be rid of him. Oh, fuck it—I'll just mace him and run if it comes to that!* Facing him squarely I put my hands on my hips just above the waist straps of my pack.

"Yes," I said, curtly, bracing myself for the worst, having no clue, though, as to what that might be.

He sighed loudly, shaking his head at me, like a teacher whose student had just given the wrong answer. "Make sure you find a group of others before you get to the Sierra section," he then said. "It's too dangerous for you to be out there alone. There's too many places you might get lost, and a wrong turn out there is serious business." I stood staring at him, dumbfounded. *Are you fucking kidding me? How is anything I do any of your fucking business? You know nothing about me. Who the hell do you think you are?* Mistaking my silence for compliance or, worse yet, perhaps gratitude, he then brushed past me, spouting one final, "Trust me on this. Find a group!" as he did.

Enraged by the fact that he wouldn't have said any of this to me had I been a man, it took me a solid mile to finally calm down. On a positive note, he had unwittingly unraveled the third and final string in the knot I'd been working on, which was that as a woman living in what felt very much to me to be a man's world, I had long ago reached the conclusion that I would never have the upper hand—not in my relationships, my place of employment, and, apparently, not even in my daily comings and goings in the world. I had succumbed to the idea that, as a female, I would never feel as safe, as strong, as capable, or as important as a male would. They were the ones, after all, to have taught me this. First as a seven-year-old. That's when the ongoing sexual abuse at the hands of a teenage babysitter started—my pale blue Holly Hobby nightgown and how he made me pull it up exposing my body, the Playboy magazines and how he forced me to pose for him like the women in them, the popcorn ceiling I counted the holes in as my young mind's way of dissociating from the shame and confusion of what was being done to me as I lay on my back on the floor. Then again at 14. I had just started high school when a night out with some new friends went terribly wrong and I was raped by two 25-year-old men. And then at 20 when I was date raped by a college classmate, in my own apartment, no less. He was too strong to fight off and held one hand over my mouth the whole time so my friends in the next room wouldn't hear me cry out for them.

I felt a strange mix of both satisfaction and sadness as I walked on. Satisfaction for the sense of clarity I now had after untangling such a harrowing thought knot. And sadness for the young girl I used to be. For all the heartache and struggle she endured. For all the wrong conclusions she came to about who she was, and wasn't, how the world worked, and what her place in it was. I imagined myself going back through the years, sitting face-to-face with her. Looking into her eyes—my eyes—and telling her, "I love you, and I promise you are worth so much more than anything that could ever be done to you."

It was late afternoon by the time I reached the town of Idyllwild. After checking in at the local campground, I made my way to the Hike-and-Bike section. Robert, the guy I'd met at the water source the day before, had beaten me there. He was in his tent with the flap open, napping soundly on top of his sleeping bag. As I was setting up my tent I met another woman who was also thru-hiking by herself. She had reddish-blond curly hair, a slight sunburn amid an array of freckles on her face, and an athletic build. She went by the trail name, Chaparral, and I instantly liked her. She was a no nonsense, outdoorsy, independent type, and at half my age I couldn't help but admire the guts it took for a woman so young to be out here doing this alone. It had taken me twice as many years to build up that much courage.

Once I finished setting up camp, I stashed my pack in my tent, left Chaparral to get back to the book she'd been reading, and walked a mile down the main road to the grocery store. Not wanting to have to put my shoes back on after taking them off, I figured I'd get my resupply done before resting.

Slowly pushing a shopping cart up and down the air conditioned isles of the store, I tossed in what I figured it would take me to get the 80 or so miles from here to the next town of Big Bear. Sticking, for the most part, with my standard selection of ramen, trail mix, protein bars, and jerky, I went with Pop-Tarts rather than oatmeal, as I'd been craving them for nearly a week now after seeing someone else eating them. I also got a bag of chips, a little tray of sliced cheese and salami, and a cute little picnic size box of red wine. Back outside, I found a bench with an electrical outlet next to it in front of one of the other shops along the strip mall lining the grocery store and sat down. I plugged in my phone and let it charge as I ate my dinner of chips and cheese, drank my wine, and people-watched as a mix of thru-hikers, summer tourists, and locals bustled in and out of the shops. As soon as my phone had enough juice I called, first Madie, and then Hailey. After having little to no cell service the whole time I'd been out here, it was a rare and welcome treat hearing each of their voices. Impatient to get back to camp so I could finally take off my shoes, I only let my inReach charge briefly, hoping that'd be enough to at least get me to the next place I could charge it.

Day 12: May 7, 2021

After sleeping in, taking a $2, three-minute campground shower, and bandaging all of my blisters, it was already midmorning by the time I made it back to the trail. I caught up with Chaparral after a couple of hours at a stream crossing where she was stopped, eating lunch. I sat with her, filtering water, as she finished up. After complaining to her about what a dud my solar charger was, she offered to let me borrow her battery pack. I was grateful, as it was already evident I'd made a major mistake yesterday, not fully charging my inReach. I plugged it in, slid the battery into the hip pocket on my pack, and did my best to keep up with her. I couldn't do it for long, though. She was a good deal faster than me. Once my device was at 80 percent I gave her battery back, thanked her for sharing it, and slowed down to my regular pace as she went on ahead of me.

Towards the end of the day, as the sun was just setting, I began to near what Guthooks had designated as the last place to camp for the next several miles. From a distance I could see a tent—someone else had already beaten me there. Ready to be done for the day, I was hopeful there'd be room enough to share. Once I reached it I saw it was Tim, the man who'd caught me sprawled out on the ground in the desert just after my little hallucination scare. I asked if he minded if I crashed his site, and he told me I was welcome to. I set my pack down, let out a big sigh, and then stretched, reveling at how good it felt to be out from under the weight of it. Then I dug my tent out and started setting it up. It was far too windy to do so gracefully, though, and after several embarrassing minutes of watching me wrestling with it Tim spoke up.

"Would you like some help?" he offered.

"No. Thank you." It was a response so automatic for me I hadn't stopped to think before I said it. *Why am I always so hell bent on not letting anyone help me?* He sat, watching me, smoking a cigarette in his foldable camp chair, with a look of mild amusement on his face. *Good lord, he probably thinks I'm an idiot.*

"Would you like a cookie?" he offered a few minutes later. *Yes—I would love a cookie!* I was still at it with my tent.

"No. Thank you." *Ugh, seriously? Now you're turning down cookies, too?* Once I finally got my tent up, I crawled in and zipped it shut. I went through my usual nightly routine of peeling off my sweaty, dusty hiking clothes, using a wet wipe to remove, as best I could, the layers of grime I'd acquired that day, exchanging my ball cap for my beanie, and putting on my slightly less dirty yoga pants and flannel shirt. All done with all that, I unzipped my tent flap and peeked my head out. Tim was still in his chair. "Any chance I could still have that cookie?" I asked him, half joking, although hopeful his answer would be yes.

"I've got two left, and I'm actually full," he said, handing them to me. "They're all yours." They were chocolate chip, and they tasted like heaven. I savored each bite as we took turns asking each other about where we were from and our lives back home. "How about a shot of whiskey?" he offered after I finished the cookies. *Seriously? This guy has all the good stuff!*

"Yes, please!" I said, smiling. He poured a shot into my tin cup, and then with him in his camp chair and me inside my tent with the flap pinned open we sat up talking until the stars were out and I was ready for bed.

The next morning, he was outside his tent boiling water as I was packing up. "You don't drink coffee?" he asked. I assured him I did, but that I'd let myself run out on purpose, in the hopes of weaning myself off of it so I wouldn't have to carry the extra weight any longer. He looked at me like I was crazy, and then told me he had plenty if I wanted some. I did. I handed him my cup, and he filled it. I could taste a hint of whiskey as I sipped it, not having bothered to rinse it out the night before.

He was still sitting in his camp chair drinking coffee by the time I took off down the trail. I got about a quarter of a mile before I started noticing all the dusty footprints beneath me were headed in the opposite direction. *That's odd.* I stopped and looked around. *This all looks way too familiar. Like I've actually been here before.* And then it dawned on me—I'd gone the wrong way. *Oh. My. God.* I turned around, and like a dog with its tail between her legs, started back towards the campsite, and Tim. *Now I'm gonna have to walk right back past this guy who probably already thinks I'm crazy after my whole hallucinating spell. Not to mention how ridiculously long it took me to put my tent up last night.* He was just as I'd left him, in his camp chair, when I got there. Pointing my finger at him playfully as I walked past I called out, laughing, "Tell no one about this!" He laughed, and raising one hand to his mouth, made a sideways motion across it like he was zipping it shut. *Of all the times to take off in the wrong direction and I had to go and do it in front of someone. Ugh!*

By midmorning I reached the 200 mile marker. "2-0-0," again spelled out in little rocks. This time, though, it was lying right in the middle of the trail rather than off to the side. As I stopped to take a picture, the fact that I still had over 2,400 miles to go hit me like a punch in the gut so hard it took a minute to catch my breath before I could move again. For the next several miles, one nagging thought lingered tirelessly in the back of my mind. *If only one out of 10 people who attempt this ever finish it, do I have what it takes to be that one, or will I be among the other nine who try only to fail?* I wasn't worried so much about the physical aspect of it. I'd been training long and hard for years in that regard, and even with my feet being in the state they were in, that wasn't a deal breaker. No, I was pretty sure if anything was to cut my journey short, it would be how homesick I was for my girls. Already the strain of missing them—their faces, their hugs, their company—was wearing on me. It wasn't quite as bad during the day. The trail had a way of constantly directing my attention towards whichever of my most immediate needs had to be met next. Like finding the next place to get water, or the next group of shrubs dense enough to take a shit behind. The next place to camp. The next place to resupply. The next spot of shade so I could stop and rest, or even to just spot the next trail sign. Nighttime, though, was a whole different story. With my needs of the day met and my body done moving, my mind was free to focus on other things, and nine times out of 10, those other things were my girls. Were they well? Were they safe? Were they struggling? They'd been my whole world for half my life, and being so far away from them felt like torture.

Another form of what felt like torture was how dangerously low I was running on water out here in the middle of this dry heat. My mouth was dry, I was borderline nauseous, and I couldn't get the image of me guzzling water at the next water source out of my head. With the sun beating down on me and no source of shade to cool off in, I trekked on slowly, doing my best to ration what little water I had left. Unable to see too far ahead, as the trail kept winding around one big hill after another, as I neared each new bend I kept getting my hopes up that the next water source would be right there waiting for me. After a few too many times of that not being the case, I finally stopped to check Guthooks to see for sure how much further it would be.

Confused by the fact that it was saying I still had three more miles to go, I refreshed the app and checked again. And then once more. Each time, nothing changed. *What the hell?!* My confusion turned to disappointment, and then to panic. With only a few sips of water left, three more miles seemed impossible. Unsure of what else to do, I took my pack off and sat down in the dirt. I knew I'd been walking slower than usual, but to have misjudged how far I'd come by this much? *Idiot.*

I bowed my head in my hands, all set to start having a good cry over my mistake, and then thought better of it. *Sitting here crying isn't going to get me to the water any sooner. It is what it is. I miscalculated, and as much as that sucks, it isn't the end of the world. Now get up. And get moving.* As I did, I came up with a plan. With three sips left and three miles to go, I would allow myself one sip per mile. It was better than nothing, and I knew myself well enough to know that as long as I had something left, even if it was just a sip, it would keep me from panicking.

Finding it hard to think about anything other than how desperately thirsty I was as I trudged through the desert, I started daydreaming about tall glasses of water, and drinking straight out of a garden hose like I did when I was a kid. About diving into swimming pools, wading across rivers, and cliff jumping into lakes. About raindrops on my bare skin and sliding down the rides at a water park. About standing on the shore of an ocean with the waves splashing against my legs and my feet sinking down into the sand. And ice cubes—*oh man, I miss ice cubes!*—all the different shapes and sizes, and how the kind from Sonic were always my favorite, but how any kind, really, would be heavenly. My tongue felt like sandpaper.

Almost an hour and a half later, with the next water source finally in sight, I swallowed down my last sip. A handful of other hikers were already there, including Tim, who'd caught up with and then passed me about a half hour earlier. They were all gathered around one of those big metal hand pumps you have to crank a few times to get the water flowing, snacking and chatting and, of course, drinking water. I filled my filtration bag, screwed on the lid that did the actual filtering, and drank greedily directly from it. Then I filled it a few more times, filtering enough to top off each of my water bottles. It had become my new habit to carry two 1-liter Smartwater bottles, which fit perfectly in each of the outer side pockets of my pack, and a mid-sized Gatorade bottle. The shoulder straps of my pack each had a handy elastic loop you could tighten, drawstring style. Technically, these loops were meant to secure your trekking poles when you weren't using them, but they also worked great for holding a Gatorade bottle, thanks to the little indentation towards the top of the bottle. This way I could drink as I walked. Otherwise, to reach my Smartwater bottles, I had to stop and take my pack off. The other bonus of carrying a Gatorade bottle was that the mouth of it was wide enough for an electrolyte tablet to fit without having to break it in half like I had to do with the other bottles.

With all of my bottles full, I got my ball cap wet and then put it back on, shivering as the excess water trickled down over my face and the back of my neck. Then I soaked my washcloth bandana as well and draped it loosely across the back of my shoulders. Heading out from there, I walked on through an open stretch of sand in what I hoped was the direction of Interstate 10—my next major landmark according to Guthooks. There being no discernable trail here, I felt better about the erratic display of footprints I'd been following once I finally laid eyes on a long, gray strip of pavement ahead in the distance. *The interstate!* Stretching out across the entire length of the landscape, it was so flat and so straight, it looked as if someone, with one broad, boring brushstroke, had painted it there. Moving steadily across it, in either direction, was a string of what appeared from this distance to be little toy sized cars, RVs, and semi trucks. The closer I got, the noisier and more lifesize they became. To amuse myself, I made a game out of guessing who they all were and where they were off to. A young family on their way to a theme park or a campground? A group of teenagers bound for a big summer concert? A trucker running late to pick up their next load? A retired couple touring the country, one state at a time? Watching them whizzing by, I felt like an outsider, as if each step I'd taken over the past couple of weeks had landed me farther away from the world they belonged to—fast paced, busy, and complicated. The trail was anything but those things. Not that it wasn't demanding; it was therapeutically simple, though. The pace was walkably slow, allowing ample time to notice and appreciate things. It was quiet, as well, enough to hear my own thoughts. Any interactions I had were unrushed, and everything I was carrying with me served a purpose. *If only everyone could experience this.* I felt sad for all the people rushing by who never would.

The trail, still merely sand, although I had since passed a couple of trail signs, intersected with the interstate by way of an underpass. Once I got there I was in for a treat in the form of some trail magic.[9] In the shade, directly under the overpass, a trail angel by the name of Mama Bear had set up an oasis. Half a dozen camp chairs were arranged in a circle. Off to the side were trash bags we could use to unload the extra weight of whatever garbage we were carrying. There were jugs of clean drinking water, a little hand washing station, and a couple of coolers filled to the brim with ice cold sodas and beer. And best of all, a table set with a sweet spread of hiker favorites: cookies, candy, chips, hot dogs, fresh fruit, and salad. Also on the table was a trail register to sign our names in, and a stack of postcards, complete with stamps, that we could fill out and drop in a basket so she could mail them off for us. I took one for each of my girls. And last, but not least, was a well stocked hiker box,[10] which, despite recently resupplying, I was happy to see. Between my appetite skyrocketing over the past couple of days, which had me eating through my supplies far quicker than usual, and having covered way less miles than I'd been planning to yesterday, which now put me a day behind schedule for getting into the next town, I was now running surprisingly low on food. Grateful and relieved, I snagged a couple of packets of tuna as well as a few granola bars.

Chaparral showed up shortly after I did, and then Tim, along with a handful of others I recognized from the past couple of water sources. Mama Bear warmly welcomed each new hiker. I stayed for probably an hour and, at one point, about halfway through, she came up to me and asked if she could give me a hug. Surprised by her offer, "I stink. And I'm filthy," I warned. Unphased, she wrapped her arms around me, saying something as she did about being used to hikers and not minding how

---

[9] When people, affectionately referred to as "trail angels," voluntarily support thru-hikers via giving rides, stocking water caches, providing food and/or lodging; often acts of kindness, expecting no more than a "thank-you" in return (as hikers, though, it's always best to at least offer a few bucks, so as not to take advantage of their generosity or make a bad name for ourselves); what Boomerang had done for me the week before—I just hadn't known what to call it.

[10] Often plastic storage containers or, if in the wilderness, lockable metal or wooden structures to prevent animals from raiding them; full of food items and supplies (i.e., band-aids, tampons, sunglasses, books); hikers take from these what they want/need, and donate back things they've either grown tired of or no longer have use for.

dirty we were. It was the kind of hug few people other than your own mother give you—snug enough to convey you are cared for, long enough to convince you everything's gonna be alright. Not realizing how much I'd needed that, as I hadn't been hugged since my girls dropped me off, by the time she let go I was crying. She pulled up a chair beside me and the two of us got talking. I told her about how much I was missing my girls, and how divorcing after almost 19 years of marriage had been the catalyst for this journey. She then shared with me how this day was what would have been her wedding anniversary. Tears filled her eyes as she told me how her husband had battled depression. How hiking a section of the PCT had been one of the ways in which he'd sought relief from it, and how, tragically, he'd ended up taking his life. She went on to explain how helping us thru-hikers was also helpful to her, giving her something positive to focus on in the midst of her grief. Deeply moved, not only by her generosity and kindness but by her willingness to share her story with me, I left feeling grateful for the opportunity to have crossed paths with her.

From there the trail continued on through a bit of a flat section crawling with huge wind turbines before climbing, first up and then down, again and again, through the next set of mountains. Now the hottest part of the day, the sun was relentless, the air, dry and dusty, and with my stomach now full, I was moving slowly and feeling sluggish, especially on the uphill stretches. One by one, over the next several hours, every other hiker who'd still been at Mama Bear's oasis when I'd left, passed me by.

It was getting dark by the time I reached the top of my final hill for the day. Having just passed a tent with a loudly snoring hiker inside, I was brimming with envy. Whoever was in there was done for the day, whereas, I, on the other hand, still had two miles to cover, albeit—*thank god!*—all downhill from here, before making it to the river where I planned on spending the night. I slipped my jacket on, and after turning my ball cap around backwards so the bill wouldn't be blocking the light, strapped my headlamp on over it. As soon as I clicked it on the light began fading, and within minutes of starting down my first switchback it had grown far too dim to be of any real use. Scolding myself for not remembering to have bought batteries for it in Idyllwild, I took it off and stuffed it into one of my pack's hip pockets. I pulled my phone from my pocket, added "2 AA batteries" to the shopping list I had in my notes, and then turned on the flashlight app to help light my way. An hour or so later, after a hard earned total of 28 miles for the day, I finally reached the river. I couldn't see much of it in the moonlight, but I could definitely hear it. I found a bare flat spot and was digging my tent out of my pack when a bunch of tiny bobbing lights off in the distance caught my eye. Dotting different spots along the mountain I'd just made my way down, they appeared to be moving. My mind was so tired it took me a minute to make sense of the fact that they were headlamps, from a dozen or so other hikers making their way down across the various switchbacks I, myself, had just traversed. As I got to work setting up my tent, I heard a voice call out from nearby. It was Tim. He'd heard there was another round of trail magic in the form of a family style dinner happening just up the river and asked if I wanted to go with him to check it out. Although I was less than thrilled about the idea of walking any further, the sound of a hot meal was far too tempting to pass up. I finished with my tent and then the two of us made our way by the light of the moon along a winding unmarked path. By the time we found the spot, dinner was over, and everyone, aside from a single trail angel who hung out chatting with us for a bit, had gone to bed. Disappointed and hungry, we walked back to our tents and said good-night. I ate one of the tuna packets I'd snagged from Mama Bear's hiker box, along with the last of my trail mix, and then fell asleep.

Day 14: May 9, 2021

I crawled out of my tent just after sunrise, moreso because I needed to pee than out of a desire to actually get up. Getting my first good look around in the light of day now, I stared up in awe at the mountain I'd made my way down in the dark last night, then traced the path of the river, both upstream and downstream, along the bottom of the valley I now found myself in. I closed my eyes, and to the tune of its gurgling, felt the warmth of the morning sun on my face. Half a granola bar and a bottle of water later, I packed up and got going.

As I reached my first river crossing I found Chaparral eating breakfast in the shade of a large boulder with her bare feet in the water as, even though it was still morning, it was already hot. With her was a girl named Lefty, thanks to her unfortunate knack for leaving things behind, who usually hiked with a couple of guys named Brightside and Booty. I'm not sure when Booty had joined the pair of them, but she and Brightside, who it turns out had been friends since childhood, were the same pair of hikers I'd gotten briefly lost with on my first day. Since then, we'd run into each other every two or three days.

Although I was happy to see a pair of familiar faces, I was bummed not to have the place to myself. I'd been looking forward to going for a swim ever since I'd checked Guthooks a few miles back and saw there'd be an opportunity. I sure as hell wasn't gonna strip down in front of anyone though. After chatting with the two of them for several minutes, I made my way across the river along a pathway of strategically placed rocks, wondering as I did who had placed them there? Perhaps some previous hiker, a trail maintenance crew, or PCT volunteer? This, not being the first act of kindness I'd seen out here in the form of the trail being tweaked in such a way as to make things easier for all who would follow, made me feel good—like I was part of a community that was actively looking out for each other.

From the other side of the river now, I turned back towards the girls and paused for a moment, weighing my desire to cool off against my desire for modesty. I lifted my ball cap and used the back of my hand to wipe the sweat from my brow. The current, flowing past me, looked refreshingly inviting. *You're not seriously gonna pass up this opportunity to cool off, are you? Just because someone might see you without all your clothes on?* I glanced back up at the girls. Both of them were busy cleaning up and sorting their gear. *They aren't even looking at you.* I took my pack off and set it down on the ground, noticing as I did, the entire backside of my shirt, as well as the length of my pack where I'd been wearing it, was soaked with sweat. *Oh for god's sake, you're not an insecure 13-year-old girl in a gym class locker room anymore—you're a grown ass woman, in the goddamn wilderness, with a chance to cool off here. Take it!* Nodding my head in agreement from my own little pep talk, I pulled my shirt up and off in one quick motion over my head, and then crouching down by the river's edge, soaked it with water. I splashed water on my face and then up along each of my arms. Then I undid my braid, flipped my hair upside down, and on my hands and knees now, touched the top of my head to the surface of the water, and held it there until all of my hair was wet. Proud of myself and much cooler now, I awkwardly wrestled my wet shirt back on. As I finished I noticed Tim walking up. Dripping wet and embarrassed by the possibility that he might have just seen me with my top off, I offered a quick, "Good Morning," threw my pack back on, and took off.

I spent the rest of the day, once again, feeling sluggish. This time, though, it wasn't due to trudging through the heat with a full stomach, but rather an empty one. With so little food left to ration, I'd been eating far fewer calories than I was actually burning.

Feeling utterly depleted as the afternoon sun began to fade into evening, a feeling of desperation so intense it actually scared me caused me to stop. I took my pack off and sat down, cross-legged in the dirt, in the middle of the trail. Folding my hands in my lap, I slumped forward, resting my forehead down on my pack which was laying in front of me. Grateful no one was around to see me (I hadn't seen another hiker in hours), I remained like that, crying silently, as proper wailing would have required more energy, for what felt like at least 20 minutes. Sitting back up, once I was finally done, I unpacked my food bag and dumped out what was left in it onto the ground. One last packet of tuna, one snack-size pouch of jerky, two cherry-limeade electrolyte tablets, and a peppermint Lifesaver. I ate all of it, minus the electrolyte tablets. Then I got back up, put my pack on, and started walking again while I came up with a plan.

I just had to make it as far as the next trailhead. At that point, after hitching a ride, I'd be home free on my way into Big Bear, with restaurants and grocery stores and hostels galore. Granted, I still had 19 miles to go before getting there. I decided I'd walk a few more miles tonight, now that I had some fuel in my stomach. Then set up camp and go straight to bed to conserve my energy. Then wake up super early and walk the rest of the way before it got too hot. Then eat all the things once I got into town. And from there on out, to make sure this wouldn't happen again, I would always carry at least one extra day's worth of food with me.

Day 15: May 10, 2021

I'm not sure if I woke up first and then my stomach started grumbling or if my stomach had been grumbling so loudly it had woken me up. Either way, once I was awake, I laid still for a few minutes, staring at the ceiling of my tent, trying to decide which kind of breakfast sounded the best. Perhaps a nice big Belgian waffle with yummy butter and warm maple syrup filling up each little square, and a side of crispy bacon to go with it, and maybe a few scrambled eggs? Oh, and a plate of fresh fruit. And a tall glass of orange juice and a hot cup of coffee. Or, maybe an omelet with cheese and peppers and onions and ham? And hashbrowns and sourdough toast with some strawberry jam. Or a bowl of oatmeal, with walnuts and berries and cinnamon and banana slices mixed in? *Ugh, I'm so fucking hungry!*

Doing my best to push the thought of food out of my mind, I turned my attention towards getting dressed. Not having bothered with my regular nightly routine last night, I pulled out a couple of wet wipes and went about the task of washing yesterday's dirt and grime away. As I sat there, naked, on top of my sleeping bag, I was struck by how different my body was beginning to look. After two weeks on the trail, my stomach was flatter, I could see definition in my legs where two weeks ago there hadn't been, and I'd never before seen the hair on my legs, or my armpits, this long. My feet were so filthy I couldn't even tell which parts were blistered or not anymore, and there was a solid layer of dirt caked under each and every one of my finger and toe nails—all of which needed clipping. Having no mirror with me, which was probably for the best, I could tell even without one, from the amount of dirt on the wet wipe after using it on my face, that it was in need of a proper washing as well. And then there was my hair, which I'd basically given up on. Being long enough to easily reach halfway down my back, without the aid of a brush, it was far too knotty now to do anything with it, other than pull it apart into chunks, braid those chunks, and put on my ball cap.

Just as eager now for a long hot shower as I was for breakfast, I packed up and got moving. Tim passed by me after a couple of hours. Then a mile or so later, I passed him as he was stopped for a snack. The sight of him eating a granola bar had me practically salivating. *I could ask if he maybe has an extra?* Thinking better of it as I approached him, I simply nodded, "Hello again," and kept on, walking past him. *It's not his fault you're hungry. You're the one who didn't pack enough food. And it's not like you're gonna starve to death from missing a meal or two. You miscalculated, and now you know better. Just keep moving, that's all you can do.* Eventually catching back up with me, Tim once again passed me. Then I again passed him while he was resting in the shade, enjoying a cigarette.

Shortly past noon, as I finally began nearing the trailhead, I saw a dog coming towards me, and then a man a short distance behind him. He introduced himself as a local trail angel by the name of Bosco, and then, in true "the trail provides"[11] fashion, offered to drive me, as well as anyone close behind me, into town. Happily accepting as that meant sparing me from having to hitchhike, we hung out for several minutes, talking, while we waited for Tim to catch up. Once he did, the three of us made our way to the trailhead parking lot where Bosco had parked. Popping his trunk, he pulled out a tin. "Cookies?" he offered, opening the lid. Catching a whiff, my mouth started watering. Tim declined. I, on the other hand, felt my whole face light up as I reached for the biggest one.

---

[11] A commonly occurring phenomenon among thru-hikers in which, as soon as one's need or desire for something arises, it serendipitously appears.

I sat quietly in the back seat as we drove into town, too tired even to listen, really, much less contribute to the conversation the two of them were having. Marveling at how fast things seemed to be whizzing by as I stared out the window, it didn't feel natural, being back in a vehicle now, moving at this speed, after having walked for so long.

Thanking Bosco as he dropped us off in front of one of the town's main hostels, I wished Tim a good rest of his hike, and then went inside to check in. The room I was assigned to had three rows of bunk beds with three bunks in each row, most of them already taken. Choosing one of the only bottom beds still available, I tossed my pack on the mattress, washed my hands in the bathroom, and then took off towards the pizza parlor I'd spotted a few blocks back as we'd been driving in. Ten minutes later I was standing in front of a cashier, ordering myself a whole pizza and a tall IPA. Taking my first sip as soon as he handed it to me, I then sighed, because it tasted *that* good, and then I just stood there, smiling at him. Staring back at me as if perhaps he was missing something, I then nodded my head a couple times. He mirrored me back. *Good lord, go sit down. You're being awkward again.* Finally breaking eye contact, I stepped away from the counter and took another sip of my beer while I scoped the place out for a good place to sit. Finding a booth next to an electrical outlet, I plugged my nearly dead phone in, and sat down. Another thru-hiker, Kemo, was also there by himself in the next booth over. We'd met a few times in passing. Slightly older than me and married, he had a real outdoorsman look about him—like maybe he could catch a fish with his bare hands or something. He also was hiking solo. Once my phone had enough juice to send an, "I made it safely to town!" message to my girls, I moved over to Kemo's booth where we took turns sharing about what had brought us each to the trail while we ate our pizzas. As hungry as I was, though, I was full after two slices. Saying goodbye to Kemo, I boxed up my leftovers, and walked back to the hostel.

Having never stayed in one before, I was a little excited. And more so, even, once I found out Chaparral was staying there, too, as were Lefty, Brightside, Booty, and several other PCTers, including one of the few couples that were hiking together, Lemonade and Walkie Talkie. Walkie

Talkie was around my age, had a slim build, wore a sun visor, and was both chatty and friendly. Lemonade was several years younger and beautiful with long, black hair, brown eyes and a kind and welcoming spirit. After getting a proper tour of the place from Chaparral, I put my name on a waiting list to use the washing machine, enjoyed a much needed shower, slathered some neosporin I found in one of the hiker boxes there on my blisters, and then laid down for a nap.

I woke up to a big group discussion taking place in the main common room about whether margaritas were better blended or on the rocks, which in turn led to the whole lot of us venturing out shortly thereafter to a Mexican restaurant for dinner. Laughing and joking on the way there about how we all seemed to be walking funny without the weight of our packs, we took turns poking fun at each other. Outside on the patio, once we got there, we scooched several tables together to form one big one we could all fit around. Then we all pulled up a chair, ordered our first round of drinks, and in real "icebreaker on the first day of class" style, went around in a circle, introducing ourselves. After a lively, yet relaxing, couple of hours we settled our tabs and walked back to the hostel. Chaparral and I stayed up late talking about our pasts and our families, all the various societal norms and expectations being on the trail meant we no longer had to conform to, and which parts of being out here we found to be most challenging, both in general and as women hiking solo, so far. We had a lot in common, on the one hand, but we were also both very different. With everyone else already asleep by the time we finished talking, as I crept quietly to my bunk in the dark, I couldn't help thinking this whole hostel experience felt an awful lot like summer camp which, as a kid, had always been one of my favorite things.

Day 16: May 11, 2021

After waking up the next morning, I decided it was time to finally take my first zero.[12] Whereas most hikers, relishing the opportunity to enjoy a rest day, had already done so at least twice, if not three times, by this point, I was definitely the odd man out, having not taken any yet. With so many miles to cover, and only so much time to do it, the idea of taking a day off just seemed counterproductive.

I'd gotten to thinking about it last night, though—lying awake in the darkness thanks to a choir of snoring hikers. About how even back home in my everyday life, I didn't spend much time resting. I worked a lot, mostly. Two jobs, in fact, since Covid—both of them waitressing. In the mornings, through lunchtime, at a small, 1950's themed diner, and in the evenings at a fine dining restaurant in a high end downtown hotel. Before that, for years, I'd been substitute teaching, although, initially, way back in my late teens–early 20s, I'd earned a degree in psychology. I also married young—at 22—and the very next year we had our first baby, Madie. Opting to stay home at that point to take care of her, by the time Hailey came along a few years later, I was so in love with being a stay-at-home-mom, I kept it up for another decade. Once Madie hit middle school I started working full time as a psycho-social rehabilitator. Not understanding at the time, though, that as an empath[13] I wasn't cut out to handle the amount of negative and tumultuous energy that type of environment would subject me to, I burnt out after a couple of years. Shortly after that is when I started substitute teaching, which I was far better suited for. And then after my divorce is when I added waitressing to the mix.

It wasn't just about work, though. Even when I had a day off, I was far more inclined to keep busy—exercising, running errands, doing chores—than to engage in actual downtime.

---

[12] A full day in which you hike zero miles, allowing your body a chance to rest and recover from the ongoing strain of thru-hiking; otherwise referred to as "taking a zero day," or "zeroing."

[13] Someone who absorbs whatever emotional energy is around them.

As I lay there wondering why that was, a thought knot began to unravel. One piece of it was that I'd come to associate taking time for myself as being selfish, and being selfish as bad. Another was that rest, in particular, was a form of indulgence, and the right to indulge wasn't something I was worthy of, but rather it had to be earned. No wonder I constantly felt the need to be doing something productive.

Eventually I fell asleep in spite of all the snoring, and by the time I woke up, half the bunks were already empty. Everyone else was heading back to the trail. Having arrived the day before me, they'd all zeroed yesterday. Other than a quick trip to the grocery store to resupply, I pretty much just ate and rotated between the hammock on the back patio and the couch in the common room all day. As hard as it was to allow myself to rest, as I did, I could sense my body thanking me for it.

The next morning I slept in, ate a leisurely breakfast, and called my parents, my brother, Eddie, and each of my girls to catch up and let everyone know I was doing alright. Then I packed up, washed my hands just because I could one last time with soap and water, and caught a ride, once again with Bosco, back to the trailhead. With a much later start than usual, I only logged around 13 miles before deciding to be done for the day.

The highlight of the following day was reaching the 300 mile marker. This time, though, rather than the usual arrangement of rocks on the ground, someone had carved the numbers down the side of a wooden pillar that was standing upright off to one side of the trail. Of course, I stopped for a selfie. *Slowly but surely, I'm getting there.*

The day after that, thanks to the physical benefits I was feeling from having zeroed a few days ago, I was fairly painlessly able to cover close to 30 miles by nightfall. Surprised, if not shocked by this, as 30 miles in one shot wasn't something I'd done before, I was glad I'd taken the opportunity to let my body recover a bit as it was clearly rewarding me.

The best part of walking that far in a single day, especially out here where every few miles your surroundings change drastically, is that it allows you to experience a lot more variety than you ever would otherwise.

Say, for instance, you start out in a forest. One so thick you can't really see anything beyond an endless array of bark and branches. Above you, tiny patches of sky peak through an occasional hole in a ceiling of treetops, swaying slightly in the breeze. The trail itself is narrow, well defined, and so soft beneath your feet it feels practically sponge-like. The strong, fresh scent of pine fills the air as you walk on to the tune of an occasional song bird or the faint whistling of the wind through the trees.

Several miles later and each step has become a balancing act as the slabs of shale that now make up the trail shift beneath you as you put your weight on them. The rhythmic "click-click, click-click, click-click" of your trekking poles striking down upon the hard surface, ringing in your ears as you vacillate between tuning it out and being so annoyed by it that you're close to losing your shit. You're steadily traversing along the side of a mountain. A steep incline shoots up to the left of you, and an equally steep drop off to your right. There is no vegetation—just rocks and more rocks, as far as you can see. So many, in fact, at times you can't even tell where the trail is. Carefully constructed cairns[14] help direct you which way to go.

Over the next couple of hours you descend in elevation. Then you climb, and then descend again. You round a countless number of bends. You spot several different types of animal droppings and see a snake or two slithering across the trail. Eventually, you find yourself moving across a wide open flat patch of sun baked, clay colored dirt. Surrounded now by a surplus of sagebrush and an occasional brightly colored desert flower perched atop a cactus. You cross over a well established stream bed which, by the looks of it, has long since dried up. A pack of coyotes howl eerily off in the distance.

---

[14] A mound of rocks intentionally stacked, one on top of another, to form a freestanding pile; oftentimes used as unofficial trail markers.

A few more hours and you're standing on the backside of a ridge you just climbed and the views are spectacular. In every direction you look, you can see for miles. One mountain range after another, after another. Each one appearing a shade darker the further away from you they stretch. You can see the trail, winding all switchback-like, for miles ahead of you—down the side of this mountain, across a meadow lying down in the valley at the bottom of it, and then up along the side of the next mountain. As you head that way, you pass a series of alpine lakes. Each of them a slightly different, yet equally stunning, shade of blue.

And then, finally, towards the end of the day, the distant roar of a river captures your attention, growing ever louder the closer you get. The temperature drops noticeably once you finally reach it, and a light mist forms drops of dew on your skin as you continue on alongside it. All around you is greenery, so lush and dense—a cloverish type ground cover and mosses and grass, quaking aspens and pine trees and shrubbery. A lone butterfly circles around you and then flutters away as you stop to admire a rock you just spotted in the shape of a heart.

Not bad for a day if you're willing to go that far.

Day 20: May 15, 2021

Weighing heavily on my mind, from the moment I woke up, was the fact that I would be missing my brother's wedding back home today. We'd talked it over, of course, before I'd left as the dates, both for my PCT permit and his big day, had been set for some time by then, and while it wasn't ideal, obviously, me not being there, at the time we'd both felt okay about it. Now that the day had come, even though I knew that he knew how much being out here doing this meant to me, I felt like a shit little sister for not being there with him.

Once I packed up and started walking, I pulled out my phone, opened the camera, scrolled over to "video," and hit the record button. With my face front and center, a bright blue sky, some rolling hills, and the trail in the background, I said hi to my brother. I told him how much I loved him, that I wished I could be there, and how it meant the world to me that he'd found someone who made him so happy. I wished him good luck and told him to have fun and to drink a few beers for me. Then I blew him a kiss, stopped recording, pulled his name up in my contacts, and hit "send." The little blue line at the top of my screen stopped half way through sending. I didn't have service. *You've gotta fucking be kidding me.* I sat down, and, cursing my phone, started crying. It was bad enough I wouldn't be there in person, but the idea of him going through this whole day without so much as a word from me was too much.

My only consolation was the possibility that at some point I might reach a spot ahead with some cell coverage, and so I stood back up and got moving.

All morning I hustled, checking my phone every 20-30 minutes to see if "No Service" had by some miracle switched back over to bars again. Sometime around noon I finally got lucky, and as soon as I saw "delivered" and then "read" pop up under my video I felt a sense of relief. Now at least my brother wouldn't think I'd forgotten about what a huge deal today was for him.

Relaxing my pace a bit, with the stress of that behind me, I turned my attention towards what was coming up next, which, oddly enough, happened to be a McDonald's. A strategically placed one, in regards to the trail, as it was just off a major interstate we were about to intersect with, and while I hadn't seen too many people over the past several days, every time I had, it was all anyone talked about—McDonald's, McDonald's, McDonald's! Not that I wasn't looking forward to it, too. Fast food, aside from what you might find in a trail town, wasn't a luxury we were used to having out here.

Just shy of reaching the interstate I veered off onto a side trail leading straight towards the famous "golden arches." Under a couple of trees, in a patch of grass between the McDonald's parking lot and a stretch of road leading back onto the interstate, were at least two dozen hikers. Some were napping, others chatting. One of them had headphones in and appeared to be journaling, and at least two-thirds of them were drinking cans of either vodka seltzers or beer. Also there in the same parking lot was a gas station, a Taco Bell, and a little family run fruit stand. I said hi to Walkie Talkie and Lemonade—the only two there from the group who'd been at the hostel. Heading first to the restroom once I got in McDonald's, I chose the handicap stall so I'd have enough room to keep my pack with me. Sighing happily as I peed—*this sure beats squatting over a hole in the ground*—I felt my whole body relax as I sat, leaning forward with my elbows on my knees and my head in my hands, on the cool porcelain seat. *Never again will I take a toilet for granted!*

After washing my hands I stared down at the sink, embarrassed, as well as in awe of how big of a mess I'd just made. It looked like a small animal had just taken a mud bath. I cleaned it up and then, turning to leave, caught a glimpse of my reflection in one of the mirrors. Curious, I swiveled back and leaned in closer for a better look. Sure, it was my face—*duh*—but something was different. *What, though? My eyes, maybe?* They did seem a bit brighter. I'd seen that before, though. They naturally stood out more, the tanner I got in the summer. And I was looking pretty tan right now—*Unless?* I glanced down at the sink I'd just cleaned all the dirt from my hands off of. *Oh my god, is my face just THAT dirty, too?* I leaned out, away from the mirror and, studying my face again, I turned my head slightly, first to one side, then to the other. *No, it's definitely my eyes.* I leaned in again. *It isn't the color, though, it's more in the expression.* A hint of something wild or unhinged-like, I'd never seen before—at least not in a mirror, like this, staring back at me. It felt a bit dangerous, and at the same time, in some obscure way—*important?* A shiver ran through me. Then I saw myself smiling. Whatever it was, I liked it.

The main door to the bathroom swung open, bringing with it the strong delicious aroma of french fries and cheeseburgers. A woman with a toddler perched on her hip stood in the doorway, holding the door ajar. "Oh, I'm sorry," she said, staring at me—in this case, with a look I knew all too well. It was one of politeness, for my sake, and concern, for her own. Looking and smelling as dirty as I did, I assumed she probably thought I was homeless. "I was just leaving," I said, hoping to put her at ease and adjusting my pack. At that she smiled and stepped out of the way, still holding the door for me so I could get through. The little boy on her hip laughed as I made a goofy face at him and then buried his face in her chest shyly as I walked out.

After ordering a Big Mac, fries, and a Coke, I went to the gas station and bought an IPA and a Gatorade. Then I found a spot in the grass with the others and dug in.

An hour or so later, feeling more full than rested, I returned to the trail where an underpass, complete with overgrown vines and a small creek running through it, led me safely across to the other side of the interstate. Continuing on from there through a fairly flat stretch, I cross a series of dirt roads, dried up creek beds, and railroad tracks. At one point, I even passed through an underground tunnel, the inside of which was lined with corrugated steel. Running my fingers along the cool, bumpy surface of it, I'd made a loud "Wee-eww, wee-eww, wee-eww" wailing sort of ambulance siren type sound as I passed through—smiling as I did at the thought of my girls and how, ever since they were little, anytime we drove through a tunnel or a long underpass we always made that sound just for fun. Even now, we still did sometimes.

Shortly after the tunnel, I rounded a corner and came practically face to face with the biggest rattlesnake I'd ever seen in my life. Coiled up right in front of me in the middle of the trail, as soon as I saw it, I leapt backwards—so quickly and with such force my Gatorade bottle jolted loose from the loop on my pack where, normally, it hung quite securely. I watched as it fell, too in shock at the sight of the snake to think to reach out and grab it. It hit, lid first, on a rock, bounced once in the brush, landed sideways on the trail, and then rolled in what felt like slow motion, straight towards the snake.

Weighing my options, a surge of panic rushed through me. *I don't want this snake to kill me. If I lose that Gatorade bottle, though, I'll be one container short of being able to carry enough water out here.* I decided to take my chances with the snake. Keeping my eyes on him, I lunged forward, grabbed the bottle, and ran, screaming, back towards the tunnel I'd just come through. Knowing that until the adrenaline pulsing through me finished running its course I wouldn't be able to think straight, I found a spot to sit down and took a few slow deep breaths.

With my heart rate slowly returning to normal, I examined my Gatorade bottle. The side of the lid had a crack in it. I took out my little Swiss Army knife, opening up a miniature pair of scissors on it, and a pen I had wrapped a bit of duct tape around—a little ultralight tip from some book I'd read. I unwound a strip of the tape just big enough to cover the crack, cut it off with my scissors, and then wrapped the lid with it as best I could. As I sat for a minute, admiring my truly hiker-trash[15] handiwork, I couldn't help feeling a tad bit MacGyver-ish. Now all I had to do was get past the snake.

I tried my usual strategy, approaching it, repeatedly, a few separate times. Unfortunately, he wasn't having it. After about 20 frustrating minutes, I saw a day hiker coming my way from the opposite direction. As soon as he got within earshot, I warned him about the snake and then pointed it out. Having uncoiled itself by this point, only its tail end was visible. Its head had disappeared into the bushes. As he approached it, without even pausing, the man looked at it, stepped a foot or two off the trail, and then walked around and right past it. *What the hell?* Too stunned to say anything, with my eyes wide and my mouth hanging open, I just stared at him, like he was some kind of god, as he brushed past me, smiling, and then continued on his way.

Ashamed of the fact that this man had so easily just done what I, after half an hour of trying, still hadn't managed to do, I decided enough was enough. I took a deep breath, and with both eyes on the snake, slowly began inching towards it. Suppressing the urge to scream again as I did, as soon as I got a hair past the tail end of it, I took off in a sprint with my pack bouncing clumsily on my back.

Thankfully, the rest of the afternoon wasn't nearly as eventful.

---

[15] A term used to describe thru-hikers' a) dirty appearance, and b) less than conventional, oftentimes highly creative way of doing or fixing things using whatever limited resources they have on hand.

The sun, dipping low, cast a warm, golden glow as I reached what would now be the last reliable water cache before the next town of Wrightwood. A large group of at least 20 hikers was already there—practically everyone I'd seen at McDonald's, as well as Lefty, Booty, Brightside, Tim, and Chaparral. Several tents had been pitched, but mostly it was just a sea of sleeping bags people had laid out over their sleeping pads, which, as warm as it was, and as far out as we were from any lights, made sense—it'd be a good night for stargazing. Joining the big circle a bunch of them were sitting in, I dug out my stove, made some ramen for dinner, and chatted with the group while I ate.

Knowing I still had several miles to go before hitting my goal for the day, even though the idea of staying here with everyone else for the night was seriously tempting, I hit the trail again as soon as I finished eating.

Shortly after nightfall, as I was pulling my headlamp out of my pack, I noticed it was already on and, worse still, already dim. *Well, shit. It must have accidentally switched on at some point while shifting around in my pack.* After tapping it against the palm of my hand several times, hoping that might do the trick, I shoved it back in my pack. *If only I'd thought to bring another, extra set of batteries with me when I'd replaced the old ones in Big Bear.*

To make matters even worse, I'd also already broken the only pair of glasses I had with me, and my night vision, even with glasses, was lousy.

Continuing on by the light of the moon, the trail narrowed and a dangerously steep drop off loomed to one side of me as I wound my way, slowly and carefully, around a series of mountains. Once in a while I'd stop for a minute and shine the flashlight on my phone around to get my bearings. Aside from that, though, all of my energy was spent focusing on not falling, as I clumsily kept tripping over little rocks and loose twigs. *This is crazy stupid! What the hell am I doing? Is hitting my goal for the day really worth the risk of falling to my death out here?*

While it was clear to me now I'd made an unsafe decision, pressing on from the water cache earlier, it was also just as clear that I had no choice at this point other than to keep going. There simply weren't any flat surfaces to camp in this cliffy section.

After a few more slow, stressful miles I finally reached the spot where I'd planned on camping. Far from your typical PCT campsite, this was more of a turn around area for vehicles at the end of a dirt road the trail crossed over. With very few options along this stretch, I'd picked it based solely on how much distance I wanted to cover. Most people, I found out back at the water cache, were steering clear of it, though, on account of a strange comment someone had posted on Guthooks about it a couple weeks earlier. As soon as one of the guys sitting next to me while I was eating my dinner found out that's where I was planning to camp, he pulled the comment up on his phone, and then read it out loud to me like it was some kind of ghost story.

"A truck full of drunks with guns showed up at 1am and proceeded to spray the area with bullets for quite a while. We ran down the hill and hid by some bushes until they left. Then we immediately packed up and got the heck out of there. Also there is broken glass all over the camping area. Probably best to find a different spot."

Having laughed as he read it, the whole thing was obviously way too ridiculous and far-fetched to be true.

Of course, now that I was out here, in the dark, alone, just to be on the safe side, I used the flashlight on my phone to scan the area for bullet casings. Finding none, I laughed at having felt the need to even check in the first place. Then I set up my tent, ate a snack, and was fast asleep by 11:00.

Startled and disoriented, I was jarred awake by what sounded like a big diesel truck pulling up just outside my tent. I reached for my phone to check the time. It was 1:22 am. *Holy shit! Those comments were legit?* I sat up, cross-legged in my sleeping bag, and felt around in the dark for my bear mace. *Just stay calm. It won't do you any good to panic.* Clutching it tightly in one hand once I found it, I cupped the other over my mouth to mute the sound of my breathing. *Just keep quiet.* I heard the engine turn off and the creak of a door opening. *You're okay.* Then another door opening, then both of them slammed shut. Then a man's voice and footsteps. *You're okay!* Then two mens' voices, and then laughter.

I could feel my palms sweating and my stomach start churning. *Are they gonna start shooting? What if they don't see my tent? But what if they do?* I couldn't decide which was worse. If they did in fact have guns and were about to start shooting, maybe the sight of a tent would keep them from aiming in this direction? If they weren't planning on shooting, though, my only hope then would be that, in a two person tent like this (which is why I hadn't opted for a one person), they'd be less inclined to mess with whoever was in it based on the assumption they weren't alone. *What if these two are the worst kind of bad guys, though?* The kind who, for whatever reason, had such an extreme lack of conscience, not only did they have no problem forcing people to do things against their will, but inflicting cruelty was nothing more to them than a way of keeping things interesting. Having already been caught in the crosshairs of just such a man more than once in my life, I knew all too well the kinds of things they were capable of. *Please, God, don't let them be those kinds of men! I promise I'll be more careful, and I'll take all of the comments on Guthooks more seriously from now on!*

I have no idea how much time passed—it could have been two minutes or 10, or 30 seconds—but at some point, again, I heard doors creaking open. And then, slamming shut, the roar of an engine starting, tires rolling on the dirt slowly past me, then picking up speed, and getting farther away. I let out a big breath of all the air I'd been holding in.

As soon as they'd gone far enough I could no longer hear them, I unzipped my tent and peeked out. There was a thick foggy mist, but no men and no truck. *Thank you, God! Thank you.* With warm tears of relief streaming down my cheeks I frantically packed up. *If they decide to come back, I'm sure as hell not gonna be here!*

The same thick mist that, quite possibly, had just kept me hidden from the men in the truck, formed tiny beads of moisture on my face and my hands and the outside of my jacket, as I walked as fast as I could down the little stretch of dirt road leading back to the trail.

With nearly five miles to cover now until I reached the next campsite, as soon as the adrenaline wore off, it may as well have been 50. A mix of desperation and anxiousness quickly set in. Every noise I heard, as well, seemed to startle me—the aftermath, I was sure, of being so frightened earlier.

After the first couple of miles a deep weariness hit me. So deep in fact that, for small spurts at a time, I was literally sleepwalking. With my eyes fluttering closed, my head would then start to lower, and then bobbing back up, jerk me somewhat awake again. Over and over, this continued to happen until what felt like an eternity passed and I finally—*finally!*— reached the next campsite.

After tiptoeing quietly around all the tents, I saw no room for one more. Knowing I didn't have it in me to go any farther, I laid my ground cover down along the edge of the site next to one of the tents, and then put my sleeping bag on top of that. As I then sat down and was untying my shoelaces, someone in the tent next to me stirred. I quietly apologized for crashing their site. He groggily mumbled that it was no trouble and asked if everything was okay. Then he sat up with me for a few minutes, listening sympathetically, as I explained what had happened.

"You wanna smoke some weed?" he offered, rummaging quietly through a small bag once I'd finished my story.

"Nah, but thanks," I said, laughing, wondering what my girls would think, knowing this was probably the third, if not fourth, time out here so far that I'd been offered, "the marijuanas," as I jokingly referred to it with them.

"Suit yourself," he said. "Just thought it might help calm your nerves." Illuminated briefly by the flame of his lighter as he then lit a joint, I caught a glimpse of his face. A good 10-15 years younger than me, he was dirty, of course, and handsome with curly shoulder length hair. "I guess since I'm up—" he sputtered, coughing, after he exhaled. Then shrugged his shoulders and added, chuckling, "I might as well."

"Go for it," I said, laughing as I slid into my sleeping bag. Then, bunching my jacket up to use as a pillow, I laid my head down and let out a long, heavy sigh.

"Home, sweet, home," he then said to me. "You're safe now."

Grateful—not only for his kindness, but for the fact that for every bad guy out there wreaking havoc and spreading misery, there were also just as many, if not more, perfectly decent, well meaning, good ones—I closed my eyes and fell asleep.

A few hours later I woke up just before dawn. A slight chill in the air had me eager to get moving. As no one else was up yet, I stuffed my sleeping bag and ground cover back into my pack as quietly as I could. I felt bad enough for crashing these peoples' campsite in the middle of the night—the last thing I wanted to do now was wake any of them up.

As I made my way along a ridge near the top of what appeared to be one of the highest peaks in the area, a fantastical sea of puffy whiteness stretched out before me. Unsure as to whether it was more of a thick, misty fog or an actual cloud formation, whatever it was, it was both massive and impressive—filling the entire expanse between where I was and what I could just barely make out in the distance as being the tips of the next closest mountain range. Studying it as I walked, I was surprised to discover that, not only was it moving, but it seemed to be drifting along two different currents, with some of it heading in one direction, and some in the other. Soon after that, thick golden rays began shooting through from beneath it, fanning both up and out across the horizon. At the centerpoint of these rays, over the course of the next 10-15 minutes, like a bright orange, rubber ball underwater bobbing up to the surface, the sun itself began to appear. I stood still at this point, watching, not wanting to miss it—a kaleidoscope of colors, blending and shimmering, first this way and then that, as the sun slowly inched its way higher. As quickly as they'd appeared, the colors then faded, leaving the sun, now too bright to look at, on its own for the day now against a backdrop of blue.

A mile or so later, Walkie Talkie and Lemonade caught up with me. I was happy to see them, especially after last night. Doing my best to keep up, as not only were they faster than me but I was running on fumes, I tagged along with them for a couple of hours. We talked as we walked, freely and openly about pretty much everything—from our childhood dreams and least favorite jobs, to best date ideas and bad date horror stories, to our favorite foods and vacation spots and all the names of all the pets we'd ever owned.

Later that day, once I got into Wrightwood, my first stop was the hardware store where I'd mailed the first of my resupply packages[16] to. Having shipped it off a day or two before I'd left for the trail, I couldn't even remember now what I'd put in there. After signing for it I took it outside and sat on a wooden bench behind the store. Using my fingernails, I scratched at the edge of the packing tape until I had enough of one corner to pull the whole strip off. Among the jerky and trail mix and dehydrated meals, all of which, as soon as I saw, I clearly remembered, I saw something I hadn't put in there. A small piece of lined notebook paper, folded into a neat little square, with my sweet Hailey's handwriting on it. Instantly homesick as soon as I saw it, I felt an ache in my chest and tears welling up. We'd mailed the package together, which meant she must have slipped this in without me seeing it somehow just before I'd taped it shut.

"Dear Momma," it read. "First, I wanted to tell you that I'm extremely proud of you for embarking on this hike—you're such a badass! Over these last few months, I've watched you go to incredible lengths to make your dream of hiking the PCT come true. That's one thing I love most about you—your dedication and passion. I'm so thankful you passed those traits onto me.

---

[16] Unlike a care package someone else fills and then sends as a gift, a resupply package is one a thru-hiker puts together for themselves ahead of time and then ships (or arranges for someone else to ship) to certain predetermined points along the trail so they can pick them up later.

I know being away from each other is going to be hard, but know that you'll be in my heart every step of the way.

Please have fun and be safe, but most of all, I hope this journey shows you just how strong you really are. You are the strongest woman I've ever known and I hope this hike allows you to see what I see in you everyday. You are strong, brave, and caring, and you are such a bright light in my life—I'm going to miss having that light around me. But most of all, I'll just miss you.

You know I've had reservations about this hike, but I need you to know that I will <u>always</u> love and support you, and I'm so happy and excited for you to be able to complete this dream of yours.

On the hard nights, the nights that you are homesick, look up to the moon, and know that I will be looking at the same moon, thinking of you. I love you more than you will ever know. Be safe, and come back home to me. You can do this, Momma.

Your forever friend and loving daughter, Hailey"

I read through it three times—not once without crying—then folded it back up, and tucked it away for safekeeping inside my pack.

In spite of having been offered several potential trail names by now from various fellow hikers, at this point I was still simply going by Amy. There had been one, though, thanks to something Hailey said in her letter, I was now thinking I might actually consider. A young guy named Baby (because at 18 years old, he was the youngest among us) had been the one to suggest it—the first time I met him, in fact. He'd just finished taking a break as I was about to walk past him. We said hello and introduced ourselves, and then ended up walking together for the next couple of miles. He was friendly and talkative and seemed genuinely curious which led to a fairly deep conversation about life and expectations and choices. It was the kind of conversation that, by the end of it, you really feel like you've gotten to know someone.

A trail this long, I was discovering, had a knack for being good at that—the way it constantly seemed to present opportunities for those traveling it to share openly and honestly with each other. About the reality of our pasts, the ins and outs of our current situations, our jobs and relationships. About things we've learned, mistakes we regret, and things about ourselves we're trying to work on. Of course, the sheer magnitude of time you have at your disposal out here plays a huge role in facilitating this, but what ultimately allows for this level of transparency to happen as often and as easily as it does is how the trail itself, unlike anything else, puts everyone on a level playing field. All the things that normally define and, quite often, divide us back in the "real world" are irrelevant in regards to the one thing being able to walk the trail boils down to. Whether or not you have what it takes to make it from point A to point B? That's all the trail cares about. Not what religion you are. Not your gender or race. Not what you do for a living, how educated you are, your marital status, your sexual orientation, or your political affiliation. Not whether you own your own home or what kind of car you drive or how much money you have. As far as the trail is concerned, we are all simply thru-hikers—united by one common goal and a sense of adventure. Period.

The trail name suggestion from Baby, though, came up, not during that first conversation we had but just after it—at the very next water source where we stopped to find Walkie Talkie and Lemonade and another young guy named Itsy Bitsy (for the "Itsy Bitsy Spider" song, due to his deep fear of spiders). With the five of us all sitting in the shade near a stream, filtering water and snacking, the topic of me still not having a trail name came up and they all started brainstorming. Baby made a comment about thinking I was the most bad-ass mom he'd ever met. At which point Walkie Talkie chimed in, suggesting BAM for Bad Ass Momma. I'd turned it down at the time, thinking it sounded a bit too hardcore for me, but now, after reading what Hailey had written— hearing she thought that I was a badass, as well, plus the fact that she actually does call me Momma, rather than Mom—it was enough to seal the deal. And now, just like that, I finally had a trail name!

Having successfully retrieved my package, I went next to the grocery store and bought a few snacks and a bottle of wine. Then, having happily accepted an invite to stay at an Airbnb with Walkie Talkie, Lemonade, and Tim for the night, I punched the address for it into my phone and took off towards it.

Lemonade let me in when I got there, as she and Walkie Talkie had beaten me into town by an hour or two, and Tim, by the sounds of it, was still a ways out from arriving. After a quick tour of the place, guided by Walkie Talkie, Lemonade led me over to one of the closets, giggling like a child about to tell me a fun little secret. The gist of which, apparently, was that as thru-hiking houseguests, one of the perks of staying here was that, for a small fee, of course, someone would come pick up our laundry and do it for us. "The best part, though," she said, grinning as she swung open the closet, "are these loaner clothes we get to wear while we're waiting!" She pulled out two bathrobes, one plaid and one white one.

"Nice," I said, nodding my head, a little confused as to what she thought was so funny. "These look comfy," I added, stroking the soft fabric of one of them with my fingertips. "Although, whoever wears them won't be leaving the house for a while." She nodded back, raised her eyebrows, smiled mischievously, and then turned around. Now with her back to me, she pulled something else out of the closets, held it up to herself, and then spun back around.

"Oh my god—no way? That's fucking awesome!" From just below her nose, all the way down to the floor, hung an adult sized, Christmas themed, pajama style, onesie. It even had a flap in the back you could unsnap open to go to the bathroom.

"I know, right?" she squealed. "There's even another!" Swinging back around, she pulled out a second, this time, solid red one—the same style but even longer and bigger.

"Take your pick," she said, laying our options out on top of one of the beds.

"Well, *I'm* not wearing those." I said, pointing at the onesies as I snatched up one of the robes.

"We'll make the guys wear em," she said, winking at me as she claimed the other robe for herself.

The three of us sat outside on the back patio in the sunshine, drinking wine and snacking, until Tim showed up. Then we each took turns showering, changed into our loaner clothes, and waited for our laundry to be done. Thankfully, the guys were good sports about allowing us girls the robes, especially since Walkie Talkie's onesie was ridiculously short on him, and Tim's, being bright red, in combination with his salt and pepperish stubble leaning heavy on the salt side, made him look just like Santa Clause—which, seeing as how he was the only one among us now still in need of a trail name, was too much of a coincidence to overlook considering that I'd actually suggested he go by Santa during a previous discussion at some point. Although my reasoning behind it hadn't had anything to do with his looks. It was more because of his knack for giving gifts—what with the cookies and the whiskey and the coffee he'd shared with me on the night I'd shared a campsite with him. After warming up to the idea over the course of the afternoon in his Santa-style onesie, the decision was unanimous, and "Santa" it was.

Once our laundry was done, the four of us ventured out to get dinner, after which we spent the rest of the evening at one of the local bars, shooting pool and drinking with a bunch of other thru-hikers who were also in town. Walking back to the airbnb at the end of the night we had a good laugh over the fact that I'd randomly kept asking what town we were in. Apparently, being drunk, in combination with having been in a new place every day for the past three weeks now, I'd temporarily and repeatedly lost my bearings.

"What town are we in?" I'd ask, straining to remember.

"Wrightwood, BAM—we're in Wrightwood," they'd kept answering me, laughing.

Day 22: May 17, 2021

After a comfy night's sleep, I had a dilemma in the form of a trail closure to sort out—the next 22 miles were completely off-limits due to fire damage. With my two options being either to arrange for someone to drive me around it, or to walk an alternate route of 20 plus miles along a two lane highway, I went with the former and lined up a ride for myself for later that afternoon. Santa, Walkie Talkie, and Lemonade, all planning to take a zero day and stay in town for another night, scheduled themselves a ride for the following day.

As I said my good-byes and gave them all hugs, I felt a bit torn. On the one hand, I was anxious to get back to the trail but, on the other, we'd all had such a good time together, I was sad to be leaving without them.

Once I got to the grocery store where I was soon to be meeting my ride, I popped in and bought some sushi, a bag of chips, and a bottle of Gatorade. Then I went back outside to wait in the little hiker-friendly rest area in front of the store. A few minutes later I got a text saying that the woman who'd agreed to give me a ride had changed her mind, and that she wouldn't be coming. With that option off the table now, as she'd been the last trail angel in town with an open seat in her car for the day when I'd called around earlier, I made up my mind to do the road walk instead.

As I was finishing up my sushi, another hiker sat down beside me. Also solo, slightly younger than me, and with a full, long, mostly white beard reaching down to his chest, he introduced himself as Nivil, "For 'Livin' spelled backwards," he said. We hit it off as we got talking. So well, in fact, that not only did we agree within the first 10 minutes of meeting each other to do the road walk together, but within less than an hour we'd gotten a hitch to the highway and started out.

Having never walked along a highway before, in spite of how dangerous it sounded, the first big chunk we covered was closed off from traffic because of construction, so it felt safe enough. And even after that, during the middle of the night, it was so dark and quiet along the road that anytime there was any traffic, we could see headlights approaching and hear the humming of engines in plenty of time to get out of the way.

As I walked along the yellow stripes of paint running down the middle of the road, Johnny Cash's "I Walk the Line" kept playing in my head.

> *"I keep a close watch on this heart of mine / I keep my eyes wide open all the time / I keep the ends out for the tie that binds / Because you're mine / I walk the line*
>
> *I find it very, very easy to be true / I find myself alone when each day is through / Yes, I'll admit I'm a fool for you / Because you're mine / I walk the line"*

Over the course of the night, our conversation took as many turns as the highway itself. We shared story after story about ourselves—some lighthearted, some serious. We laughed. We ranted. We had stretches of silence. At which point I'd once again go back to walking along the line down the middle of the road, humming mostly, but occasionally singing softly out loud to myself.

> *"As sure as night is dark and day is light / I keep you on my mind both day and night / And happiness I've known proves that I'm right / Because you're mine / I walk the line*
>
> *You've got a way to keep me on your side / You give me cause for love that I can't hide / For you I know I'd even try to turn the tide / Because you're mine / I walk the line"*

At one point, in the early, yet still dark, hours of the morning, we came across a car full of people parked along the side of the road, sounding all rowdy and playing their music super loud. Spotting us, most likely from the lights of our headlamps, one of them called out in our direction. I couldn't make out exactly what it was he was saying, but the way he was saying it—more obnoxious than friendly sounding—had me worried they might be trouble. Nivil answered back, and, thankfully, that was the end of it. Feeling especially grateful in that moment that he'd chosen to come with me, my imagination ran wild as we walked on from there—playing out one horribly tragic scenario after another of various ways I could have been mistreated and brutalized had I been alone and those people come after me.

A mile or so later, we stopped along the shoulder of the road to rest for a bit and eat something. Sitting in the dirt with our beanies on and our jackets zipped all the way up to keep out the cold, we dug through our food bags. Out of nowhere, Nivil jumped up, and pointing out into the darkness behind me yelled out, "What the fuck?!" Startled, and terrified it might be a bear, I jumped up, too, and turned around to see what he was looking at.

"Do you see that?!" he asked, still pointing.

"See what?" There was no sign of a bear. *Thank god.* But I couldn't see anything else, either.

"Over there!" He said, still pointing. "Those lights. Is that—like, aliens?"

I saw it now. A string of small lights from some satellites or aircrafts or something off in the distance, shining brightly against the dark night sky. "Some lights, Nivil? Seriously? You scared the hell out of me!" I glared at him—half playfully, half serious, although mostly just relieved we weren't in danger of being eaten alive.

"Oh, sorry," he laughed sheepishly, explaining that he was worried his tired eyes had betrayed him and he'd just wanted confirmation he wasn't losing his mind. He seemed genuinely relieved, as well, once he knew he wasn't the only one seeing them.

A few hours before daylight, after covering over 20 miles, we finally reached the campground where the trail resumed again just past the closure. Exhausted, we said good-night and good-bye, set our tents up, and went straight to sleep.

PART TWO

Into the Thick of It

"We depend on nature
not only for our physical survival,
we also need nature
to show us the way home,
the way out of the prison
of our own minds."

−Eckhart Tolle

Day 23: May 18, 2021

I rose with the sun after only a few hours of sleep, anxious to get as early of a start as possible. Having found out that Lefty had set a new record (at least among those of us I knew) by covering 40 miles in a single day, at some point during my road walk last night, seeing as I'd already have over half that done by the time I finished, I decided that this would be the perfect time to try and beat it. Checking the time as I quickly got dressed, I then counted how many hours it had been since Nivil and I started out. Nearly 12, which meant I now had just over 12 hours left to do roughly 20 more miles. *Totally doable.*

As I climbed out of my tent there was no sign of Nivil. Impressed by the fact that he'd already gotten a head start on me, I wasn't surprised—after sharing my plan with him last night about wanting to try and beat Lefty's record, we'd bet a milkshake as to which of us could log the most miles today. With no time to waste, I ate a protein bar and chugged the last of my water while I packed up my tent.

As I walked down to the water spigot near the entrance to the campground to fill my water bottles, a police car pulled up. The officer rolled down his window, asked if I was alright, whether I was alone, and which direction I was headed. A bit taken aback by how concerned he was acting, he then told me a hiker had recently gone missing nearby. He described what the man looked like and what he'd last been seen wearing. Then he asked me to keep an eye out for him and told me to be careful. Standing there watching, as he then drove away, I felt oddly vulnerable, as if a whole new element of danger had just been thrown into the mix of what I was doing out here. I filled my water bottles, hit the "start tracking"[17] button on my inReach, and started out.

All I could think about for the next couple of miles was the man who'd gone missing. *Was he injured? Was he scared? Had he taken a wrong turn?*

---

[17] A function available on various Garmin devices that allows you to record specific routes and locations. This data can then be uploaded onto their website in the form of a map that can be shared with others.

Did he have children? A wife? Were they all out of their minds with worry right now? Was he out of food? Would he ever make it home again?

Eventually, after exhausting every possible scenario I could imagine he and his loved ones might currently be facing, my thoughts took a turn towards something more personal.

Today was the 18th of May, the date of what would have been my wedding anniversary. And even though five years had come and gone now since my divorce, I knew from years past that this would be a day involving a steady flow of memories and self reflection. I also knew the forward motion of literally walking myself through it would be the best thing for me.

Having entered a stretch that had recently fallen prey to wildfire, it was charred and desolate, which seemed perfectly fitting given the significance of today. As I walked, various events during my relationship with my ex played out like a movie in my head. Like the first time we met. It was during my final semester of college. I'd gone out to a club with some classmates to celebrate how well we'd all just done on a particularly difficult exam. He was sitting at the table next to me with a girl he introduced me to as his sister. It wasn't until a few weeks into the two of us dating that I found out the truth—not only was she actually his ex-girlfriend, he didn't even have any sisters. And so began a long, baffling string of lies he then spent the next 19 years feeding me. A string I found myself constantly choking on, although I could never quite see it for what it was.

Overwhelmed by a flood of emotions as one memory after another rose to the surface, I found myself grateful there was no one around. It felt cathartic to be able to cry freely without having to worry about anyone else. I felt sadness, first and foremost. For the things I'd lost, like our home and our little family being intact and my ability to trust, not only a partner, but my own intuition. And a fair bit of remorse, as well—for not recognizing sooner the toxic nature of our marriage or the negative effects it was having on our girls, and for staying as long as I had in a situation where I'd been made to feel I wasn't deserving of things like loyalty or attention. And longing, for what might have been if things could have been different. And frustration, that all these years later I still had thought knots that needed unraveling in regards to him and the life we'd shared.

Just shy of 24 hours from when Nivil and I had started on the road walk, I finally stopped for the day. I'd covered 42 miles, which meant I beat Lefty's record. Having not run into Nivil again, or anyone else for that matter, there was no way of knowing whether he'd gotten off the trail at one of the road crossings or had gone on even further than me. Utterly exhausted, both physically and emotionally, it was all I could do to set up my tent, choke down a protein bar, and take a few selfies to mark the occasion. Then, lying down inside my tent, I watched in silence through the open flap as the sun sank down below the edge of the horizon for the night.

Day 24: May 19, 2021

With yesterday behind me and a whole year before I'd have to face the 18th of May again, I woke up relieved. I was now free to focus on what and, better yet, who I had in store for myself tomorrow. Another, pretty major trail closure being the what, and the who being Hailey, as she'd agreed to drive all the way out here again from Idaho to help get me around it—my own personal trail angel. Having been over a month now since I'd last seen her or Madie, I was so excited I could hardly stand it.

Yet again, I got an early start. Coupled with the fact that I was now in a pretty remote section, that meant the only tracks I was seeing this morning had been left, and recently, by animals. And by animals, I mean bears. And by bears, I mean one big one. So big, as soon as I saw the size of its paw prints just a few steps ahead of me in the dirt, I dug my phone out to get a picture of it. And then I listened, as intently as I could for the next mile or so. If he, or she, was still in the vicinity, the last thing I wanted was to be caught off guard.

In general, so far, the PCT as a whole was pretty well traveled. It was more common than not, throughout the course of any given day, to come across at least one or two other people. There were, of course, exceptions, especially in some of the more remote areas. Today being one of those, as well as yesterday, too—other than the sound of my own voice either talking out loud or singing, the wind blowing through the trees, or an animal scampering through the brush, I spent the whole time in silence, alone.

By midday I reached a section of the trail that clearly had not been maintained for some time. Left to grow wild for who knows how long, the brush on either side of it was so overgrown that not only did I have to physically part some of it with my hands in order to see the trail on the ground in front of me, but walking was now more like pushing my way through a field of seven foot tall branches, many of which had prickly thorns. Soon covered in scratches, I even tried going backwards through parts of it so my body wouldn't have to take the branches straight on.

Most hikers, due to a heads up on Guthooks about this section being so bad you'd have to bushwhack to get through it, were bypassing it completely by skipping ahead. I myself, being BAM now, and eager to live up to it, hadn't even considered not embracing this challenge.

After a sharp jab in my left eye from the tip of a branch I was seriously regretting the fact that I hadn't, though. Immediately blinded, a wave of panic swept through me as I stood, hunched forward slightly with both hands cupped over my eye, wondering how far away I was from being able to access any sort of medical help. A little alarmed by how much it was watering, I did my best to stay calm as I kept it closed for a few minutes. Then, standing up straight again, I lowered my hands from my face, and slowly opened my eye. *Oh, thank god—I can see!* It still hurt, badly, and while I wasn't out of the woods yet as far as perhaps having damaged it permanently, at least I could see. I put my sunglasses on as a precautionary measure, and from there on out I was three times as careful.

Eventually making my way out of that section, I reached a KOA[18] in the teeny-tiny town of Acton towards the end of the day. I stopped in at the little store there for a few snacks and a Gatorade and then, joining a big group of other PCTers at one of the campsites, sat for a bit and ate dinner. None of the other hikers were people I knew. Having done so many miles in the past couple of days, they'd all previously been ahead of me. One of them, the guy who'd actually called me over and invited me to join them as I'd been walking by, was there trail angeling. After offering me a beer and introducing me to everyone, he told me about his love for the trail and how, in spite of several failed attempts, he was still hoping that, one day, he'd be able to complete it.

Although tempted to stay put for the night, I still had quite a few miles to cover to get to where I'd be meeting Hailey the next day, and I didn't want to take a chance on not making it to her in time.

I continued walking until I felt myself growing too tired to be able to keep up a good pace. At that point I figured it'd be smarter to sleep for a bit—I could log more miles, faster, once I rested. Not bothering to change out of my clothes once I set up my tent, I laid down on top of my sleeping bag, and crunched some numbers. I'd done 31 miles today. Not bad after yesterday's 42, but I still had, roughly, another 37 to cover before reaching Hailey tomorrow. And I only had until 6:00 pm to do it.

Day 25: May 20, 2021

With my body's desire to sleep being no match for how excited I was to see Hailey, I woke up well before my alarm had a chance to do the job for me. Soon after I got started, the trail began winding through Vasquez Rocks County Park. Like nothing I'd ever seen before, a fascinating array of otherworldly looking rock formations of all different shapes and sizes stretched on throughout the length of the park. Ranging in color, from burnt orange and peach to a charcoalish-

---

[18] A chain of campgrounds called "Kampgrounds of America."

brown, they varied in texture, as well. Some, as I ran the tips of my fingers along them, were smooth, like big chunks of matte marble, while others had more of a scratchy, porous feel to them. Finding myself awestruck by such natural beauty, I kept stopping to take "just one more" picture—briefly, of course, as I had a long way to go yet and the clock was now ticking.

By noon, I'd covered 20 miles. With my legs beginning to feel slow and heavy and my feet now starting to throb, I stopped for a quick lunch and checked in with Hailey. Trying my best not to panic as she let me know she was making better time than expected and was most likely going to be early, I checked my map one more time in a desperate, albeit futile, attempt to find a spot closer to me where the trail intersected with a road she could access. With nearly 17 miles to go and the strain of the past few days now taking an obvious toll on my body, I wasn't sure I could even make it on time at this point, let alone get there early. Feeling the weight of discouragement drain what little energy I had left in me, I hugged my legs into my chest, rested my head on my knees, and pictured Hailey, standing next to her car, having driven all the way out here from Idaho, waiting for me. *If you wanna see your girl, you have to keep moving.*

I got up and kept going. *Don't worry about the 17 miles you have left. Just focus on this one, and just keep putting one foot in front of the other. There's no room for "can't" or "maybe" here—this is Hailey we're talking about, and she's gonna be waiting for you. And you WILL get there.*

A few hours later she messaged to say she was almost to our meeting point. I messaged her back letting her know I was still eight miles out. She told me she'd hang out in a park and read a book for a bit. Knowing she was so close but that it would most likely take me another two and a half hours to get to her felt cruelly unfair.

Willing myself to dig deep, I cinched the waist and shoulder straps on my pack as tight as I could get them and started running. It was more of a slow jog, really, thanks to the weight of my pack, but fueled by my desire to see her, I kept it up long enough to shave at least 40 minutes off my expected time. Bubbling with excitement as I rounded the final bend, my heart sank as my mind tried to make sense of the fact that rather than a parking lot full of cars and my daughter's sweet face, another set of hills lay in front of me. *You have got to be shitting me.*

I turned around, scanning the mountainside I'd just made my way across, realizing my mistake as I did. From a ways back, the outer edge of this—what I thought was my "final" big hill—had been protruding just far enough to have kept this whole additional set of hills nestled back in here, completely hidden from sight. I wasn't sure whether to scream or cry. How dare the trail so blatantly have disregarded how badly I'd needed that last corner to have been my *last* corner?! It felt unforgivable. I hung my head and took a couple of slow, deep breaths—trying hard to let the sense of defeat I was now feeling wash over and off of me, rather than settle in. I kicked a small rock lying on the ground in front of me, sending it tumbling down the side of the mountain. *Take that, you stupid neverending mountain. You're not the only one here who can be mean.* Clearly at the end of my rope, I walked on, seething, until I no longer had the energy for it. At which point I resorted to pouting.

Half an hour later, one big, dirt covered bundle of utter exhaustion by this point, I made my way down the real final hill to the trailhead where Hailey was waiting. As soon as I saw her car my relief was so intense I started crying. After walking 180 miles in the past week, 110 of which had been in the last four days, I had finally made it. And here was my sweet, precious, beautiful girl!—safe and sound, even, after being on her own in the world for the first time without me for the past month. And me, too, having survived so far on my own in the wilderness—I was proud of us both.

"I'm filthy and smell terrible," I warned as she reached out to give me a hug.

"I don't care," she said, squeezing me tight. Hugging her back, I then held her at arms length for a minute while we both stood there smiling at each other and laughing through happy tears. After so many days, so many miles, and so many new and different experiences, it felt surreal to have her—a part of the world I'd known before the trail—here now with me in this one, like nothing had changed, when, in fact, so much had. Too tired to make any more sense of what I was feeling than that, I hugged her again and then sat down on the ground by her car. I watched in amusement as she stood looking me over—doing her best to take in this new hiker trash version of her mom.

"Wanna see my feet?" I asked, pulling my shoes off, desperate to be free of them. "They're gross," I warned. As I gingerly finished peeling my socks off, she gasped, horrified, clasping both of her hands up over her mouth.

"Oh my god, Mom!" Her tone was so firm it was as if she were scolding me. She crouched down beside me to get a closer look, as if she wasn't quite sure what she was seeing was real or not. "They look terrible," she said, her tone softer now. She wasn't wrong—they had definitely taken a turn for the worse—even I hadn't seen them look this bad. Any parts that weren't either oozing puss or actively bleeding appeared to be stained, a dark brown-maroon mix of dried sweat, blood, and dirt. And there were scrunched up, blood soaked bits of KT tape that, by the looks of them, had rubbed loose hours earlier—some with tiny flaps of blistered skin hanging from them. Not to mention that the stench was so bad, if you weren't plugging your nose you'd be gagging. With tears in her eyes she looked into mine. "Are you okay, Momma?" she asked, half whispering, half crying.

"I am now," I said, smiling. "I can't believe you're here! It's so good to see you."

She helped me up off the ground, gave me another hug, tossed my shoes on the floor in the backseat of her car, and handed me a pair of flip flops. Wincing as I slid them on, "They look worse than they feel," I lied, trying to sound convincing. She gave me a look letting me know she knew better, and I couldn't help laughing. Apologizing in advance for how bad my feet were about to stink up her car, we then stuffed my pack in the trunk and drove to the closest hotel we could find. Not having bothered to even try and shop around, it ended up costing twice as much as I'd budgeted for, but I was so tired and ready to rest I didn't care.

After showering, I sat on the bed in a clean pair of clothes Hailey had brought me from home while she and I took turns brushing the tangled knots out of my hair, which, after nearly a month now of neglecting to care for it, took at least 20 minutes. Next up were my feet. Now that I'd washed as much as I could of the stain off, the sight of the state they were in was almost too much to stomach. There were so many blisters—some just beginning to form, some ripe with fluid and warm to the touch, and some recently popped, leaving loose flaps of skin to expose raw looking, tender, little sores underneath. And they were everywhere, too—between my toes, on the bottoms of my feet, along the backs of my heels, and even up along the sides of my feet. I could also see a few spots where there were calluses forming, as well as a toenail that, by the purplish-black look of it, would be falling off soon. Every bit as painful as they were gnarly looking, I slathered them with neosporin, covered them in band aids, slipped on my flip flops, and headed out with Hailey in search of a hot meal.

We spent the whole next day catching each other up on all that had happened over the past several weeks, and per my request, the only walking we did was from our hotel room to the pool area and back, and a lap around Wal-Mart so I could resupply. Aside from preemptively already missing her, it was a perfect day.

Day 27: May 22, 2021

The next morning, aside from my pants and my ball cap, I stuffed pretty much everything I'd been wearing so far out here into our little hotel room trash can. Too sweat stained and dirty to come clean even in the washing machine now, I'd asked Hailey to grab some things from my closet so I could just swap them out. A long-sleeve workout shirt with little thumb holes to replace my flannel, along with a fresh tank top and bra, and several new pairs of undies. And a thin, long-sleeve, white, cotton, button up, collared shirt, which I figured would be good sun protection, without being too hot. Holding it up to my nose before putting it on, I breathed in the scent of home—clean and familiar. Then the two of us each braided our own hair in front of the bathroom mirror together, packed up, and checked out.

After a leisurely breakfast at a bagel shop down the street, we then drove around the trail closure. The last half hour or so was along a bumpy, old, forestry road. Stopping once we reached where the trail picked back up, we got out and took a selfie together next to a fairly new looking PCT trail marker. Then we hugged each other and, with both of us crying, said a painful good-bye.

Once again now I stood, just as I had at the border, all alone, watching as her VW Bug made its way, slowly, down a dusty dirt road. A saying I heard a long time ago came to mind—that having a child is like having your heart walk around outside of your body. Aching now for this piece of myself as I watched it drive off and away from me, I thought back to how that saying has always rung true for me. Ever since Madie had been born and my midwife was bathing her in the sink, I remember feeling as though she was too far away from me. And that same feeling, rather than dividing equally by two when I had Hailey, instead multiplied—whenever either of them wasn't physically with me, a part of me ached for them.

And now here I was with Hailey gone again, right back to aching double.

When she'd gotten far enough down the road that I could no longer see her, I turned around towards the trail and started walking. Looking ahead at the well-trodden path as it stretched on for miles in front of me, winding this way and that over one hill after another, I found myself wondering—*How many other moms had walked this same trail before me? Had they been missing their kids as much as I now missed mine? Had it all been worth it to them in the end? Am I doing the right thing being out here?* I imagined myself in the seat beside Hailey. Zipping down the interstate with the music turned up and the two of us singing—happily headed home to our apartment together. Surely, going home would be the only real remedy for how badly I was missing her and Madie. *But wouldn't I be disappointed in myself if I didn't finish?* I already knew the answer to that. I also knew I owed it to my 16-year-old self to at least try.

Way back now, at 16, during my junior year of high school, I'd been a cheerleader. There wasn't anything about it I hadn't enjoyed—making posters, going to practice, decorating the players' lockers on game days, cheering in front of the fans, leading pep rallies, doing fundraisers like car washes. The best part by far, though, was how I hadn't even had to suffer through tryouts to be on the squad. This having been one of the few perks, in my young opinion, of attending a school so small my graduating class had less than 30 students in it—with there being so few of us, the numbers had been in my favor. It took eight people to make up a full squad, and with exactly eight of us wanting to participate that year, there'd been no need for tryouts.

The following year I wasn't so lucky, though. With more than eight of us vying for spots on the squad this time, as soon as I learned we'd have to try out, I made the choice not to. The fact that, as a senior, it'd be my last chance to participate hadn't even factored into the equation. My fear of rejection was so far through the roof that the possibility of not making the squad was more than I thought I could bear.

I spent my entire last year of high school regretting that decision, wishing I'd chosen differently, disappointed in myself for not trying, and secretly envious of each girl who had. I'd learned a valuable lesson, though, that had stuck with me since, and while there was nothing I could do now to change the fact that my 16-year-old self would never know if she'd had what it took to make the squad, I sure as hell wasn't gonna stand in the way of letting myself find out now if I could conquer this trail.

Between being lost in thought about all this, and on and off again bouts of crying from having just said good-bye to Hailey, I was a bit of a mess and somewhat startled as a small group of hikers approached from behind me. It was the same threesome I'd first seen during my second week out here, right before making my way over the big, scary rock slide. As their pace was faster but I usually went farther, I'd since learned their names as we'd done a fair bit of leapfrogging.[19] The girl went by Dirty Knux, as in "dirty knuckles" thanks to her camp spoon being too short for the standard size pouches many of the dehydrated backpacking meals came in, so her fingers kept getting covered in food when she ate. Hoops, for his love of basketball, was the younger of the two guys, and Just Kyle, who's real name actually was Kyle, was the same one who'd rubbed me wrong by commenting on what I'd been wearing. Not realizing they were behind me until they were practically trying to pass me, and embarrassed to have been caught crying, I stepped to the side of the trail and stood silently, staring straight ahead, awkwardly. They each looked at me funny as they passed by, and then Dirty Knux turned back around with a concerned look on her face.

"Are you okay?" she asked.

No. No, I'm not.

"Uh-huh" I lied, nodding. I could tell by the way her eyes narrowed as she stood there examining me that she wasn't buying it. Trying my best to make it believable, I stood a little straighter and flashed a too-big-not-to-be-fake smile long enough to get her to turn back around and catch up with the boys.

Once again alone with my thoughts, I walked on the rest of the way to my next stop of "Hiker Town." It was midafternoon by the time I got there, and Lemonade, Walkie Talkie, Santa, Itsy Bitsy, Hoops, Dirty Knux, and Just Kyle were all there, sitting together around one of the picnic tables in the center of the "town." It wasn't actually a town at all, but more of a compound really. A plot of land lined with a variety of one room, handmade, shack type structures, the entire perimeter of which was gated in by a tall chain link fence. The whole place had the look and feel of an old, abandoned, wild west ghost town type movie set.

---

[19] When you repeatedly take turns passing each other.

I said a quick, "Hi–Bye," and, "Goodluck!" to Santa, who was on his way out to start the "Hiker Town to Tehachapi 50-mile Challenge." With the upcoming section between here and the next town of Tehachapi being fairly flat, especially a long stretch along the LA Aqueduct, this challenge had been designed to take advantage of that. To do it successfully though, you had to walk the full 50 miles in 24 hours. Perfectly content at this point with my 42 mile record, this was one challenge I was completely fine passing on. Nor did anyone else, apparently, other than Santa.

After resting there for an hour or so I spent the next two days making my way first, across the aqueduct, and then over the dry and windy, wide open landscape into Tehachapi. As I neared town and got back within range for cell service, I saw I had a message from Santa. He'd nailed the 50 mile challenge, was zeroing in town for a couple of days, and had an extra bed in his hotel room if I wanted a place to crash. I messaged him back, taking him up on his offer. Having not seen a single other hiker in the past couple of days, it'd been a long, lonely stretch, and I was ready for some company.

Once I reached the main highway I found another lone hiker, a bit discouraged by this point, as he'd been waiting around for nearly an hour now trying to hitch a ride into Tehachapi. Of the three cars he'd seen so far, none of them had even been heading in the right direction. He was young, around Hailey's age, and by the sound of it, even less comfortable with the whole hitchhiking scene than I was. After agreeing neither one of us would leave the other behind, we took turns egging each other on to stick our thumbs or a bit of leg out—trying different techniques to get drivers' attention, and then poking fun at each other after each failed attempt. Between each random car passing we chatted about how long we'd been on the trail and what our favorite parts were so far. And then we took bets on how long we'd be out here, and on which of us would be lucky enough to finally secure us a ride. A little over an hour later, an elderly gentleman in an old, beat up, two-seater, pickup truck finally pulled over. We tossed our packs in the bed of his truck and then, laughing, squeezed both of our bodies into the one empty seat next to him. Luckily for us, it wasn't too far of a drive and neither one of us was very big.

After getting dropped off in front of a grocery store and thanking our driver for his kindness, we wished each other the best of luck, said good-bye, and parted ways. Eager to get my resupply over and done with, I went into the store, washed my hands and face in the restroom, threw my pack in a shopping cart, and made my way through a maze of aisles as I gathered supplies. After such a long stretch, alone, out in what felt like the middle of nowhere, it was a little overwhelming to suddenly be surrounded, not only by so many people, but by such a surplus of *stuff*. So many shelves lined with boxes and bags and bottles and cans. Produce and pet supplies, clothing and toys, jewelry, sporting goods, tools and appliances, diapers and formula, cleaning and office supplies, a bakery, a deli, a pharmacy. Anxious to get back outside and away from the sensory overload I was experiencing, I made a beeline for the self checkout as soon as I had what I needed.

From there, I walked over to the hotel where Santa was staying. Having messaged me that he was with Hoops doing laundry at the laundromat, I checked in at the front desk, showered, and laid down for a nap. Waking shortly after as he entered the room with Hoops, the three of us then met up with Lemonade, Walkie Talkie, and Dirty Knux at the pool. After swimming and hot tubbing for an hour or so, I went back to the room and got dressed, and then walked over to the post office to pick up a care package that a couple of my co-workers had sent me. Waiting to open it until I got back to the hotel, the others were as excited as I was to see what was inside. A huge, bulk size bag of gummy bears, and a big box of cinnamon flavored Hot Tamales were the highlights. We opened them up and dug in. A sweet note of encouragement was in there, as well. After reading it over a couple of times, feeling grateful for the gift, of not only the care package but their friendship, I sent a message to each of them, letting them know I had gotten it.

Then we all walked down to a sports bar where a whole slew of PCTers had apparently made plans to meet up—so many of us, in fact, we took up over half the restaurant as we spent the evening watching basketball, drinking beer, eating dinner, and enjoying each other's company.

Afterwards, Santa and I, as well as Hoops, who had also taken Santa up on his offer for a place to crash for the night, walked back to the hotel together. With Santa in one of the two double beds in the room, and my stuff on the other, I offered to share with Hoops once I saw him laying out his sleeping bag on the floor. "As long as you sleep on top of the sheets and keep your hands to yourself," I warned playfully, having no doubts neither one of them would be anything less than perfect gentlemen.

Day 30: May 25, 2021

After a good night's sleep, I called a taxi the next morning to get me back to the trailhead. With no one else wanting to leave that early, I didn't want to have to risk hitching alone.

The air was hot and dry as I walked on through a stretch of rolling hills littered with wind turbines. I'd never seen a wind farm before, and the only turbines I'd ever laid eyes on had been from a distance. This close up, as I was practically walking right underneath them, I was shocked by how massive they were. And scary sounding, too, as they made a loud, eerie, *swoosh, swoosh, swoosh*, over and over, above me. I couldn't help worrying about what a dangerous spot I was in if by some chance one of the blades were to accidentally come loose and break off.

As the heat of the day intensified, and with zero shade in this stretch to provide any kind of relief, I rolled my pant legs up to help cool me down. Of course, most people were in shorts out here. Thanks to being highly allergic to seemingly all types of grass, though, I pretty much always hiked in pants, no matter the temperature—the discomfort of running a little too hot being a far cry less miserable than a horribly itchy rash. Within minutes of my lower legs now being exposed, I kept having to swat away what I thought were no-see-ums.[20] Until, that is, I realized what was actually happening, at which point I couldn't help laughing at my mistake. Rather than a swarm of tiny bugs biting me, I was really just feeling my own leg hair brushing against my skin in the breeze. Having not shaved once the whole time I'd been out here, my leg hair hadn't been as long as it was now since I was 13—before I first started shaving. It was an odd sensation, to say the least, and it took me the next several miles to get used to it.

I spent the rest of the afternoon climbing out of the valley I'd just passed through and up into the next range of mountains—happily exchanging the sight of wind turbines for pine trees as I did.

After 20 something miles, feeling tired, but still wanting to get a few more hours of hiking in, I made an extra strong cup of coffee once I stopped to eat dinner. Stretching for a bit after I ate, I then looked over my map while I waited for the caffeine to kick in. Just as I was packing up, Walkie Talkie and Lemonade caught up with me. Tagging along with the two of them from that point, I listened intently as Lemonade gave me the lowdown as far as what to expect over the next couple of months—things to watch out for and places to be sure to stop at. Explaining beforehand that, aside from the very end of the trail, which they were planning on doing next summer, and the part they were doing now, from the southern border to Mt. Whitney, they'd already done the whole rest of the trail, piece by piece, over the past several years.

"That's strange," I said, stopping her, practically mid sentence, at one point as she was telling me all of this. "I met another couple my first day out here who also said they were planning to get off around Mt. Whitney. What are the odds?"

"That is weird," she agreed.

"I never saw them again though," I added, "other than that one time I met them."

---

[20] Annoying gnat-like bugs, practically too small to see, that bite like crazy and usually hover near the ground.

Walkie Talkie, who'd been walking a few yards in front of us this whole time, turned his head to the side so we could hear him and said, laughing, "That was us, BAM! We've known you since day one."

Lemonade and I exchanged a quizzical look as our minds made sense of this new-to-us information, and then we both burst out laughing. "What the hell, Walkie Talkie? You knew that this whole time, and you didn't say anything?"

"I thought you guys knew," he said, shrugging his shoulders.

A few miles later we caught up with Hoops and Santa who, despite my getting a fairly decent head start on them that morning, had both easily blown past me a few hours earlier—as was more often than not a regular occurrence with most of the hikers in the bubble[21] surrounding me. They'd set up camp and had a fire going just off the trail in a sweet spot overlooking the valley. Having shown up just in time to catch the tail end of a gorgeous sunset, we took our packs off and all stood, shoulder-to-shoulder, out along the edge of a ridge, admiring the show. Then we all moved over to the campfire where, within 10 minutes of sitting down, our initial, "How 'bout we stop for a quick rest?" turned into, "Ah, fuck it, let's just stay the night here."

We pitched our tents next to Hoop's and Santa's and then gathered back around the fire. Continuing to live up to his trail name, Santa pulled some goodies from his pack to share with us—a family size bag of caramel M&Ms and a big bottle of pink lemonade flavored vodka. As the night sky grew darker we sat under an ever growing canopy of stars, laughing and talking, as we passed around the booze and the chocolates.

---

[21] Trail lingo for a group of thru-hikers traveling roughly the same distances in the same general proximity.

Day 31: May 26, 2021

I woke the next morning to the stale stench of puke and the sound of someone snoring. Like right next to me, in my tent! *What the fuck?!* With my head throbbing and my stomach churning, I slowly turned over to see who it was. *Santa?* It was definitely him, stretched out and lying face up in his sleeping bag between where I was and the door of my tent. *But why?* A wave of panic washed over me. *Good lord, how much vodka did I drink last night, and did I come on to him? Why else would he be lying here in my tent right now?*

Two unfortunate facts when it comes to me and drinking are that a) my threshold for blacking out is uncommonly low (as in, it doesn't take much), and b) my hangover anxiety is usually somewhere between moderately high and severely disabling. At this point it was off the charts. Grateful he wasn't awake yet, as I had no idea what, if anything, I should say to him, I stared at the ceiling of my tent, picking crusty little chunks of dried puke from my hair (at least now I knew where the stench was coming from) as I tried my best to recall how the night had gone down. I remembered everyone except for me and Santa having gone to bed. Then me drunk-crying about how hard it was being so far away from my girls and how much I missed getting hugs from them because "I never get hugs out here." OMG, *did I really say that?* And then asking Santa if he'd move his sleeping bag into my tent and sleep next to me because I didn't want to be alone. I also vaguely remembered, although it was more like an image from a movie clip rather than an actual memory, leaning out the door of my tent at some point to throw up. What I couldn't remember, though, was whether or not Santa and I had done anything other than fall asleep once we'd gotten in my tent. *Fucking vodka…*

As he began to stir I made a stupid joke about waking up to find a man in my tent, and then, like I always do when I'm nervous, started laughing. And not good laughing, either, but in that awkward, uncontrollable way that, even while you're doing it you (along with everyone around you) wish to god that you weren't. He turned to look at me. I could tell he felt uncomfortable. And then in all seriousness, with a tone that seemed to suggest he was hoping this would jog my memory rather than be new information, he said that I'd been insistent last night that he sleep next to me in my tent.

Instantly ashamed that my lame attempt to lighten the mood had caused him to feel the need to defend himself, I nodded in agreement to let him know I at least remembered that much.

"Yeah," I said, as he climbed out of my tent, "I can be pretty insistent when I'm drunk."

He popped his head back in and smiled at me as he reached for his sleeping bag. "You sure can."

Although tempted at that point to get to the bottom of what we had or hadn't done last night, I was too embarrassed to ask. I zipped my tent cover closed instead, cleaned myself up a bit, and changed into my hiking clothes. Then, bracing myself for a round of questions from the others as to why Santa had slept in my tent, I climbed out. To my surprise and relief, as I looked around, Santa was the only one there—sitting in his camp chair, smoking a cigarette, sipping his coffee. Everyone else had already cleared out. With no idea as to how early they'd all left, or whether anyone had even noticed Santa wasn't in his own tent, I figured we had a 50/50 chance of either being off the hook completely, or starring in the next up and coming bit of juicy trail gossip. I had no idea how we were gonna find out, though. If Santa knew, he wasn't saying, and I sure as hell wasn't going to ask.

Eager to put the site of my dumbass drunkenness behind me, I packed up as quickly as I could considering how hungover I was feeling, and then, leaving Santa to enjoy the rest of his morning in peace, I set out.

With my mind racing as my legs trudged on, the idea that I may have behaved in such a way last night that my friendship with Santa might now be in jeopardy felt like a self-inflicted stab wound, straight in my heart. I hadn't realized until now just how much he and the others and this sense of community we'd unknowingly been building out here had come to mean to me. And while I didn't want to lose any of it, I couldn't help wondering if I already had. *What if I had come on to him? And what if he thinks that I don't really like him—that I was just using him to keep me company?* The truth was, I did like him—very much. I wasn't sure if that made this whole thing worse, though, or better. *What if I've hurt him and he's sitting there right now cursing my name as he's drinking his coffee? He's been nothing but kind to me, and this is how I repay him?*

I got no further than half a mile before my self-shaming thoughts got the best of me. Hiding behind a bush just off the trail, huddled up and sobbing, I felt so out of sorts, for the first time since I started, I was seriously contemplating the idea of going home.

A few miles later, at the next water source, Santa caught up with me. We took turns filling our water filters from a slow pouring spout above an old trough full of water so nasty looking you wouldn't want to dip your toes in, let alone drink it. Not only were there things floating in it, but swimming, crawling, and growing, as well. I wasn't in the habit of using water purifying tablets in addition to my water filter, but in this case I did.

After 5-10 minutes of awkwardly attempting to make small talk, I decided to take what felt like a huge risk. "Can I ask you a favor, Santa?" I said, looking straight at him.

He looked at me inquisitively for a few seconds before answering, "Yeah."

"Will you let me walk with you? I know you're faster than me, and I don't wanna slow you down, but if you'd just let me try and keep up with you for a bit–" I paused, catching my breath. I'd been talking too fast, hoping to say what I needed before losing my nerve. "I– uh. I just–" *Why is this so hard?* "I could– um." *Oh my god, really? Just say it. The worst that could happen is he'll tell you no.* "I could use a friend," I finally managed, immediately embarrassed that it sounded more like a confession than a statement.

He gave me a look in that moment that not only assured me our friendship was still solid, but seemed to suggest that no matter what the favor was, if I was the one asking, the answer would always be yes. It caught me by surprise and left me feeling as if he'd just found a chink in my armor. *How did he do that?*

"Yeah," he nodded, smiling. "You can walk with me."

As we made our way from there, we took turns asking and answering all the usual get-to-know-you questions. Where'd you grow up? How many siblings do you have? What's your favorite holiday? We shared stories about our childhoods, our college years, and our past relationships. We compared our likes and dislikes. The more I found out about him, the more I liked him, and when we ran out of things to talk about we made up games to play and started keeping score.

Grateful for his company and pleasantly surprised by how at ease I felt around him, I kept up (thanks in large part, I'm sure, to him slowing down) until late in the afternoon, at which point I hung back as he went on ahead. Feeling much better by then, I'd completely forgotten about how, just hours earlier, I'd been upset enough to consider throwing the towel in.

The sun was just setting as I reached the 600 mile marker. I stopped for a selfie next to it and dug out my headlamp. It was still a couple of miles further until the next water source, and seeing as how I was down to my last few sips now, I had to at least make it that far before I could stop for the night.

As soon as it grew dark my focus shifted to staying upright, as in, not tripping over something and falling flat on my face on the ground. This was a hard enough feat in broad daylight given the number of roots, rocks, holes, pinecones, and dead branches likely to be lying across the trail at any given point in time. In the dark, though, especially in heavily wooded areas like this, where the trees were so thick they blocked out any extra light you might otherwise get from the moon, in addition to my already terrible night vision, it became downright dangerous.

With about a quarter of a mile left to go, a terrifyingly, wild-animal sounding screech pierced the silence. I stopped midstep, frozen. *What the fuck is that?* Straining to see in the darkness, my eyes searched desperately for some sort of answer. I couldn't see anything. I could hear it, though, breathing—loud, labored breaths. Whatever it was it sounded agitated, and close, although I couldn't tell where exactly, or worse, which way it was heading. With my heart pounding so hard I could feel the rhythmic throbbing of my pulse in my ears, I stepped, slowly and carefully, off to the side of the trail. Then, as quietly as I could, I slid my pack off and felt around for my bear mace. Not that I thought this thing was a bear, although it was definitely large enough, based on how big of a scuffle it had made in the underbrush. It's voice, though, sounded more like that of a cow or a horse or a big wild boar or something. With my finger on the trigger of my mace now, I debated as to whether or not my next move should be to try and scramble up a tree. A few seconds later, it tore off, noisily, through the brush—thank god, away from me. Once it was far enough away I could no longer hear it, I felt my shoulders relax, down and away from my neck. After a few slow, deep breaths I put my pack back on and got moving. This time though, rather than stuffing my bear mace back in my pack, I cinched it around my waist strap for easier access. Just in case.

Despite a rough start, by the time I finished for the day, I'd covered 24 miles—thanks in huge part to Santa for managing to help get me out of my head. This being the only water source within quite a few miles, there were already a dozen or so other tents set up by the time I got there. Although it was far too dark to be able to make out who all of them belonged to, I pitched mine in between Dirty Knux's and Santa's. Then I filtered some water, made some ramen, and fell asleep.

I hiked alone over the course of the next several days, through a dry, wideopen, sunbaked stretch ripe with cacti and sagebrush and Joshua trees. I logged 22 miles the first day, 27 the next, 22 on the third day, and then just over 26. All of which I spent lost in my mind—wandering further into the wilderness of my own irrational thoughts as the days and miles wore on.

My "Vodka Night" as I had since come to refer to it, had done a real number on me, and while walking with Santa had initially helped me feel better, without anyone else around to help me keep things in perspective, I was struggling. For one thing I was doubting my sense of belonging. And not just in regard to the trail itself or my fellow thru-hikers, but to life in general. In addition to that, I was also wrestling with the question of what exactly had driven me to be out here in the first place. Why in god's name was it so important to me to be doing this?

Knowing these questions would continue to haunt me until I could answer them, I kept sorting through old thought knots, desperately attempting to make sense of things. On the rare occasion I thought I might have just unraveled something useful, I would take a minute to record it on my phone.

> iPhone note May 28, 2021 at 8:30 am:
>
> *I think this is why I spend so much time alone. And why I isolate myself from other people and especially the possibilities of romantic relationships, especially long-term. I'm complicated. I'm messy. I'm constantly changing my mind. About some things. Other things I never change my mind about. I'm a walking oxy-fucking-moron… and that's exhausting. Hard enough for me to deal with, I can't imagine someone else volunteering to put up with it.*
>
> *I'm out here for a reason. I'm not sure what that reason is, but I have a suspicion this has something to do with it.*
>
> *I'm tired of trying to prove myself. I'm tired of trying to act like I'm okay. I'm not okay. I hurt. I'm scared. I don't want to feel like I'm always the odd man out…the one who doesn't belong. I'm trying to prove myself. I'm trying to prove that he was wrong in what he did to me. That I am worth loving. That I am worth having. That I am worth cherishing.*

In tears by the time I finished typing, I looked around for a flat spot, and sat down. Having just climbed a series of switchbacks, I was pretty high up at this point along a dusty, shrub-covered ridge. A quiet little valley stretched out below me. Leaning back against my pack, as I hadn't bothered to take it off, I read over what I'd just written. Again in tears by the end of it, a quote I'd come across a few years earlier came to mind. "When it hurts—observe. Life is trying to teach you something" (Anita Krizzan).

What is it you're trying to teach me, Life? In all of this pain.

I saw myself, five years ago. Lying on the floor in our bedroom closet, half of which now stood empty. His half. I was curled up in the fetal position, sobbing so hard I was gasping for air. The sight of the stark white, bare shelves, where that very morning all of his things had been, had sent me into a state of shock too intense for my mind to remain present with. I felt myself, falling, through a deep, black hole, as if an abyss of darkness was swallowing me. Had I been in my right mind, I would have been conscious of the floor beneath me, but I was not. I have no idea how long I laid there. It might have been 10 minutes, or it could have been several hours. I had lost all sense of time, along with my only chance at happiness, and all hope of ever truly being loved. *If he doesn't love me, no man ever will.*

I took my ball cap off and tilted my head up to the sky. Closing my eyes, I let the morning sunshine warm my face until my tears had dried. Then I plucked a sprig of sagebrush from the bush beside me, bent it in half, and rubbed it between my fingers to release its aroma. As it fell to the ground, I brought my hand up to my nose and breathed in the familiar scent, allowing it to bring me fully back to the present moment. *Had that really been five years ago now? And what had you taught me, Life, in the midst of all that pain?* I sat for a few more minutes, trying to connect the dots, until I felt as if I'd hit a wall. Too emotionally spent to keep at it any longer, I stood back up, brushed myself off, and got back to walking.

I had no idea if I would ever find the answers I was looking for. But the chance to be out here, asking these questions, and having unlimited amounts of time to be able to think things through and process all these emotions, felt like progress—and however slow my pace was with it, at least I knew I was heading in the right direction.

With just a few miles to go before reaching the junction that would get me into the next resupply town of Kennedy Meadows, a text came through from Santa. It said for me to come to a place called Grumpy's. That it was a blast and all the other hikers we knew were already there and that he had a bottle of wine with my name on it waiting for me. Anxious for a shower, as my hair still smelled faintly of puke, and more than ready for some company, I was tempted to press on. As soon as I found a place to sit down and cook dinner, though, I decided to stay put for the night. Having already covered 26 miles, I just didn't have it in me to go any further.

Day 36: May 31, 2021

I woke up early the next morning. Hungry for a real meal and excited for a shower, I wasted no time packing up. Once I passed the 700 mile marker, Just Kyle caught up with me. We walked together, single file, until the trail finally intersected with the main road heading into town. From there we hitched a ride together to Grumpy's with the first car that happened to pass us.

Unlike your usual run of the mill resupply stop, Grumpy's was a full on *experience*. A thru-hiker's paradise, in every imaginable way. The main building was a restaurant with a bar and a huge outdoor patio. It also served as a post office and had a little gift shop. As soon as a fresh-from-the-trail-hiker walked in through the door, the whole place stopped what they were doing, called out the person's trail name, just like they used to do for Norm on "Cheers," and then started cheering and clapping for them. It made you feel like you were some kind of celebrity. Like no matter what had transpired over the past 700 miles, the fact that you made it this far meant you'd earned your stripes, and all of these people, well, they were your people now. In fact, as soon as I walked through the door and was greeted with my own hearty, "BAM!" complete with hoots and hollers and "We're so happy to see you!" faces, the weight of how alone I'd been feeling began to lift.

The smell of bacon frying and fresh coffee brewing was so strong and enticing that my mouth started watering. And while it wasn't much past 10 in the morning, the whole place was packed with semi clean, already half drunk thru-hikers, drinking Bloody Marys and pitchers of beer, and eating giant plate-sized pancakes smothered in melting butter and syrup. After a round of hugs I got in line and ordered a breakfast burrito, a coffee, an orange juice, and a beer. Then I had a seat out on the patio between Lemonade and Santa and dug in while they caught me up on all the various shenanigans that had gone on there the night before.

Out behind where we were sitting was a covered wooden platform with a washing machine on one side and a couple of makeshift shower stalls on the other. And clothes lines running back and forth between there and the back of the restaurant—not an inch of which wasn't covered with washed, but not quite clean, sweat stained and/or tattered hiker laundry. Further out beyond that was a seemingly unlimited amount of wide open space where dozens of tents were pitched. Some by themselves, and others in little clusters. Granted, it was a bit of a dustbowl out there, it was flat and it was free so no one was complaining. Just up the nearest dirt road a little ways was a big, portable storage container that had been set up to serve as a gear shop with all the basic necessities a thru-hiker could want: jackets, base layers, hats, gloves, socks, shoes, water filters, dehydrated meals, protein bars, trekking poles, fuel canisters, sunglasses, chapstick, batteries, and ibuprofen.

Once I finished eating I braved the outdoor shower, slipped into my rain gear, and tossed my clothes into the washing machine. Then Santa and Lemonade showed me and Just Kyle where they'd set up camp, along with Hoops and Dirty Knux, and we pitched our tents there, as well. The next and final thing on my to-do list was to pick up my resupply package. Hailey had been kind enough to ship it off to me a couple of weeks ago. The General Store, where I'd arranged for her to send it, was a few miles up the road. Not wanting to walk there, I took a local up on his offer to give me a ride—telling me along the way all about how he was a former thru-hiker who'd decided to stay put after getting hired on at Grumpy's.

Along with all the usual provisions—food, body wipes, electrolyte tablets, chapstick, and sunscreen—this package also had my bear canister[22] in it, which, from this point until we made it all the way through to the other side of the Sierra Nevada mountains, we were all required to carry any scented items we had with us in one of these. That meant not only food and toiletries but trash, as well.

After signing for my package, the same friendly local drove me back to Grumpy's. Not having a free hand to open the door with once I got there, thanks to how big and bulky my box was, I went to push it open by backing up into it. Just as I did, someone on the other side of it pulled it open for me. A gentlemanly gesture on his part, but with no door to catch my weight I fell straight to the floor—so hard I actually bounced. His eyes got big and his face had, "I am SO sorry!" written all over it as I stared up at him in shock. I recognized him right away as I'd met him in passing a week or so prior—he wore a hat that was unmistakably unique, like a Chinese fisherman hat with a string under the chin to secure it if need be. He was in his early 20's most likely and looked athletic, like he probably played sports all through high school (as did the majority of those doing the trail). The whole room had gone quiet and all eyes were on us. Too embarrassed to be upset, I burst into laughter. As did everyone else at that point, himself included. He reached out his hand to help me up, and after dusting myself off, I playfully warned him, "If you don't have a trail name yet, this just earned you one."

---

[22] A heavy duty plastic container with a locking lid.

And from there on out, he was Doorman. That wasn't the only trail name awarded that day. Just Kyle became Prime, thanks to the hilariously excessive amount of supplies his boss had just shipped to him there through Amazon Prime. It was seriously enough food to feed multiple hikers for at least two full weeks. As he opened one package after another, everyone in the place gathered around him, cheering and calling dibs on various items as he held them up for us to see.

A little later that afternoon I wandered over to the gear shop and picked out a few things I thought my girls might like. Then I wrote each of them a letter, boxed everything up, and shipped it off. Then I called, both them and my parents, to check in and catch up.

And then, with everything done, I spent the rest of the day in party mode. We all did. It felt like summer camp on steroids having everyone I'd met along the trail so far (as well as loads of others I was just now meeting for the first time) all here in the same place at the same time. We ate. We drank. We laughed. We played games. We shared stories about the trail. And when the topic turned to our starting dates, we discovered a bunch of us had actually all started on the same day. The 26th of April. It was me, Dirty Knux, Lemonade, Walkie Talkie, the newly named Prime, Hoops, Music Box (a kind hearted, energetic, good-looking, 20-something I first met back at the hostel in Big Bear), and Santa, who we unanimously decided to include, even though, technically, he started the day before us. Dubbing ourselves "The 26ers Club," we declared ourselves tramily,[23] posed for a group photo, and raised a glass to our shared success of having completed the first 700 miles.

With the desert section now behind us, next up was the Sierra Nevada mountain range. Famous for its challenging to navigate, yet awe inspiring, scenery we all knew we were in for a treat. So much so, as we sat around a big table on the patio that night discussing it—long after the bar had shut down—our excitement was palpable.

---

[23] Trail lingo for a closely knit group of hikers, combining the words "trail" and "family."

As I sat there, polishing off my final beer before heading to bed, I was overcome with gratitude. How this group of total strangers had managed to form such a deep sense of community out of nothing more than the shared experience of traveling this trail was beyond me. All I knew was that I was happy and honored to be a part of it. I stretched out my legs and rested them across Santa's lap. He'd been in the seat next to me throughout most of the night. As I leaned my head back to catch a glimpse of the stars I felt him rest his hands on my shins. Having no reason to think of it as being anything more than a comfortable gesture between friends, until that is, Walkie Talkie, raising his eyebrows and pointing playfully at us, made me wonder if perhaps there was a chance Santa was beginning to fall for me—in the same way I was beginning to fall for him.

PART THREE

Tramily Ties

"Everything in nature
invites us constantly
to be what we are."

–Gretel Ehrlich

Day 37: June 1, 2021

We all slept in the next morning. All of us 26ers, that is. Along with someone Dirty Knux had recently befriended who'd also joined us in our camp spot, named Shit Kit. By far the funniest trail name I'd heard yet, she'd earned it, embarrassingly enough, after losing the bag she used to carry her trowel and toilet paper in. Whoever had then found it had seen fit to return it to its rightful owner by shamelessly holding it up in front of a large group of hikers while yelling out, "Who lost their shit kit?" In claiming her bag, the name had stuck.

After packing up, with Santa and I being the only ones among us wanting to head out yet, we decided to catch a ride together back to the trailhead. Once the guy we got a hitch from dropped us off, Santa turned to me and asked if I would sit with him for a minute. "There's something I want to ask you," he said.

"Sure." I rested my pack on the ground and sat next to him on a log on the side of the road.

"We're heading into the Sierras now," he began.

"Uh-huh," I nodded, curious and confused as to where this was going.

"How would you feel about doing the Sierras together?" he asked. I felt a fluttering in my stomach, and my palms start to sweat.

Are you kidding me? I would love to.

"I'd be game for that," I said, shrugging my shoulders, attempting to act nonchalant. Like the idea of having a 400 mile chunk of time to get to know him better wasn't as big of a deal as I thought it was. Certain the smile on my face was far too big to conceal my excitement, I turned away, pretending to look through my pack for something.

Between the heat, the hangovers we were nursing, and the newly added weight of our bear canisters, we didn't make it too far. A measly five miles up the trail from where we started, in fact, we found a nice, quiet, shady spot along the river and set up our tents. Not that I was complaining. On the contrary, having swapped out the trail runners I'd started in for the hiking boots I'd sent myself in my resupply box yesterday, it was nice to have a chance to ease my feet into wearing them.

First Hoops, then Dirty Knux and Shit Kit, and then Itsy Bitsy all stopped as they caught up with us and pitched their tents, as well. After cooling off in the river we all sat around brainstorming different types of food options. We were far enough into this now that people were beginning to grow bored with their regular routines. The tricky part, though, was trying to come up with things that not only tasted good, but were lightweight enough to carry, and high enough in calories to make it worth the effort.

We all turned in early, just after the sun set. I laid in my tent, unable to stop smiling, as I replayed my conversation with Santa about doing this next section together, too excited by the prospect of getting to know him better to sleep.

The next day was another hot one. Unlike the day before, though, Santa and I were the last in our group to pack up and get moving. It wasn't until midday that we caught up with the others, at a river crossing where a huge group had congregated in search of relief from the afternoon heat. Lining both sides of the river, a few were napping, some were swimming, and others, just chatting amongst themselves in the shade.

Leaving Santa to join the others, I found a shady spot in the grass where I could rest on my own. I was in a weird mood for some reason and wanted a few minutes alone to try and figure out why. I had just dug a snack out of my bear canister when an older man I hadn't met before introduced himself as Paco and asked if he could join me. Not wanting to be rude, I made space for him in the shade beside me. His English was broken and his accent was thick as he explained how he was from Hungary and that his wife had sent him out here to lose some weight for the sake of his health. He was funny and interesting and easy to like.

Spotting an empty, sandy bit of beach on the opposite side of the river, as Paco prepared to nap, I set out for it. With my boots and socks in my hands and my pant legs rolled up, I waded barefoot across the river and then upstream until I reached it. Setting my pack down, I then took all of my clothes off, and waded back in. Finding a shallow pool of sorts where a wall of river rock formed a bit of a dam, I laid down in it. As I lay there naked, floating weightless on my back, I stared up at the sky. It was bright blue with a soft white halo around the sun and not a cloud in sight. I took a few slow deep breaths. With my ears under water each inhale and exhale was amplified and dramatic sounding as the muffled gurgle of the current flowed past me. A warm gentle breeze blew across the few parts of my body bobbing above the surface—my toes, hands, breasts, and face. Smiling as I took it all in, I felt as if whatever weird mood I'd been in had just washed away. All I felt now was a sense of freedom, and very alive.

Back up on the sandy beach, I used my shirt to sit on and my pack as a pillow while the sun dried me off. I thought about how far I'd come since I started. And not just in miles. For one thing, I never would have swam naked in broad daylight with a crowd of people no more than 100 yards away. Hell, I'd never even been comfortable being naked in front of a lover unless it was in the dark. It felt liberating. It felt like progress.

Santa wandered over after a bit. "Can I join you, or would you rather be alone?" he asked, tentatively.

"Join me," I said, looking up at him, patting the ground next to me with one hand and shading my eyes from the sun with the other. As he made himself comfortable his question got me thinking—about what the weird mood I'd been in before had been all about.

As a somewhat introverted empath, not only did spending time around other people ('people-ing' as I call it) require a certain amount of energy, but, quite frequently, I need time alone in order to recharge. Seeing as how the whole time I'd been at Grumpy's I'd been surrounded by people it made sense, now that I thought about it, that my mood had been a byproduct of feeling worn out and depleted. Of course, that's not to say I hadn't thoroughly enjoyed my time there with everyone, especially those in my new little tramily, I'd just temporarily had my fill in the people-ing department.

Santa, understanding this about me, as we'd already had a couple of different conversations about this very thing, stopped halfway through untying his shoelaces, and asked hesitantly, "Are you sure you don't need a break from people?"

"You're not 'people' to me, Santa," I said, a little surprised by how comfortable I felt being candid with him. "Nothing about being around you feels intrusive or "too much" to me. It's kinda weird—," I confessed, shrugging my shoulders and smiling at him, "but I like it." Unsure how else to explain it, the truth of the matter was, no matter how much time I seemed to spend with him, I never wanted to not be around him. Hoping my transparency hadn't made him uncomfortable, I was relieved to see him smiling, too, as he finished taking his shoes off.

By the end of the day we covered 13 miles.

And then 13 more the next.

The terrain was changing, and while we hadn't encountered any extremely high passes yet, the smaller ones we'd been making our way up and over were beginning to offer some stunning views. I saw marmots for the first time—such cute, chubby, curious things. And with it being warm enough to cowboy camp, we'd simply been setting up our pads and sleeping bags in lieu of bothering with our tents. Priding himself on his ability to find the best campsites, Santa took the lead as far as planning where to stop each night.

The spot he'd chosen for us tonight was along the edge of a ridge near the peak of a mountain we'd just spent the day climbing. We set up camp and then scrambled up a steep set of rocks until we got to the highest point. With a view of the valley below stretching out before us for miles, we sat, side by side, together on what felt like the top of the world, watching the sun set.

Day 40: June 4, 2021

There was no denying Santa and I had two very different styles of hiking. Not that we hadn't both been in the habit of logging fairly big miles, but our paces were radically different. Santa, being faster, had established a routine of sleeping in, walking until mid-late afternoon, and then setting up camp with plenty of time left to hang out and relax before heading to bed. I, on the other hand, having a much slower pace, was used to waking up early and hiking all day, oftentimes well into the night. In an effort to merge our two styles we'd been keeping Santa's schedule, but at my pace. The upside of this was how much more enjoyable the whole experience had become. The downside, though, was that the number of miles we were covering each day had decreased significantly.

I couldn't help feeling bad, as it was my pace that was slowing us down. *If only I could walk faster.* And while my biggest fear associated with no longer being able to stick to my daily mileage schedule was that I'd run out of time before making it to Canada, I was also beginning to worry if I kept slowing Santa down he'd change his mind about wanting to hike with me.

The more I thought about it, the more I worried. Not the legitimate kind of worry that stems from anything that's actually been said or done, but the wildly imaginative, subconsciously self-sabotaging, making-things-up-as-I-go-along kind. Like in regards to the fact that Santa and I hadn't left each others' sides since Grumpy's. *Are you kidding me? Who wouldn't need a break from me by this point?* Or, that he'd even asked me to hike with him through this next section in the first place. *Maybe he just thinks he likes me because he doesn't really know me yet? Give him long enough and he's bound to change his mind.* And my pace, of course. *Who in their right mind would sign up to walk this much slower than they had to?* After doing so much of this to have genuinely convinced myself I was doing him a favor, I suggested, rather adamantly, that he go on ahead at his regular pace, and that I would catch up. Although initially reluctant, in the end he agreed, and for the next several hours we each hiked alone.

Once I finally caught up with him, he was with the rest of our tramily (minus Walkie Talkie and Lemonade) at Chicken Spring Lake. Having stopped there to wait for me, I was glad he'd had company. After saying good-bye to the rest of them, as they were all heading out again just as I got there, Santa and I then decided to stay put for the night. It was a beautiful lake, and with just enough sun left that it was still warm enough to go for a swim, we couldn't resist. We set our tents up next to one another in the sand along the shore, and then stripped down, and got in. The water was far too cold to stay in for long, although as always it felt good to at least be able to rinse off.

As the sun began to set, the wind started to pick up. Chilled and shivering, as I'd gotten my hair wet, I slipped into my yoga pants, a dry pair of socks, and the new long-sleeve, base layer shirt I'd, thankfully, picked up from the gear shop near Grumpy's. Whereas, up until now, it had always been warm enough to just sleep in my underwear and a tank top, unfortunately that wasn't going to cut it anymore as the elevation out here got higher. Then Santa grabbed his sleeping bag and climbed into my tent with me to warm up and escape the mosquitos while we ate dinner.

As night fell the wind grew stronger and colder. With both of us still in my tent at this point, we laid in our sleeping bags, next to each other, listening as it blew through the trees behind us, further up and away from the shoreline.

Being dark enough now we couldn't see each others' faces, and in a somewhat serious tone, Santa broke the silence, saying, "There's something I want to talk to you about."

Oh good lord, here it comes. The inevitable, "I don't think we should walk together anymore," or, "You're not actually as cool as I thought you were," talk.

"Okay," I said, bracing myself.

Much to my surprise, that wasn't it at all. Instead, he went on about how we obviously liked each other, and what would I think about taking things to the next level? Like dating, but trail style?

I was flattered, for sure, but also, conflicted. On one hand, I did like him—very much. But on the other, I didn't want to risk losing his friendship by giving this a go and having it not work out between us, romantically. There was also, of course, the issue of our friend group to consider. The thought of a future breakup potentially causing anyone out here to feel the need to choose sides seemed hugely unfair.

Aside from all of that, though, was perhaps the biggest reason. Plain and simple, I was scared. Of repeating old patterns. Of being the shiny new toy, and that once that newness wore off, so would his interest in me. I knew I had no trouble getting a man's attention. It was the keeping it part I had doubts about. And after close to 20 years of being married to a serial cheater, those doubts ran quite deep. As in, "I'll now have trust issues for the rest of my life, thank you, very much," deep. There hadn't been a time since, in fact, that these doubts hadn't plagued me. So much so, in the years since my divorce, my dating habits had consisted of letting a man get to know me all the way up to a certain extent (the point at which I began, on some level, to feel vulnerable) and then calling the whole thing off. Two weeks had been the average length of my relationships, if that short of a time even counts as such. The longest was a few months. And it's not even as if some of them weren't great guys who, most likely, would have been perfectly willing to stick around, and quite possibly grown to have loved me. I just never gave them the chance.

That wasn't something I could do to Santa. I knew him too well by this point and valued his friendship far too much to chance hurting him in that way. Not that I'd ever intended to hurt any of the guys I'd dated, I just had a better understanding now of what was at stake.

After taking a bold risk by sharing some of this with him, we laid there for a few minutes in silence. *What if I've been wrong all along, thinking of myself as unlovable? What if someone really could love me and the only reason it hasn't happened yet is because I always have my guard up? What if I were to do things differently this time, though? What if this here is a real shot at finding love and I pass on it and end up missing out? If I do give this a try, the worst that could happen is he changes his mind about me somewhere down the line. I can survive that—I've done it before. On the off chance, though, that this could work out, that he could love me, and that I could love him, and that we could be happy together—it could be the best thing ever.*

As if reading my mind, Santa broke the silence by suggesting, "If you take a chance on me, you won't regret it." Wanting nothing more than to believe him, I chose right then to do just that. After sharing the sweetest first kiss in all my years of first kisses, he then held me, close enough I could feel the warmth from his body, as we both fell asleep.

I woke the next morning feeling lighthearted and giddy, both excited by and optimistic about this new romantic twist. Santa made us both coffee, and then we packed up and headed out. We spent the next several hours going back and forth about whether to summit Mt. Whitney or not. One factor was that it wasn't actually part of the PCT, which, of course, meant we had the issue of my utter disdain for doing extra miles to consider. It was, however, *the* highest mountain in the Lower 48, which made the opportunity to summit it hard to turn down. So hard, no one else we knew was even considering not doing it.

Santa was ultimately leaving the choice up to me. Having already been to the summit on a previous trip, he was happy now to either take it or leave it.

More so than the extra miles, my biggest concern, really, was the increase in elevation we'd begun to experience. Or, more specifically, how my body was choosing to react to it. Over the past several days, as we'd slowly begun climbing higher, I was noticing that any time we got above around 9,500 feet, I was feeling it, big time. Shortness of breath, lightheadedness, and nausea mostly, but also, at least on the ups, every step seemed to require twice as much effort. Having heard about people suffering from elevation sickness before, this was my first time ever personally experiencing it. And the higher we climbed, without really ever descending much, the worse it seemed to be getting.

It was late afternoon by the time we reached the clearing where a side trail splitting off towards Mt. Whitney was waiting. Having still not made up my mind, and knowing we couldn't go any further until, one way or the other, I did, we stopped and set up camp. After soaking our feet for a bit in a nearby stream, we made dinner. Unable to find my spork[24] and too tired to properly search for it, I wiped off two of my tentpegs and used them like chopsticks. We then did one more round of pros versus cons regarding Mt. Whitney, made the decision (finally) to pass on it, and went to bed. With Forester Pass just ahead, which would have us climbing clear up into the range of 13,000 feet, I knew the elevation was gonna be a struggle. It felt like the smartest choice, at least for me, would be to reserve whatever strength and energy I had for actual trail miles.

I fell asleep thinking about Lemonade and Walkie Talkie. About how we hadn't seen them since the day we left Grumpy's. And about how, with Mt. Whitney being this year's finish line for them, now that we'd reached that spot, we wouldn't see them again. It made me sad. As if a little piece of what had made this whole experience as sweet as it had been so far had just been taken away.

Day 42: June 6, 2021

With the morning sun sparkling off droplets of dew in the grassy meadow surrounding us, we sat on a downed log outside our tents, drinking coffee and mapping out the day ahead of us on Guthooks—namely, how far between water sources and where to camp for the night. I made a packet of oatmeal while Santa had a granola bar, and then we packed up and set out.

Gaining nearly 3,000 feet in elevation over the next 13 miles, slowly but surely, we climbed to the summit of Forester Pass (with an emphasis on

---

[24] A spoon for all intents and purposes, with little fork-like prongs at the end of it.

"slowly," as I had to keep stopping, either to catch my breath, keep my dizziness in check, or wait for a wave of nausea to pass so I wouldn't throw up). As dumbfounded as I was annoyed with this still new-to-me phenomena of elevation sickness, what normally would have taken me five hours took roughly eight. Not that I wasn't used to being somewhat slower than most, but this was downright ridiculous. Even Prime, Dirty Knux, Hoops, Itsy Bitsy, and Shit Kit had blown past us along the way up—after already having summited Mt. Whitney that morning! Assuring us as they did that they'd wait for us at the top, once Santa and I got there, I was honestly a bit surprised to see they had, considering how much longer it took us. There they all were, though, clapping, whistling, and cheering us on as we took our last few victory steps. And there we all stayed for a good long rest, celebrating our newest accomplishment with sighs of relief, smiles of joy, and an overall feeling of pride, both in ourselves and for each other. And then, with our first major pass in the background, next to a sign reading, "Entering Sequoia National Park. Forester Pass. Elevation 13,200 ft," we posed for a group photo, and then began our descent.

Still not feeling great, as soon as we started descending, I began to notice my symptoms weren't nearly as bad. My pace, as well, began to improve, shifting back more towards normal. The only explanation I could think of for this was that perhaps the severity of my symptoms was somehow linked to my level of exertion. Whatever the reason, now that I was free to focus on something other than how miserable I was feeling or how drastically I was slowing Santa down, I began to take in the scenery. Void of any vegetation, as, at this elevation, we were well above the treeline, we made our way through a grayish-brown sea of rock and dirt. Here and there, in some of the smaller crevices and along the flatter, less sun prone areas, bright white patches of snow, still lingering from the previous winter, stood out in stark contrast. In some of the larger crevices lie dark blue pools of water with not yet melted ice of various sized chunks floating around on the surface. And out beyond us in the distance, for as far as you could see in every direction, was an endless array of mountains, as rugged and unyielding as they were majestic. *Now this is wilderness.*

Day 43: June 7, 2021

With another new pass to climb on the agenda today, this one named Kearsarge, the good news was that by the end of it we'd be in the next resupply town of Bishop—freshly showered, bellies full, drinking beer in some pub with our tramily. The bad news, unfortunately, was that my elevation sickness had now reached a new peak. If yesterday's summit was grueling, today's had more of a this-may-very-well-kill-me feel to it. The higher we climbed the more frequently I had to keep stopping (every 5-10 feet in some places) just to get enough oxygen. I had a splitting headache, and my stomach was churning, nonstop. My breathing sounded more like wheezing. My legs felt like they had 50 pound weights strapped to them, and I was so lightheaded I kept leaning to whichever side looked like it'd have a softer landing, in case I passed out.

As bad as I was feeling, though, I felt worse for Santa. With people, one after another, shuffling past us on their way to the top, I knew, if it weren't for me, he could just as easily be one of them. He insisted on staying with me, though. Even after offering several times to meet him up at the top if he wanted to speed up, he never went any further ahead of me than he could without keeping me in sight. As much as I hated the fact that I was holding him back, it was a comfort having him near— his constant reassurance that I was doing okay being the only thing preventing my frustration at my body's inability to adjust to these new heights from turning into a total meltdown.

What felt like an eternity later, we finally reached the summit. Excited about the idea of spending a zero day in town with him, and now, more than ever, ready for some downhill action, we began our descent into Onion Valley. Once we got to the parking lot at the bottom we hitched a ride into Independence. From there we got a second hitch into Bishop with a couple of guys in the weed business who, in the end, sent us on our way with a hefty free sample of their product to try.

We then checked into our hotel which, thankfully, Santa had lined up for us ahead of time, as, apparently, the whole town was booked solid now thanks to a big traveling rodeo. Everywhere you looked, the streets were lined with people wearing cowboy hats and Wranglers.

Having called dibs on taking the first shower, I did just that while Santa took a walk to the store. Among the many bags of snacks and drinks he came back with, was a gift. "For you," he said, grinning, hiding whatever it was behind his back.

"Aw, Santa, how sweet! Lemme guess what it is first, before you show me." Three wrong guesses later, he handed it over to me. It was a pretty, purple, plastic hairbrush, designed specifically, the label boasted, to help with tangles. Having not brushed my hair in so long that, more than once, I'd gone on and on about what an unruly mess of knots it was becoming, the fact that he'd been paying attention and then done something about it made me feel special.

Later that evening, a bunch of us met up for dinner at a Mexican restaurant. Santa and I, being the last to arrive, were ushered by one the hosts into a private room in the back to find everyone already gathered, family style, around one large table made up of several smaller ones that had been pushed together. The whole room suddenly got awkwardly silent.

"Well," Prime finally spoke up, a sheepish grin on his face, "we've all been talking. Would you two like to go by BAMTA for BAM plus Santa, or Santam for Santa plus BAM?" We all burst out laughing.

"They're onto us, Santa," I said, turning towards him, my face flushed with embarrassment.

After agreeing to BAMTA, Santa put his arm around me, and, leaning in for a kiss, whispered, "Guess this means we're official now." After dinner we all wandered over to the bowling alley, which was packed, for the rest of the evening.

The next morning, after sleeping in a bit, Santa and I planned out our meals for the upcoming stretch and did our resupply shopping. Then we spent the rest of the day lounging around, doing laundry, and catching up with our families over the phone. We wrapped up our last night in town swimming in the hotel pool and soaking in the hot tub where we met a group of girls participating in the rodeo and swapped PCT stories for tales of their rodeoing adventures.

Day 45: June 9, 2021

The next morning, as several of us were waiting to catch a shuttle together back to the trailhead, Dirty Knux pulled me aside. Because her tent had recently broken and she'd had no luck finding a new one in town within her budget, she was considering taking Santa up on his offer to give her his. Knowing that if she did, he and I would then be forced to share mine, she wanted to make sure I was okay with it first and let me know that she understood if I'd rather he hung onto his, in case things didn't work out with us.

Assuring her that Santa and I had discussed it and were on the same page, I thanked her, gave her a hug, and told her I was okay with it. Not that it wasn't a big deal. It was as big of a step in our relationship, actually, as moving in together would be back in the real world. We both felt comfortable with it, though—during the time we'd spent together so far we'd gotten to know each other quite well. Of course, we had the trail itself to thank for that. Things never would have progressed nearly as fast if we hadn't been out here.

Whereas normally in a new relationship, with schedules to work around and responsibilities to tend to, you only ever see each other for a few hours at a time, once or twice a week maybe, out here you pretty well have access to one another, nonstop. And when all you have to do each day is walk, you're in a very unique position to learn a whole lot about someone in a very short time. Like how they act when they're stressed out or tired and hungry. How they interact with other people, and how compatible the two of you are. If they know how to compromise. How they handle disappointment. Whether they're a pessimist or an optimist, introverted or extroverted, spontaneous or more rigid. What their interests, beliefs, and priorities are. Whether they're prejudiced and rude, or open-minded and kind. What scares, what excites, what motivates, and what calms them. What kinds of music and movies they're into. Their capacity to push themselves or deal with challenges, and their ability to relax. If they snore, how they sneeze, their go-to phrases, favorite swear words, and whether or not you can count on them. All of which might otherwise take years to discover, you can potentially find out in a matter of weeks, if not days, out here.

After tackling the long, winding trek back up and out of Onion Valley, we entered the legendary John Muir Wilderness. Being one of the few sections of the trail I'd actually heard first hand stories about from people, I was excited for the chance to finally be able to experience it for myself.

As we neared the top of Glen Pass towards the end of the day, the weather, unexpectedly, took a turn for the worse. The temperature, previously pleasantly warm, quickly plummeted to more of a shivering-cold-with-a-hint-of-incoming-wind-gusts that grew in intensity the higher we climbed. With no one, ourselves included, being properly dressed for it, I kept tugging my shirt sleeves down over my fingers and stuffing my hands in my jacket pockets. As a long time sufferer of Raynaud's,[25] I knew all too well the risk I was running in not keeping them warm enough. Having had no use for my gloves until now, though, the thought of standing around in the cold, pulling my gear out in search of them felt like too much.

As if racing us to the summit, as we continued our ascent, an ominous looking storm system we'd initially seen building off in the distance began heading straight for us. Doing our best to beat it there, and with Santa just a little ways ahead of me, we made our way as quickly as we could, back and forth, along the final set of switchbacks. Looking down as I heard someone call out, "Where the fuck did this come from?!" I

---

[25] An uncomfortable, unsightly phenomenon, triggered either by stress or the cold, in which a decrease in blood flow, turns one's fingers and/or toes, first red, then purple, and then stark white as a painful tingling-burning sensation progressively escalates until reaching the point of complete numbness; also referred to as Raynaud's Syndrome or Raynaud's Disease.

saw a guy by the name of Big Red huddled in the corner of one of the switchbacks digging his coat out of his pack.

"Right?" I answered back, taking comfort in the fact that as scary as it was to be walking straight into a nasty storm at this elevation, at least we were in good company.

Having lost sight of Santa for several minutes as he'd reached the top before me, I found him at the summit, shivering uncontrollably and eager to get moving. He'd chosen to wait for me, but in this bone chilling kind of wind that can turn your sweat soaked clothes against you in a matter of minutes, I felt bad that he had. Having grown far too cold now, myself, to put it off any longer, I rummaged through my pack for my gloves while he started out. By the time I found them and had swapped out my jacket and ball cap for my puffy coat and beanie, my teeth were chattering, and a few of my fingers were beginning to tingle. Taking a quick look around as I hoisted my pack back on, I stood, breathless—captivated by the sight of storm clouds melding into mountain ranges. Equal parts beautiful, dangerous, and exhilarating, it was the kind of scene that puts you in your place as one tiny human being, reminding you a single lifetime is but a blip on the timeline of the planet's history as a whole.

A deep rumbling of thunder brought me back to my senses. It was directly above me. *I've gotta get down from here.* Before I could, I first had to make my way across a narrow ledge of jagged rock spanning the length of the summit. It looked as sketchy as a tightrope considering how steep of a fall you'd be in for on either side of it should you misstep on a loose rock or, god forbid, lose your balance. There was no way around it, though. *Just start moving. And take it slow.* I took a deep breath and tightened the waist strap on my pack. *But not too slow—up this high is the last place you wanna be if lightning starts striking.* Within my first few steps the wind picked up so much that I was fearful it might actually blow me over the edge. I crouched down, my heart racing. Inching my way forward, I made it two or three feet when the wind, again, grew even stronger. Deafeningly brutal now, all I could do to keep from falling was to lean into it as I sat all the way down and gripped the rocks in front of me with both hands. *Fuck. I can't stay here. But I can't move, either, if this wind won't let up.* My eyes were watering, and I could feel my palms sweating inside my gloves. *Just don't look down.* Of course, then I did—my imagination painting a gruesome picture of my body tumbling in slow motion over the rocks on the way down to the bottom from this point. *Please, don't let me die here.* I took a deep breath. And then another. Looking up and ahead at how much further I still had to go, I saw Santa, turned back towards me, watching and waiting. *Just imagine yourself on the other side of this—safe and proud of yourself and getting the hell off of this mountain. Just because you're scared doesn't mean you can't do this.* Continuing to lean into the wind, I released my grip and, again, crouching, inched my way forward.

Once I made it all the way across I gave Santa a thumbs up that I was all good. He nodded, gave me a thumbs up in return, and then started off again. I breathed a sigh of relief, tugged my beanie further down over my ears, and took one last look at the death trap I'd just conquered. *I made it!* Another rumble of thunder and the fact that it was now beginning to snow were my cues to get going.

Wanting to put as much distance between myself and the summit as quickly as possible, I ran-walked as best I could on my now wobbly-from-the-strain-of-crouching legs.

A mile or so later, with Santa still a little ways ahead of me, I stopped to put my rain jacket on over my puffy, as well as my packcover. Now that we were getting lower in elevation and the temperature was rising slightly, what had been snow at the top was now sleet.

By the time I caught up with Santa it was a light, steady rain, which we continued on through together until we reached the next water source—a beautiful lake nestled deep in a valley at the bottom of the pass. The first thing we did was find a flat spot to set up camp. Although the 12 miles we'd managed to cover was a lot less than we'd been aiming for, Santa was in bad shape and needed to warm up. His hands had gotten so cold he was worried a few of his fingers might even be frostbitten, as he could no longer feel, much less move them. I set the tent up as quickly as I could while he stood, silent and shivering miserably, watching me. Once that was done I laid out his sleeping bag and helped him get into it. Then I lit the stove to start making our dinners and we each had a sip of vodka to warm us up on the inside. As he began to thaw out he started talking, telling me how impressed he was with my heartiness and how much better I was at handling the cold than him.

"Thanks for the compliment, Santa, but if you hadn't been standing around freezing your ass off waiting for me at the summit, you never would have gotten so chilled. So really, it's my fault," I told him.

He didn't agree. And while I refused to be swayed from my opinion on the matter, I was grateful for the chance to be able to help him. Especially considering all the times he'd been there for me with my elevation sickness—cheering me on, keeping me company, offering to lighten my load by carrying things from my pack for me. It felt good being able to take care of him for once.

By the time night fell he'd warmed back up and was feeling all better. Safely out of the woods from any possible threat of frostbite, as all of his fingers looked and felt normal now, we had a good laugh (or, at least I did as he kept saying, half joking, "It's too soon, BAM. Too soon!") at what he said he would from here on out refer to as his near death Glen Pass experience.

We woke the next morning to beautiful blue skies, ate breakfast, and packed up. Admiring the lake as the trail wound us around it, we then made our way out of the valley. After reaching the 800 mile marker, we summited Pinchot Pass. Thanks to my well developed fear of disappointing people, I continued to worry about how much I was slowing Santa down. He, on the other hand, continued to try and reassure me that he was fine with it and was happier taking his time with me than rushing ahead without me. By the end of the day, we'd made it 16 miles.

And then another 14 the next. This time through beautiful green valleys, across trickling streams, and over fields of fallen rocks as we made our way up and over yet another pass—this one named Mather. Well before nightfall, having descended far enough below the campfire restriction zone, which, in this section, was any elevation at or above 10,000 feet, we found a spot with a firepit and set up camp. Santa gathered wood while I set up the tent and then filtered some water from the creek below our site. After dinner we shared a couple of cocktails in front of the fire until we were both sleepy enough to head to bed.

At some point in the middle of the night I woke up to the sound of Santa shouting my name, "BAM!" Startled and confused, I sat up. "BAM—" he called out again, "where are you?!" His voice sounded frantic, but I had no idea why. I was clearly right here next to him.

"Santa?" I said groggily, rubbing my eyes, trying to understand what was happening. I could see him in the moonlight. He was sitting up, too, and his eyes were open, but he was staring straight ahead. *Is he talking in his sleep?*

"BAM!" he called out, now for the third time.

I reached over and, touching his face, turned it towards me. "Santa," I said softly, "I'm right here." He stared at me, blankly. "Santa?"

Finally seeing me, he put his hands on my shoulders, as if he needed to touch me in order to prove I was real. "BAM, you're here!" he said, genuinely sounding both surprised and relieved. "And you're okay," he added, quickly looking me over.

"Yeah, Santa," I said, still confused, "I'm alright." Pulling me to him, I could feel his heart beating, hard and fast, as he held me close for a minute. "You must have had a bad dream, Santa," I said. Wide awake now and with my eyes having better adjusted to the darkness, I noticed a streak of blood running down the side of his face. "Santa, you're bleeding!"

"What?!" he said. "Really?" Raising his fingers to where I was pointing, he winced as he touched his cheek. "What the hell?" He seemed just as confused as I was. We sat in silence, staring quizzically at one another. After a few too many awkward seconds, I spoke up.

"Santa, what's going on?" I asked. "How'd you get all bloody?"

"Okay," he started, "but just—" He paused, as if searching for the right words, and then took a slow deep breath before continuing. "Can you just answer something for me first?"

I nodded, now curious as well as confused.

He looked at me, intently, as if to make sure he had my full attention. "Did we—," he began, "did we— did we— go — somewhere? Just now?" I could feel my face scrunching up, into one of those involuntary expressions you make when something leaves a bad taste in your mouth. "Or—" he continued, "or, have we been here— the whole time?"

Trying hard to relax my face so he wouldn't think I thought he was sounding like he'd lost his marbles, it occurred to me that perhaps I just didn't understand the question. "Here?" I repeated. "Do you mean 'here' like, as in, in the tent? And 'the whole time' like, as in, since we went to bed, and we've been asleep?"

He nodded.

Is he fucking with me? Studying his face for any sign I could find to help me figure out whether or not he was serious, all I could tell for sure was that he was still waiting for me to answer. "Yes, Santa," I said sternly, hoping to put an end to this game, if that's what it was, "we've been here. The whole time."

As he let out a long, slow, deep breath I saw his shoulders relax, down and away from his ears. I felt bad for not noticing he'd been so tense he'd been holding his breath. "I had to have been dreaming," he said, finally explaining, "but man, it was so real! We got a hitch. At a trailhead. From some people—some rough looking people. And I'm not sure where we were going, but we were in the bed of a pickup truck. You, and me, and a bunch of other hikers. But then—" he paused, as if not wanting to revisit what his mind was remembering, "they were kidnapping us. And then, you—you weren't there. And I was calling out to you because I needed to find you—because you weren't okay."

"Aw, Santa, it's okay, I'm right here," I said, reassuringly, placing one of his hands on my face. He stroked my cheek with his thumb and smiled back at me, sleepily. "And nobody's kidnapped us," I added.

"And—" he paused, raising his eyebrows and cocking his head to the side, as if a little unsure he should even be asking, "I've been here the whole time? And you—you've been here the whole time, too?"

"Uh-huh," I said, nodding, a tad bit unsure all over again whether or not I should be taking him seriously. Rather than overthink it, I reached for my headlamp and turned it on to get a better look at his face. He had about an inch and a half long scratch across his right cheek. It didn't look serious, and the blood had dried. "We'll clean it up good in the morning," I assured him. "You must have gotten out of the tent to pee while you were in the middle of your dream, like sleepwalking, and cut your cheek on a branch while you were walking around in the dark."

Needing to pee, myself, at that point, I gave him a kiss as I climbed over him and out of the tent. By the time I got back in, just a few minutes later, he was already sound asleep again.

Day 48: June 12, 2021

The next day was a hot one—a far and welcome cry from our time on Glen Pass a few days earlier. We stopped along a river around lunchtime, found a calm spot where the water was pooling behind a large pile of rocks, stripped down to our underwear, and went for a swim. Then we laid out, side by side, on top of one of the larger, smoother, boulder type rocks, leisurely allowing the sun to dry us as we discussed underwear style preferences and compared our hiker trash tan lines.

Feeling refreshed, we set our sights on Muir Pass. Santa, having previously done the John Muir Trail,[26] had been telling me stories about his past adventures and pointing out landmarks ever since the PCT had joined up with it back at Forester Pass (all but 41 of the JMT's 211 miles overlap the PCT). Feeling as if I had my own personal tour guide as we began our ascent, he described a cool hut waiting for us at the summit, and then gave me a bit of history about John Muir himself. Happy enough to listen, as talking on the ups made me feel winded, I was grateful for the distraction.

About halfway to the top, we rounded a bend to reveal a scene so picture perfect and serene looking it stopped me in my tracks. Overcome with emotion by the sheer beauty of it, tears filled my eyes as I slowly took it all in. Against the backdrop of a bright blue sky was a jagged, grayish, granite type mountainside speckled with pine trees. A shallow, slow moving stream gurgled past me before dividing itself between several small ponds. And all around me, a bright green, grassy meadow was dotted with cheerful little patches of fuchsia colored wildflowers.

Having forgotten for a moment that I wasn't alone, I hollered ahead to Santa to get his attention, and told him I needed a minute. I then took my pack off and sat down in the grass beside the stream. As tear after tear dropped from my cheeks, leaving little wet spots on my pants, I took a few slow, deep breaths to help ground myself. Plucking a petal from one of the wildflowers next to me, I rubbed it softly between my fingertips before bringing it up to my nose and inhaling deeply. Although faint, it had a comfortingly familiar, sweet, earthy scent to it. Then, dipping my fingers in the water I drew a figure eight, around and around, sunlight sparkling playfully along the surface. The fact that all this natural beauty was here and continually happening, regardless of whether anyone was, or would be, present to witness it, felt like a cruel misfortune. Pondering how few people in the world would ever get the chance to see this, I found myself wishing I could share it.

---

[26] Commonly referred to as the JMT.

Santa, having backtracked in my direction, gave me a slight look of confusion when he got close enough to see I'd been crying. As he sat down next to me, I did my best to explain my tears to him, "It seems surreal that after so many years of planning and dreaming about this, that I'm finally out here. It's overwhelming, Santa. In a good way. I feel so lucky to be doing this—and with you."

He gave me a big hug and a slow, soft kiss. "I feel lucky, too," he said, smiling. Wiping away what was left of my tears with the back of my hand, I drank some water and then took a few pictures before putting my pack back on.

Following behind Santa as he led the way, I stopped to take one last look as we approached the next bend—knowing this had been one of those rare moments in life when, even as it's happening, you know you'll never forget it.

The higher we climbed, the more snow we started to see. Thankfully, not much along the trail itself, though, and the few patches we did end up having to walk through were neither soft enough that we had to posthole, nor slick enough that we had to dig out our microspikes. All the lakes we were passing still had thin sheets of ice floating around in them as well.

Once we reached the summit, we took our time checking out the hut Santa had told me about. He was right about it being impressive. And not just because it was a rarity to see a manmade structure of this size out here in the middle of nowhere, but because it had been built well enough to have withstood the test of time. Close to 100 years old now, people were still using it, quite frequently by the looks of it, as an emergency shelter. Complete with a wood burning stove and a chimney, it was a sturdy looking, octagonal shaped room constructed out of granite slabs. The only way in or out was a big wooden door that was split in half, horizontally, allowing you to swing the top half of it open while keeping the bottom half closed. Fastened to a rock lying on the ground near the entrance was a plaque dedicating it to the memory of

John Muir. "Muir Hut," I read aloud from it, tracing the letters with the tips of my fingers as I crouched down beside it.

After seeing all there was to see, taking a few photos, and chatting briefly with a group of JMT hikers, who, unlike us, were headed south, we began our descent.

We got a couple more hours in before deciding to stop, putting our grand total for the day at 18 miles, once we did. With that being the furthest we'd been able to manage since entering the Sierra section, it appeared that my body—*thank god*—had finally risen to the challenge of acclimating to the elevation.

Santa scoped us out a sweet spot to camp. We had to scramble a bit to get to it, but the lakeside view we had from our tent once we did was well worth it. A mirror image of the gigantic mountain towering in the background, lay perfectly still on the water's surface. We sat, watching the sky turn a blood orangish-pink as the sun set, and then planned our mileage goals for the next few days over dinner.

Day 49: June 13, 2021

I woke up feeling energized. Although even my pre-elevation sickness pace had been much slower than Santa's, the prospect of finally being able to log a more normal number of miles again was exciting.

In an effort to get our mileage back on track we'd decided to try a new strategy—one that would play to both of our strengths. With Santa, of course, being able to go farther faster, and me, being more slow and steady, I was also a morning person who had no trouble getting started as soon as I woke up, whereas Santa was, well, not. All things considered, the plan was for me to start out early, by myself, getting enough of a head start on him that by the time he got going and eventually caught up with me we'd be in a much better position to be able to cover more miles.

Eager to put our new strategy to the test, I packed up, and then gave him a kiss. "See you in five minutes, Santa," I said, joking, as I cinched up my pack straps.

"Five minutes, huh?" He laughed. "Might be more like an hour. But I'll catch you," he said, as he winked at me.

"You'd better," I called out playfully over my shoulder.

After scrambling my way back up to the trail, I waved down to him. Sipping his coffee and enjoying a cigarette, he smiled up at me and waved back.

I started off, quickly finding my rhythm, as in the sky, to the east, the sun began to peek up over the highest ridge. Soon casting its light on the lake, a million tiny sparkling diamonds appeared to dance on the surface. Once it rose a bit higher I stopped for a minute, turned my face towards the sun and, closing my eyes, allowed myself the simple pleasure of feeling its warmth on my skin.

After an hour or so, the trail crossed a river where a row of rocks had been set up as a means of getting from one side to the other. Scanning the opposite shore to see where the trail would pick back up once I got there, it occurred to me that I hadn't crossed a river without Santa by my side since we'd left Kennedy Meadows. The mere thought of him being enough to make me start missing him, I maneuvered my way across, wondering when he'd catch up to me and hoping it was soon.

Surprised by how quickly I'd gone from enjoying my own company to longing for his, as I walked, I thought back over the past month and a half since we first met. About how, right from the start, he'd been nothing but kind to me. About how, each time I'd learned something new about him, like the fact that he was left-handed, or originally from England, or preferred milk chocolate to dark and thought white chocolate was disgusting, I'd only grown to like him more. About all the miles and the meals we'd shared, and all the fun we'd had together in different resupply towns. About how well we worked as a team to make a plan or solve a problem. About how accepting he'd been and how much tenderness he'd shown me each time I'd risked being honest with him about something I was thinking or feeling. About our first kiss, and each one after, and how his touch made me feel both safe and alive. About how, the more time we seemed to spend together the more connected to him I felt. And about how, by this point there was no doubt about it—I was falling in love with him.

After much longer than either of us had been expecting, he finally caught up with me. Not that it had taken him so long because I'd suddenly become *that* fast, although my pace was certainly improving. He'd actually taken a wrong turn after the river crossing, and not realizing his mistake until he'd gone far enough to hit a dead-end, then had to backtrack.

Happy to have him back by my side, we continued on, together—managing another 18 mile day by the time we stopped to set up camp for the night.

The next day, as well, was another 18 miler, as we exited the John Muir section and then summited Selden Pass.

Day 51: June 15, 2021

Around noon on the following day, in keeping with this section's theme of, "another day, another pass," we reached the top of Silver Pass. Doorman, who we'd spent the better part of the morning passing and being passed by, was there. We found him sitting alone on a ledge overlooking a huge valley, playing, of all things, a harmonica. The tune he was playing sounded hauntingly beautiful. We sat, listening quietly, until he was finished. Then we all dug our food packs out and ate lunch, sharing with each other as we did about what had prompted us to do the trail in the first place.

As Santa and I continued on our conversation shifted, as it always did heading into the next resupply town, to the many luxuries of civilization we were looking forward to—things that, back in the real world, are so readily available they're usually taken for granted. Like running water and electrical outlets and fresh fruits and veggies. Having chairs and benches to sit on. Toilets and showers and ice cream and wifi. Proper mattress with clean bed sheets, warm blankets, and comfy pillows. The taste of a cold beer, the feel of carpet between your toes, the smell of laundry detergent. Menus and tables, utensils and napkins. Being able to wash your hands in a sink, see your face in a mirror, or drink from a glass.

When thru-hiking, the most crucial element in regards to being able to successfully engage in these types of mental indulgences, especially food cravings, is timing. You cannot do it too soon. Allowing your mind to drift anywhere near these types of thoughts when you're still days away from being able to satisfy any of them, and you run the risk of pushing yourself to the brink of a mental breakdown. It's just simply too much for anyone to handle. Only once you know for certain that you're no more than a matter of hours away from being close enough to somewhere your cravings can be met, is it then safe to do so.

Thankfully for us, with getting into Mammoth Lakes being the first item on our agenda in the morning, we were good to go at this point.

We reached the 900 mile mark later that evening. *900 miles—Holy shit! Only 100 more till 1,000. And 1,000 miles—now that's gonna be impressive.* After taking a few selfies and congratulating each other on having made it this far we pressed on a little further, getting ourselves as close to Mammoth Lakes as possible without actually getting off the trail. Having pushed past our recent daily average of 18 miles, to 22 this time, I then set up the tent while Santa made dinner.

Day 52: June 16, 2021

By the time we got down to the trailhead parking lot the next morning, at least a dozen other thru-hikers were already there, all of them anxiously awaiting rides into town. With so many of us there all at once, only a lucky few were finding hitches. Not that the parking lot wasn't full of cars, but considering most of them belonged to day hikers who likely wouldn't return soon, the odds of us hitching out of here weren't looking good. Thankfully, unlike any of the other resupply towns we'd made our way into yet, Mammoth Lakes had a trolley service that ran hikers all the way into town right from the trailhead.

As we waited for the next one to arrive, we made ourselves comfortable at one of the picnic tables, and started talking with a few other hikers we hadn't met before. One of whom, a somewhat younger single dad who's trail name was Soccer Mom, had some pretty funny stories about his experiences so far on the trail.

Our first stop, unsurprisingly, once we got into town was a diner. Music Box, Hoops, Dirty Knux (now just "Knux"), and Prime were all waiting for us and had saved us seats. The next table over was full of other hikers we'd all become friends with as well. There was Produce, a big-hearted, easygoing, friend-to-all kind of guy. And Delayed, who, having already hiked the whole PCT before, had been given his trail name thanks to the fact that, for one reason or another, he'd kept getting held up and having to delay his plans. And then there was Craftsman, who was from Germany and in his mid 20s. He had a thick accent and was a fast hiker, although never in such a hurry that he wouldn't chat for a bit as he passed you. He'd earned his trail name, impressively, because he'd handcrafted much of his own hiking gear, like his trekking poles and his pack. It was fascinating to hear him tell how he'd thought to assemble things and how sturdy and functional they ended up being. And a girl named Leathermaid, who'd started the trail carrying a Leatherman tool (she'd since ditched for something lighter).

Santa ordered the biggest breakfast on the menu, as always, and I splurged on a plateful of pancakes smothered with soft, still-melting butter and warm maple syrup. After cleaning our plates, we said goodbye to Music Box. Having beaten us all there by a few days, and only sticking around for as long as he had so he could say hi to Santa, he was now heading back to the trail.

With our stomachs satisfied, we made our way to where we'd be staying. Santa had reserved a suite large enough for Hoops and Knux and

Prime to join us. We spent a fun couple of nights there—hot tubbing, watching movies, eating, relaxing. The hotel had a public washer and dryer, too, which was a nice switch from having to make a whole separate trip to a laundromat. After planning our meals for the next stretch, we all ventured out, using the town's bus system, to resupply. On our last morning there, Hoops volunteered to cook us all breakfast, as our room was equipped with a kitchen. Gathering around the table once he had everything ready, to a family style feast of blueberry pancakes, scrambled eggs, bacon, banana bread, fresh mangoes, orange juice, and coffee, we were all quite impressed. We all cleaned up afterward and then Santa and I stayed behind while the three of them caught a trolley back to the trail. There was something he wanted to do that could only be done in town. That "something" being to watch his beloved home country of England play Scotland in the Euros that afternoon. Having learned early on that he was a diehard football (as in soccer) fan, and with this match in particular being especially important to him, I'd agreed to hang out and watch it with him before we made our way back to the trail. Possessing very little knowledge of this sport, myself, he patiently explained things as the match progressed. At halftime we FaceTimed his dad and younger brother who were watching it as well. After getting a chance to meet them both, I let the three of them talk football. We ate lunch during the second half in the little pub where we were watching it. Then, once it was over, we caught the next trolley back to the trail. Sadly for Santa, the game was a goalless draw.

Day 55: June 19, 2021

The Devil's Postpile National Monument was our first stop the next morning—a fascinatingly unique geological structure made up of countless hexagonal shaped columns. Being close to a main road as well as a major campground, the whole place was swarming with tourists. We wove our way through them, stepping to the side when necessary, and taking a few pictures of our own as we explored.

From there, the landscape made it nearly impossible not to notice the fact that we were easing out of spring and into summer. Bright pink and yellow wildflowers were blooming all over the place. And everywhere you looked, from the grassy meadows, to the leaves in the trees, to the many shrubs and bushes, the whole earth appeared to be clothed in one shade or another of green.

Sixteen miles later, towards the end of the day, we reached Thousand Island Lake. Knux, Hoops, and Prime, as well as the two most recent additions to our tramily, Soda Pop and Matt, were all already there, hanging out on a big rock overlooking the lake. Soda Pop, not much older than my girls, was an easygoing ginger who'd just graduated from college, and Matt, closer to my own age and the even keeled, dependable kind, was one of the few hikers left to make it this far without a trail name.

Santa scoped out a spot big enough for all of us to camp together for the night, complete with a firepit. Eager to get in the water before the sun started setting, I hurriedly pitched our tent, and leaving everyone else at the campsite, ventured down to the lake. Ever since seeing a little blue and white duck icon on Guthooks that morning, indicating there'd be a sizable lake ahead, I'd been daydreaming about going for a swim. Stripping down to my underwear, I left my clothes on the shore, and waded in. Not for long though, as the mountains surrounding us were still capped with snow, and the water was freezing. As always, it still felt good to rinse off, though. After a long day of sweating under the weight of a full pack, a lake like this or a river was the next best thing to being able to shower out here.

Back up on the shore I laid my shirt out and sat on it. Studying each wave as it rolled in and broke on the sand, I had the whole place to myself as what was left of the late afternoon sun warmed me back up.

After a while a woman came down to where I was to filter some water. Her name was Shawnté, and the more we talked, the more I liked her. She told me about the multi-day, all girls, backpacking trip she was on with some friends. And how, not only had she also done a big chunk of the PCT, she'd actually written a book about it.[27] After introducing her to the rest of the tramily once they finally came down to the beach, she stayed with us while they went for a quick dip and then Santa fixed a cocktail that we all passed around. All of us minus Prime, that is, as he didn't drink. Impressed with what the rest of us had by now come to regard as Santa's signature trail drink, she asked him what was in it.

"It's like a hiker trash version of an Old Fashioned," he answered, sounding flattered that she had asked him. "First, you take a 1-liter sized Smartwater bottle," he said, holding one up. "Fill it about two-thirds full of filtered water. Then add a lemon-lime electrolyte tablet, and a couple shots worth of honey flavored Jack Daniel's whiskey."

"You should call em 'Old Trashioneds,'" Shawnté suggested.

After voting unanimously in favor of adopting this new name, we enjoyed one more round before parting ways with our new friend and heading back up to our campsite. We ate dinner as the sun set and then gathered around the fire for the rest of the evening, discussing the various highlights and challenges the next section of the trail had in store for us.

Once we'd all gone to bed, with Santa snoring softly beside me in our tent, I thought about Shawnté and how fun it was to have met her. Then I thought about Knux and Hoops and Prime. And Walkie Talkie and Lemonade. Chaparral and Mama Bear and Nivil and Music Box. Doorman and Boomerang. Baby and Produce. Booty and Bosco and Itsy Bitsy. And Santa, of course—especially Santa. I'd met so many amazing people out here. Each of them with a unique backstory, set of strengths and abilities, and reason for being out here. For all their differences, though, I couldn't help thinking it was the one thing they all seemed to share that had drawn me to them. Because I shared it, too. Born out of a desire to feel alive rather than merely exist, they all possessed the same adventurous, open-to-new-experiences type of mindset. It was something I deeply admired, and because of the many years it had taken me to learn how to cultivate it in myself, it was something I could easily recognize now when I saw it in others.

---

[27] "Hiking the Pacific Crest Trail: Southern California" by Shawnté, Salabert.

Not that I'd signed up for this journey in the hopes of making friends. On the contrary, I'd come out here to be alone. And I'd done that. Initially. Somewhere along the way, though, through my interactions with each of these people, something had shifted. Especially since I'd left Grumpy's and teamed up with Santa. And not that I wasn't still intent on finishing—I very much was. But my emphasis was no longer on simply logging miles and proving to god knows who that I was strong enough and smart enough to be out here doing this by myself, but rather on embracing the entire experience as a whole. Most notably, the people. And my tramily in particular, who, to my amazement, genuinely seemed to want me here. Until now, I couldn't remember a time in my life when I hadn't felt like an outsider. I'm sure more often than not, at least to some degree, that this had been my own doing. I'd chosen to keep my distance as a sort of self defense mechanism to avoid the possibility of getting hurt or being rejected. Out here, though, things were different. There was nowhere to run off to, for starters. You couldn't just leave or not answer your phone or unfriend someone on social media like you could back in the real world when you felt uncomfortable or someone rubbed you the wrong way. We were all walking the same trail, stopping in the same towns, and sharing the same resources. Which meant, to a certain extent, we all needed each other. And because of that, we had all grown accustomed to helping each other. Whether by leaving comments on Guthooks about water sources drying up, sharing food with someone who was running low, or keeping someone company for a few miles when they were struggling. And we were all, at times, struggling—for different reasons and in different ways—as the trail repeatedly insisted on testing our limits, pushing us farther out of our comfort zones than some of us had ever dared to wander before. It was no wonder this incredibly taxing, sometimes terrifying experience had served to solidify us as a unit. We had come to know and even grown to love each other over the course of the last almost 1,000 miles, and the respect we now held for each other was undeniably mutual. *What a rare and beautiful opportunity it is to be out here doing this*—was my last thought before finally falling asleep.

Day 56: June 20, 2021

With today's mission being to get ourselves up and over Donahue Pass, one by one, everyone started out as they finished packing up after breakfast.

It also happened to be Father's Day and, as I currently had no cell service, I was hopeful we'd reach a spot at some point during the day where I would so I'd be able to call my dad.

All morning long, we passed one pristine lake after another, each more inviting than the last, especially as the temperature began to warm up. Finally giving in to the temptation to stop and enjoy one, we treated ourselves to a quick (on account of the water being freezing cold) swim and a picnic around lunchtime.

Checking my phone every quarter to half mile eventually paid off as we began to near the summit and the little bars in the top corner of my screen indicating I had service lit up. We found a large rock to sit on and tried Facetiming my parents. Once they popped up on the screen it occurred to me that I hadn't seen their faces in over 2 months. It felt good to finally connect. I wished my dad a Happy Father's Day, and introduced them to Santa. They sounded both relieved and excited that, now that I'd found myself a hiking partner, I wasn't out here alone. We didn't talk too long, as they were out at a restaurant, and after ending the call we pressed on to the summit, and then began our descent.

Day 57: June 21, 2021

Next up on the map was Tuolumne Meadows—a small, yet welcome resupply point nestled inside Yosemite National Park. All within one building, was a convenient store on one side, selling grocery items and souvenirs, a post office in the middle, which was simply a window you walked up to, and on the other side was the "Tuolumne Grill," which served things like burgers, grilled cheese sandwiches, and chili dogs. Off to the side there was also a big outdoor area with picnic tables and sun umbrellas and public restrooms.

Santa and I grabbed a few things at the store once we got there. Then we ordered some lunch and joined Delayed, who was already sitting at one of the picnic tables. As the three of us were talking, a group of women at the table next to us apparently overheard us. After apologizing, first for eavesdropping, and now for interrupting, they took turns asking questions about what doing the PCT was like. Having just finished up a weeklong backpacking trip themselves, they told us they admired us for being out here for as long as we had, offered each of us a beer, and wished us good luck on finishing. Feeling a bit like celebrities as we pressed on from there, Delayed kept us company for the next several miles.

We stopped again once we reached Tuolumne Falls. The waterfall, being as impressively big and beautiful as it was, was crowded with hikers—taking pictures, making videos, and cooling off in the water. After setting up camp a little further down the trail, we backtracked to a swimming hole that had caught our eye as we had passed it. Not nearly as crowded as the larger falls, it had a big sandy beach, and its own, much smaller, waterfall.

It had pretty well cleared out by the time we finished swimming, other than another couple who were car camping nearby. We got talking with them about where we were all from, and once they found out we were doing the PCT, they, too, offered us goodies—this time in the form of weed. Having never been a real fan of smoking pot (although in all fairness, I'd only ever tried it once, back in college), I would have happily preferred another beer—not that the generosity behind their kind gesture wasn't appreciated. Santa added it to our ever growing collection of just such "donations" once we got back to our campsite. Then he built us a fire while I set up our bedding, and after dinner we called it a night.

Day 58: June 22, 2021

Having hiked together for the past three weeks now, Santa and I were definitely finding our groove. Every morning he'd sit, just outside the tent, and make us coffee while smoking a cigarette. Then he'd ask for my tin cup, fill it up, and bring it back to me, where I'd sit, still in the tent in my sleeping bag all cozy and warm, and take my time drinking it. Then I'd get dressed and pack up the tent. He would carry the bulk of our food supply, and I would carry the tent and our sleeping bags. Most days, I'd start out before him, and he'd catch up an hour or two later. During that time, while I was walking alone, I'd often find myself thinking about him. Marveling at how open I was to letting him get to know me, especially considering how guarded I'd been in all of my previous, post divorce, attempts at romantic relationships. And without any of the normal trappings of everyday life back home, even. No make-up or no nail polish or jewelry or perfume. No outfits other than the same one I wore every day out here. No income coming in, no vehicle, no home full of furnishings. No way to hide the complexity or the messiness of my moods or emotions. And the fact that he still seemed to like me, in spite of my utter inability out here to try and impress him as I normally would, by showing him only the parts of myself I felt confident enough about to risk sharing with everyone, that's what amazed me the most. And the more this kept happening, as he consistently kept meeting this realest, rawest version of myself with acceptance, the more I could feel my fear of rejection lessening, as if an old wound was finally healing. It made me feel beautiful and special and capable of anything, and knowing that I had him to thank for it, made the feelings I was beginning to have for him grow.

Once he caught up, he'd often share one of his earbuds with me, and we'd listen to music or a podcast together. He'd even started creating a playlist of all my favorites on Spotify, titling it, "BAM's Jams." And then, in the evenings, he'd boil the water to make us our dinners while I inflated the air mattresses, set the tent up, and laid out our sleeping bags.

Today being no different, we followed our routine to a T, logging 18 more miles and finding a private little riverbed island to camp on. The only downside to this site was the mosquitos, which, despite dousing ourselves in bug spray every 15-20 minutes, as well as lighting a campfire, eventually got so bad we hung out in the tent to escape them.

Day 59: June 23, 2021

It was no better the next morning. If anything, they seemed to be worse. As soon as we stepped foot outside the tent we took turns spraying each other all over with bug spray. Santa made us coffee as I hurriedly packed up the tent and then filtered enough river water to get us through the first half of the day. We drank our coffee much quicker than usual, swatting and swearing as they continued to swarm, and then started out in the hopes of outrunning them.

It wasn't until the trail finally led us away from the river that we experienced any sort of relief, though. And even then, it was only temporary. For the rest of the day, every time we got anywhere near water, which, given the surplus of rivers and lakes in this section, was surprisingly often, there they were again, as numerous and bothersome as ever. Buzzing, loudly and tirelessly, in and around our ears and our faces, with such spitefulness and tenacity it was hard to focus on anything else. Landing on any little section of bare skin they could find—on our hands, ankles, forearms, the back of our necks. The initial sting of each bite giving way to another itchy red bump—the worst of which, by far, considering no part of the human body was off limits in their savage, little, bloodthirsty minds, was, god forbid, when you had to pee and there you were with your pants down surrounded by them.

As the muscles in my arms began to ache and tire from all the swatting I kept accidentally hitting the brim of my hat, jamming my sunglasses into the bridge of my nose. Annoyed more than anything, although it was also beginning to feel as if my nose might be starting to bruise, I found a small branch covered in pine needles to use as a fly swatter. Entirely unsure after a while as to whether I was spending more energy trying to protect myself from the mosquitoes than actually hiking, for the first time, I began to dread the sound of water flowing each time we got close enough to the next stream or river to hear it.

At some point near midday the trail had us crossing a river with so much debris, both over the top of it and around it, aside from the muffled sound of water flowing underneath, you could barely even tell there was a river. Santa, after crossing first, was on the other side waiting for me. Normally, creek and river crossings were kind of my specialty. I'd breeze across them quickly like they were no big thing. This one had me spooked, though. It looked a little too unpredictable, with a thick cluster of logs lying precariously in various stages of decay. I stood on the shore sizing up the one log that looked to be the surest bet for a successful crossing—as in, no part of me, including my shoes, would be wet by the end of it. It was the same log Santa had just used to make his way across. It was perched pretty high, though, on top of so much other debris, I wasn't sure I could hoist myself up there, especially with the extra weight of my pack. With Santa being 6'6" all he had to do was step onto it. For me, though, being 5'4," it was a whole different story. I made a half-ass go of it, and then stood back on the shore giving Santa a "What now?" look while shrugging my shoulders.

"You got this, Girl!" he called out to me.

Easy for you to say, Tall Guy.

My usual strategy, once I came to a crossing, was to envision myself standing safely on the other side, and then go for it. All I could envision this time though were logs shifting and crumbling beneath me, and then falling though, and getting tangled up in the debris and being pulled under, not being able to breathe, and— My hesitation, having led me to fear, meant I was now downright scared.

In search of another option, I spotted a section in the lower debris that it looked like I might be able to inch my way across. If nothing else, if I did end up falling through, at least it wouldn't be as far of a drop. I took a couple of steps in that direction, and then stopped. *What am I doing? Taking the easy way out, just because you're afraid? In a matter of minutes, one way or another, this is gonna be over. Do you wanna walk outta here feeling proud of yourself for the rest of the day, or like you let yourself down by shrinking away from a challenge?*

I looked back up at Santa. He was still standing there. Patiently watching me. "You got this!" He called out again.

He thinks you can do this.

I think I can, too.

I took a deep breath. Reaching both of my hands up I gripped the log Santa used, and imagined myself standing on top of it. Then, with everything in me, I pulled myself up.

I did it. A bit shocked, I stood, beaming. Halfway across, though, another wave of fear hit. I froze, laughing nervously, and looked in Santa's direction. "I'm scared," I confessed.

He gave me a nod. "You got this."

I nodded back, as if by choosing to agree with him I could be made to believe it, too.

I got this.

My feet, though, refused to move.

"You got this, Girl," he called out again. Half expecting there'd be a hint of irritation with me in his voice by this point, as I was annoyed with myself for making this crossing so much more of a big deal than it needed to be, I was grateful not to hear any.

Finally able to picture myself standing there next to him, I took one more slow, deep breath, and started moving. Steadily making it the rest of the way across, I gave him a big goofy smile and a hug once I reached him. "I did it!" I announced, more out of astonishment than pride.

"You sure did," he said, smiling back at me. "Good job!"

The rest of the day, even with the mosquitoes, was a breeze after that, and we managed an even 16 miles before calling it quits.

PART FOUR

Not All Heroes Wear Capes

"Love takes off masks
that we fear we cannot live without
and know we cannot live within."

–James Baldwin

Day 60: June 24, 2021

After rummaging around in my pack the next morning for the pot I'd been using as a coffee mug, I came to the sad realization that I'd left it behind. I could see it now, right where I'd left it, lying upside down on a rock to dry, yesterday morning. We'd been in such a hurry to get away from the mosquitoes I'd failed to be as thorough as usual in my final sweep of the place before we left. It was gone forever now. *Damn it.*

Not that this was the only thing I'd lost so far out here. I was also down one bandana and a pair of gloves. Not too bad, considering. The fact that I'd sent my little titanium mug home during a shakedown[28] at Grumpy's, though, meant I now had nothing left to drink coffee or eat oatmeal out of. Thankfully, at least to the drinking coffee part, Santa had a solution. The main element of his stove unit had a lid that doubled as a cup. This was normally what he used to drink his coffee out of, but he said I could use that now, and that he'd use the larger, main part that he boiled the water in to drink his.

"Boyfriend benefits," I joked, as he handed me the lid, now full of coffee.

"What?" Santa asked, confused.

"You know," I said, explaining, "like, one of the perks of having a boyfriend is that you get to borrow his stuff, wear his hoodies, have him do things for you." Laughing at that, he joined me with his own coffee on the log where I was sitting, and with a chipmunk making a ruckus in one of the trees just a few yards away, we mapped out the day ahead on Guthooks.

Rather than me getting my usual head start, we spent the morning walking together, through a thick section of forest, listening to a podcast. It was talking about the climate crisis—an issue Santa was not only passionate about himself, but, as a professor, actually covered in some of his classes. Every once in a while he would pause it, either to explain something further or answer a question I had.

---

[28] When you rid yourself of non-essential items in order to lighten your load.

Eventually the trail opened up into a clearing with a lush green meadow and a good sized lake. As we stopped there to rest and have a snack we noticed a storm system building off in the distance. By the looks of it, the trail had us heading straight for it. Santa, who, if given the choice, would 100%, always prefer to hike in dry, hot conditions, was dreading the possibility of getting rained on. I, on the other hand, found being out in wet and stormy conditions exhilarating—summer storms in the mountains, especially. Feeling a little disappointed he didn't share my enthusiasm as we geared up for this one, I made it my goal for the day to help him enjoy it. And while he was thoroughly unconvinced I could do so, he agreed to at least be a good sport about letting me try.

After passing the rest of the way through the meadow, we were right back to being surrounded by pine trees and, not long after that, the rumbling of thunder began. As soon as rain started falling, I announced that we were stopping—it was time to put my plan for Santa to enjoy this storm into action. We'd been steadily climbing anyway, which meant it wasn't a safe idea to go any higher until the chance of lightning had passed. I dug the tent out of my pack, and as we went about the task of setting it up, I enlightened him with the details as to how I planned on helping him to enjoy being out here in the rain. We climbed in and zipped it shut just as it started pouring. I dug out our sleeping bags, spread one out for us to lay on and the other to drape over the top of us, stripped both of our clothes off, and made good on my plan.

After enjoying our "tent time," as we then playfully dubbed it, we fell asleep in each other's arms to the sound of raindrops pitter-pattering on the tent cover until the storm passed.

Feeling rejuvenated after our nap, and in the clear now from the threat of lightning, we shook the rain from the tent, secured it to the outside of my pack so it could dry out as we walked, and continued on.

Having taken the lead, with the tent flapping behind me in the breeze like a cape, "You look like a superhero, BAM," Santa teased from behind.

"Well, Santa," I teased back, "are you a little more inclined now to be a fan of the rain after today?"

He grinned, sheepishly, "Yeah."

"Then I feel a bit like a superhero," I said. Laughing at that he then asked me to stop for a minute. Part of my "cape" had come loose and he wanted to tie it back up for me so I wouldn't accidentally trip on it. I'd already stumbled twice in the past several minutes, as the rocks we were now making our way over were all slippery from the rain.

"Can't have you twisting an ankle or falling to your death out here, can we?" he said, turning me around to face him once he was done.

"Thanks, Santa," I said, looking up at him, appreciatively.

"Not all heroes wear capes, Bammer," he said, pretending to tip his hat to me while he curtsied.

Shortly after making our way up and over Dorothy Lake Pass, we hit the 1,000 mile marker. Santa stood pointing at it as he called me back to come see it. Too hungry at that point to be paying attention to anything other than how hollow my stomach was feeling, I'd walked right past without even noticing it. We took a few selfies and congratulated each other. Then we stopped just before crossing the next creek to make dinner as it was becoming evident, even to Santa at this point, that my hunger was now bordering on the edge of hanger. This was the one part of hiking with someone else I still hadn't grown accustomed to. Deciding when it was meal time. When I'd been on my own I would just stop and eat at whatever point I got hungry. It didn't much matter where, and sometimes I wouldn't even stop at all, I'd just chew as I walked. Santa was more in the habit of waiting. For lunch, that meant until he found a good resting spot, and for dinner, not until he was done for the day and had set up camp. Aside from the rare occasion like tonight when I just wasn't having it, we'd been doing it his way.

Day 61: June 25, 2021

The next day we made it to Kennedy Meadows North—a campground style resupply spot, not entirely unlike Tuolumne Meadows, only a whole lot bigger and with way more facilities. Like a laundromat and a full size restaurant, a bar with a jukebox and dance floor even, and a bunch of little one room cabins those not wanting to tent camp could rent.

The place was jam packed, and not just with PCTers, but with all kinds of summer travelers, lots of them families with little kids. We checked in at the main office, left our devices to charge at a big communal charging station, and found a spot to pitch our tent in the designated hiker section. I changed into my rain gear and did our laundry while Santa hung out with Matt, as he had beaten us there. Once the laundry was done, I showered and changed into my (once again, finally!) clean clothes. The whole rest of our tramily having arrived by then, we all met up in the restaurant for a meal, laughing and eating, sharing story after story about the many mishaps and adventures of the past several weeks.

After that I picked up a care package I had waiting for me at the general store. This one, my third such package so far, was from my ex, of all people. Curious as to what he had sent me, I carried it outside, set it down on an empty picnic table, fumbled with my pocket knife until the blade finally came out and—frozen, with my knife poised to cut through the tape, I stared at the shipping label. Caught off guard by the sight of my name spelled out in his handwriting, an old ache gripped my chest— the same one I'd felt all the time, every day, going through my divorce. A sadness, so pervasive and powerful, I've only ever felt it in conjunction with the permanence of grief. The shape and slant of each letter, unmistakably his. How something that hadn't been a part of my daily life for so long now could still feel so familiar was beyond me. Seeing as how we only ever texted or talked in person or on the phone anymore, I hadn't seen his actual handwriting in years.

Three little girls brought me back to my senses. Each of them barefoot and sunburnt with a beach towel thrown over one shoulder and wearing a brightly colored swimsuit. They were arguing over which flavor was the best as they walked past my table sampling each other's popsicles.

I sliced through the tape and then opened the box. Surprised by how much he'd managed to fit in it, as I sorted through what appeared to be a whole week's worth of food, I thought about how strange it was that he and I still maintained some sort of friendship. Not that our divorce had been hostile or messy. We hadn't even used lawyers. After agreeing to terms that seemed as fair as possible to us both at the time, we'd drawn up all the paperwork ourselves, and had even done a cordial job co-parenting.

That I'd chosen to pardon so much in the name of remaining on good terms with him, that's what was strange. And confusing. *Who does that? Is it healthy? Or a form of denial?* I honestly didn't know.

What I did know was that it had taken almost a year of working with a therapist before I was able to understand, let alone admit it out loud to anyone, that he'd been emotionally abusive. Having been my "normal" for so long, I'd failed to recognize the toxic nature of our relationship. I knew the main reason I'd chosen to stay with him as long as I had was that I'd been raised in a religious culture where divorce wasn't an option. Come what may, once you made your choice to marry, you stuck with it. I knew, as well, that I didn't hate him—although I did hate the pain he'd caused, not only me, but particularly our girls. I knew I hadn't been a perfect wife. I knew he was, and always would be, the father of my children. I knew that every time I'd faced the dilemma of whether or not to believe him, regardless of the amount or the extent of evidence against whatever story at the time I was getting from him, I'd chosen to buy into the Bible's, "Love always trusts," approach to being a "good Christian wife," rather than listening to my own voice of reason.

And after the divorce was initiated and he finally came clean, at long last, about all the times he had cheated on me, oddly enough, more than anything, what I felt was relief. To finally know that, for all of those years, it hadn't been, "all in my head," meant that I wasn't crazy after all. Or any of the other things he'd accused me of being when I had questioned him or aired my suspicions—like, "so insecure I was imagining the worst of him," or overly jealous, or making shit up, or overreacting. My gut had been right all along. *If only I'd listened to it from the start.*

And lastly, I knew forgiving him would be the only way to move forward without bitterness and resentment, which make people ugly and miserable, so, that's what I did.

All things considered, when he messaged me before I set out for the trail, asking if he could help in any way, I suggested he send a care package. As I read over the note he included, asking me to be safe and saying he was proud of me, again I felt that same ache. I thought back to a time when it would have meant the world to me to have heard those words from him. Along with so many other things from the life I'd lived before my divorce, that was all in the past now. Not that I didn't appreciate his support, or that I wasn't grateful we still got along as well as we did, especially for the sake of our girls.

Joining me at the picnic table with a basket full of his own resupply items from the general store, Santa sorted through his things while I sorted through mine, and then we planned out our mileage for the upcoming week. This also happened to be the spot, with the Sierra Nevada Mountains officially behind us, where the majority of us were now shipping our bear canisters home. Glad for the opportunity to be rid of the extra weight of it, I wiped mine down, slipped a note inside for each of my girls, along with a pair of socks and a shirt I hadn't been wearing, and my crampons, which I'd been carrying since day one and still hadn't used. Then I locked it shut, stuck an address label right on the lid, and shipped it off.

The next morning, after sleeping in, we treated ourselves to a big, hot breakfast at the restaurant. Then we waited for the next shuttle with two empty seats available to take us back to the trailhead, and got a small handful of miles in before nightfall.

Day 63: June 27, 2021

After covering close to 17 miles over the span of what felt like an unusually long day, we stopped at a campsite with a nearby stream so we could refill on water. I grabbed a few empty bottles, along with my water filter, as it was my turn to do the collecting, and left Santa to rest while I took off towards the stream. Flowing lazily through a bright patch of grass in a crevice between two hills, each covered in pine trees, it was like stumbling across a hidden treasure once I found it. Wildflowers lined either side of it—some bright orange, some deep yellow, some plain white, some soft purple. With butterflies fluttering back and forth between the purple ones, mostly. And the sound of crickets all around me, signaling the coming of dusk. Feeling lucky to have stumbled upon such unexpected beauty, I took my time as I filtered the water, and then recorded a little video on my phone of the place so I wouldn't forget it.

Back up at the campsite with Santa, we debated as to whether or not we wanted to press on for a few more miles. On one hand, it was getting late in the day, and we were both feeling tired and hungry. On the other hand, we had been talking quite a bit lately about wanting to start upping our daily mileage. In the end, we decided to stay put. I set up the tent and changed into my base layer while Santa built a fire and fixed us an Old Trashioned. After relaxing for a bit, he started dinner and I wandered down to the stream again, loading up on enough water this time to last us through the first half of tomorrow.

Once night fell, after dinner, we sat listening to the crackling of the fire and watching the flames glow in the darkness. Santa lit himself a cigarette. Nothing unusual there. Oddly enough, though, I felt a strong urge to light one up for myself. Knowing it'd been nearly 10 years since I'd given the habit up, and wanting no part in being in any way responsible should I end up getting hooked again, it took some serious convincing on my part to talk him into sharing one with me. After several minutes of going back and forth about it and a promise on my part that, come what may, I wouldn't hold him responsible, he eventually did.

I was 17 when I first started smoking. After thinking it looked cool I'd talked a friend from school, who I knew smoked, into teaching me how to do it. "If you end up hooked and getting cancer because of this, I'll kill you!" she'd warned me, only half-jokingly, at the time. I had gotten hooked, and all through college I went through a pack of cigarettes every 2-3 days.

Once I found out I was pregnant with Madie, I quit, cold turkey, all the way until I finished nursing her. Once my body was entirely my own again, I'd gone right back to it, though. Until, that is, we started trying to get pregnant for a second time, a year and a half or so later. At which point I again gave it up throughout my pregnancy, this time with Hailey, all the way until she'd finished nursing as well. From that point on I'd been a closet smoker, attempting to keep my socially frowned upon, dirty, little secret hidden, from my own children even, as best I could.

It wasn't until I made my mind up that I wanted to start being a runner that I was finally able to kick the habit for good. I figured I couldn't do both, and not only was I tired of feeling like a slave to my nicotine addiction, but my girls were reaching the age where me telling them smoking was bad while still doing it behind their backs felt shamefully hypocritical. Having never been a runner before, I bought a good pair of shoes, began to train for a marathon, and, somehow mustering the will to swap my old nasty habit for this much healthier new one, never looked back.

Until now, that is. Between being out of my normal routine of running 3-4 times a week, and the ultimate freedom associated with there being no one around I felt the need to be setting a good example for, once *Why not just have one?* entered my mind, I simply went with it.

Day 64: June 28, 2021

The next day was pretty much the same. We covered 18 more miles. At the end of which, I again gave into the urge to have "just one more" cigarette. Knowing, already, that first one yesterday had done me in, I rationalized my choice to indulge by dismissing it as a luxury I'd allow myself on the trail, then swap it out for running as I had in the past once I got home.

Day 65: June 29, 2021

Since leaving Kennedy Meadows North, we'd been running into far fewer hikers than usual, and with none of them being people we knew, I was beginning to miss our tramily. Today being a perfect example of this, we saw no one aside from each other until we stopped for the evening. Shortly after we set up camp, we heard the faint sound of voices coming up the trail. Unable to see who it was, as our site was tucked back away from the trail in a thick patch of pine trees and boulders, once they got close enough I recognized one of their voices. "Knux!" I called out, ecstatic, as I jumped up and ran towards her.

"BAM? Is that you?" She could hear me but she still couldn't see me yet. Our voices were echoing off the boulders surrounding us.

"Knux!" I called out again, spotting her first. "And Prime!" He was behind her. I greeted them with hugs and then led them over to the campsite and Santa. Just as excited to see us as we were to see them, we all filled each other in on the happenings of the past several days as they set their tents up next to ours. Then we all climbed up on top of one of the huge boulders surrounding us to get a better view of an impressive looking double rainbow the late afternoon drizzle had left behind for us.

After climbing back down from the boulder, I was surprised to see I had missed a call from Hailey. Three missed calls, actually, and a voicemail. With how remote this stretch had been, we'd rarely been getting cell service. I played back her message. She sounded upset and said nothing more than for me to call her as soon as I could. My stomach churned with the heartwrenching, panic inducing kind of worry no mother is a stranger to. Scrambling back up onto the boulder, as I figured the higher I could get, the better chance I'd have at getting a signal, I tried calling her back. It was ringing. *Thank god.* And ringing—*Come on Hailey, pick up!* No answer. Just a recorded message telling me her voice mailbox was full. *Seriously?* I tried again. Still no answer. I typed out a text telling her that the service here was spotty but to call me back as soon as she could. Then I stood there staring impatiently at the screen until the little "sent" message finally changed to "delivered." Turning the volume on my ringer up as high as it would go, so if she called again, this time I would hear it, I climbed back down off the boulder.

Growing more and more worried as the hours passed with still no word from her, I tried calling one more time before we finally went to bed. Still no answer. As I lay there, wide awake on my back in my sleeping bag, feeling sick to my stomach, images portraying any number of scenarios she might be facing began to flash through my mind, like clips from a movie—each one more disconcerting than the last.

After a miserably long, restless night, as we were packing up the next morning, my phone finally rang. Hailey's picture popped up, filling the screen. She was smiling and her hair was several inches shorter than it was now. We'd taken it on Mother's Day, some three or four years ago, and it had remained as her contact photo on my phone ever since. Bracing myself for the worst, I tapped the "accept incoming call" button.

Far from the horrifyingly gruesome, worst case scenarios I'd been up half the night imagining, it turned out she'd been having a bit of car trouble. As soon as I heard her voice and knew she was alright—that nothing life threatening or dangerous had happened to her, and that she wasn't lying unconscious in a hospital bed somewhere—I lost my shit.

"Don't you ever leave me a message like that again unless you're in serious trouble!" I warned.

"Are you seriously gonna talk to me like this right now?" she snapped back in a tone that sounded more like a challenge than a question. "I called three times! And you didn't answer! I knew a message like that would get your attention."

"Get my attention?" I balked. "Do you have any idea how worried I've been?!"

"I needed you!" Her voice sounded shaky. My heart sank. Missing an opportunity to be there for my kids when they need me is one of the worst feelings ever. "I'm hanging up," she said after a short pause. I could tell by the way she said it, she'd reached her limit. "I'll call you again later," she added. I started to explain that if she couldn't get through to me later, it was because of the bad service out here, but she'd already hung up.

Wanting nothing more than to get her back on the phone so we could work this out while I did still have service, I knew if I pushed her it would only make things worse. I slid my phone back in my pocket. *She'll call again when she's ready.*

Knux and Prime started out first. With Santa and I not far behind, we spent the first part of the morning gradually making our way up the side of a long, open ridge. Just as we reached the top Hailey called again. I immediately apologized for losing my shit with her. She in turn apologized for making me worry. She then went on to explain what had happened with her car. How something had been wrong with the ignition and she couldn't get it to start. And how her biggest concern had been that if she couldn't get it fixed, she wouldn't be able to drive out to meet up with me in a few days like we'd planned—for the 4th of July weekend, in Tahoe, with Santa, as well, and the rest of the tramily. Santa had lined an Airbnb up for all of us, and Hailey was planning to pick us up at whatever trailhead we were closest to by then. I was excited to introduce her to everyone, especially Santa.

In the time since the worrisome voicemail she'd left me, she'd managed to arrange on her own for someone to fix it. "I'm proud of you for figuring it out, Hail, and for doing what you needed to to get it handled," I said once she'd finished explaining.

"Thanks, Momma. I'll see you in a couple days!"

Sliding my phone back into my pocket once we said our good-byes and I love you's, I walked on from there feeling weightless—beyond relieved to know my girl was okay.

Echo Lake was next up. Santa had seen on Guthooks that the trail ran right by a store there where you could buy snacks and sandwiches and such. The only hitch was that they closed at 5 o'clock. From where we were now, if we hustled, we could make it in time to snag some goodies for the night. Feeling the emotional drain from such a hard core worrying session the night before, I for one didn't have any hustle in me. Santa, on the other hand, was itching to go on ahead of me and try. "Once I get to the store I'll keep going from there until I find a spot for us to camp," he suggested. "And if it's not a place you can see from the trail, I'll leave one of my trekking poles so you'll know where to turn off to find me."

With a plan in place, he took off. One by one, the hours passed as I made my way, slowly, even by my standards. First, passing the boat launching area next to the little store, which, of course, was already closed by the time I got there. Then, up along the ridge that, for the next two miles, traced the outline of the lake. Every so often a cozy looking lake house or log cabin would appear, nestled in the wooded area halfway between where I was up on the ridge and the shoreline below. Not having stopped for water back by the store, I was down to my last few sips with no idea at this point how much further I still needed to go before I'd catch up with Santa. There seemed to be no way to access the lake to get water, though, from where I was on the ridge. A little embarrassed at being so ill prepared, but more thirsty than anything, I eventually started asking day hikers as they passed me, heading in the opposite direction, if they had any extra water they could spare. One young couple happily handed me an extra water bottle they had. And then a ways further, a group of teenage boys sweetly, albeit clumsily, tried to funnel some water from one of their Camelbak bladders into one of my water bottles, most of which ended up on the ground.

After eventually making my way past the entirety of Echo Lake, a message from Santa came through on my phone. The good news was, I'd briefly had enough service to hear from him. The bad news, though, was that the spot he'd found for us to camp for the night was still miles ahead. *What the fuck? Miles?* For the second time today, my heart sank. I took my pack off and sat, cross legged on the ground, with my elbows on my knees and my head in my hands. Uncertain at the moment as to which I felt more—frustration, exhaustion, disbelief, or disappointment? Ever since I'd gotten past the boat launch I'd been half expecting to find Santa waiting for me around the next bend. *I can't go any further. Especially not MILES!* Too tired to even cry at this point, I just sat there. Wanting more than anything to not have to go any further, it occurred to me that I had the tent. Which meant not catching up to Santa wasn't an option. Especially not with the potential for a storm tonight brewing in the sky like it was. I had to keep going. *Just get moving. And think about seeing Santa, instead of the miles.* Mustering the strength to stand up, I dusted myself off, put my pack back on, cinched it up, and started walking again.

Resisting the urge to chug what little water I still had left from the bottle the day hikers had given me, every 15-20 minutes I allowed myself one little sip. As the early evening sky gave way to dusk, I watched the storm ahead in the distance change course. No longer a threat now, I was able to relax a bit—at least Santa wouldn't be getting soaked while he waited for me. Just as it was getting dark, I finally spotted one of his trekking poles to the side of the trail. True to his word, he'd stabbed it in the dirt and draped his bandana over the handle for me. Beneath it, drawn in the dirt, was an arrow pointing down towards what looked like a little village of tents by a lake. Grabbing his pole and bandana, I followed the arrow.

It took a few minutes to find him, as the place was so crowded. Without even bothering to take my pack off, I slumped to the ground next to him in the little spot he'd picked out for us. He was happy to see me and realizing how spent I was, helped take my pack off for me as he explained he'd been starting to worry something bad might have happened, given how long he'd been waiting. "Are you hungry?" He then asked.

"Starving," I said, taking my boots off.

"I thought we'd have a picnic," he said, smiling. "I hear you like them." *Aw, he remembered.*

"Uh-huh." I nodded, smiling back at him.

Before we were anything more than just friends, we'd had a conversation about the various questions you're required to answer when signing up for online dating apps. Like what kinds of traits are you attracted to, what level of commitment you're looking for, and what your idea of a perfect date would entail. My answer to the last one, as I had then shared with Santa, would be to go on a picnic. I was touched, not only by the fact that he'd been paying attention, but by his efforts to make me happy.

Opening his pack, as he pulled out each of the items he'd managed to score for us at the store, I felt a bit like a game show contestant who was being told what her prizes were after winning the final bonus round. Holding each thing up briefly, he presented it by name, "Fresh bread. Turkey. Ham. Salami. Cheese. Lettuce. Mustard. Mayo. Chips. Cookies. Wine, for you, and beer, for me."

I could feel my mouth watering. "Impressive, Santa!" I said, smiling at the feast laid out now before us. "Thank you," I added, giving him a kiss, "this looks amazing." After constructing our sandwiches and enjoying our late night, lakeside picnic, Santa helped me set up the tent, and we called it a night.

Day 67: July 1, 2021

The majority of the terrain we covered the next day was rocky, and not just the landscape surrounding us, but the trail itself, as in the ground beneath us, actually. A little bit of which is no big thing, but mile after mile after mile of it, and the bottoms of your feet get so sore they start to ache and throb with every step. This being the case, we didn't make it all that far before deciding we'd had enough for one day.

We found a beautiful, quiet spot to camp, just off the trail, along the edge of one of the many lakes in the area. As soon as we'd set up the tent, a huge marmot appeared. Entertaining us from then on for the rest of the evening, he proved to be as bold and mischievous as he was friendly and cute—sniffing around our tent trying to get in, licking the sweat off the straps and handles of our trekking poles, and even trying to make off with one of Santa's shoes at one point.

Another entertaining feature of the night was thanks to the fact that I let Santa talk me into trying edibles for the first time. Knowing I'd never tried them before, and on the off chance I might eventually want to, Hoops had picked some out for us at one of our previous resupply stops and Santa had been carrying them with him ever since. With my curiosity finally getting the best of me, I was ready to find out for myself what all the hype was about.

Shortly after we took them we decided to swim out to the little island in the middle of the lake. The water felt amazing, especially on our sore and tired feet, and the temperature was perfect. About half way between the shore and the little island, though, I got an uneasy, sort of claustrophobic, hard-to-breathe type feeling. I'd felt it while swimming before, although rarely, and only ever in much deeper water. I laid on my back and floated for a minute, taking a few slow, deep breaths, and hoping it would pass.

"Do me a favor, Santa?" I called out to him, a little ahead of me now since I'd stopped.

"Anything," he said, turning back towards me.

"Stay with me?" I asked. "I wanna go back to the shore."

"Are you okay?" He looked concerned as he swam his way over to me.

"I just feel a little weird. And I don't think I can make it all the way out there right now. I just wanna go back," I said. "I'm sorry."

"Don't be sorry. You're okay," he said reassuringly, as we started swimming back together towards the shore.

We dried off and changed into our base layers. Then Santa made dinner while we sat on a log, watching the orangish-yellow and purplish-blue hues of the sunset reflect off the lake which was now perfectly still.

Santa fell asleep first, as was usually the case. As I lay next to him in the tent, I thought about what happened earlier in the lake. How I'd had no qualms about letting him know I was scared. And how unusual that was for me. Whereas, happy or sad, or even upset or confused, I had no problem sharing any of those feelings with other people, I had an obvious thought knot when it came to admitting I was scared. It felt risky at best, if not utterly unsafe. As if in doing so I was surrendering a certain amount of power over to them. And that made me feel small. And feeling small, in that way—I hated that, more than anything.

It was different with Santa, though. With him, I felt safe. He didn't judge me or make fun of me or cause me to feel ashamed for anything I was thinking or feeling—ever. In fact, now that I thought about it, it wasn't just that I felt safe with him, either—this whole time, what he'd really been doing, was helping me learn how to trust again. Taking comfort in the soft, steady sound of his breathing, I laid still a bit longer, until my mind finally slowed down enough I thought I might be able to sleep. "I love you, my big capeless hero," I whispered, softly kissing his cheek. Then I rolled over, closed my eyes, and fell asleep.

Day 68: July 2, 2021

Knowing Hailey would be picking us up this afternoon, we walked all morning, as quickly as we could. I was so excited to see her I could hardly stand it. And while I was excited, as well, to introduce her to Santa, I was also a little nervous, hoping they'd hit it off. I knew all too well from past dating experiences, there'd be an unbearable amount of friction in store if they didn't.

As it got close to lunchtime, the trail crossed over a dirt road where a young couple had parked their truck along the shoulder and were offering trail magic. They'd gone all out, too, by the looks of it. Not only was there a table full of food, they'd hauled an old couch out here, as well, along with a barbecue, two jumbo sized coolers of soda and beer, and a huge patio sized sun umbrella. We joined the half dozen or so other hikers who were already there, as our hosts threw a few more hotdogs onto the grill for us.

With a fairly popular trailhead being just up the road from us, in the time it took us to eat our lunch, we'd already seen a couple of cars drive past on their way to the parking lot. Torn between whether to push on for the next several hours to where we'd arranged for Hailey to meet us, or to try and hitch out from here to somewhere she could reach us more easily, and sooner—the only catch was whether we'd be able to let her know if and how the plan was changing. We didn't have cell service at this point, but we would once we got closer to town. She was also driving through some pretty remote patches, though, which meant that even if I was able to send a message out, she might not get it right away.

Between our now full bellies and how uncomfortably hot it was getting, we decided to try and hitch. I sent Hailey a message, using my inReach, letting her know we'd send an updated meeting point to her as soon as we could. Before long we got a ride with a couple of locals—a mom and her teenage daughter, who'd just finished their midmorning trail workout. Once they dropped us off at a little strip mall just off the interstate, I pinned our location and sent it to Hailey. With our packs beside us on the ground, we sat at a picnic table outside a Dairy Queen, comparing scrapes and bruises and degrees of dirtiness while we waited. Half an hour later, her little lime green VW Bug pulled up. Squealing with delight as I ran over to her car, "There's my girl!" I announced to Santa. She and I shared a big, long hug, and then she and Santa, shaking hands, officially met one another.

We stopped to pick up some groceries and then made our way to where we were staying. With it being a holiday weekend, Tahoe itself had been booked solid, so Santa had found us a place in the neighboring town of Soda Springs instead. Within a few hours the whole tramily was there—Knux, Prime, Hoops, Matt, and Soda Pop. After having told them all so much about my girls, and Hailey, so much about them, it was a fun treat for me having both tramily and family in the same place at the same time. Hailey fit right in and, even more than the batch of homemade cookies she'd baked for us, they all loved her as well.

We spent the next couple of days playing board games and watching movies. We all took turns cooking big family-style meals and then cleaning up afterwards. We sat out back on the deck together, sharing stories with Hailey about life on the trail. We slept in and took naps and ventured out to the laundromat and got our resupply shopping done.

At one point, wanting some one-on-one time with Hailey, she and I went out to lunch. Once we sat down and ordered, she got quiet and her eyes filled with tears. My heart sank at the sight of how sad she looked. "What's the matter, Sweets?" I asked, reaching for her hands from across the table so I could hold them. Her nails were freshly painted from the night before when she and I had taken turns giving each other manicures. And on various fingers, an assortment of rings she'd, for years now, been collecting—souvenirs from vacations, secondhand store finds, one, a gift from my mom, and a couple of them that had been mine when I was her age.

She opened up about how she'd been struggling. About how lonely she was being at home in our apartment, without me. How she'd never been alone for this long before, ever. And how the thought of me not even being halfway done with the trail yet felt unbearable.

I knew exactly what she meant. I was right there with her. Not "there," of course, as in physically at home, obviously, but "there" as in not a single day had passed since I'd been out here that I hadn't been missing her, longing for the familiar routine of our day-to-day life together. Sitting across from her at our wobbly, yet cozy, little second hand dining room table, sharing a meal and the details of our day. Trips to the laundromat, and hanging out in the coffee shop while waiting for the wash cycle to finish. Running beside her on the trail along the river. The way she'd roll her eyes and give me a, "Mom, please!" every time she played one of her new songs for me and I was like, "What does that even mean?" when I didn't understand the lyrics. Laying out together by the pool at our apartment complex, gossiping about what the neighbors were up to. Our once a week family dinner nights when Madie and her boyfriend would join us. Watching a movie (that usually took us longer to agree on watching than to actually watch) or an episode or two of whatever reality show she was currently into, a big bowl of popcorn between us on the couch. Our many ongoing conversations about coworkers, who we were dating, assignments she was working on, or books we were reading. All of it—every day, I was missing it.

Ever since we'd moved back to Idaho after the divorce, other than for a short time when Madie had moved back in with us from her college dorms, it had just been the two of us. She'd finished up high school and then started at the same college Madie attended. The same one, in fact, that I myself, as well as both of my parents, graduated from. With her being at a stage where she was just starting out in life, and me being at a stage where I was just starting over, we'd had a lot in common. The older she got, the stronger the bond between us grew, and the more our previous mother-daughter dynamic evolved into a best friend/roommate relationship.

I could only imagine how jarring it must have been for her to go from having a non-stop, onsite support system to being completely on her own, twenty-four seven. "Honey, I'm so sorry," I said, giving her hands a little squeeze.

"I need a minute," she said, pulling her hands away and wiping the tears from her face. "I'll be right back." Standing up from the table she quickly added, "Don't follow me. I just need a minute." Knowing she's never been comfortable with people seeing her cry, I watched her as she walked out of the restaurant. The whole front of the building was lined with full length windows. She stopped in front of one, pulled her phone out of her pocket, and turned to face the parking lot.

I looked down at my now empty hands, resting on the table. *You're the worst fucking mom. She needs you at home—you've no business being out here.*

She's 20, though—this is normal. Change and growth are painful…but that doesn't necessarily mean it's bad.

How is her struggling not bad? You're just being selfish—wanting to finish this stupid trail. You really are the worst fucking mom. Really!

How can I fix this? How can I help her?

Interrupting my little Dr. Jekyll/Amy and Mr. Hyde/BAM episode, Hailey sat back down in the seat across from me. I'd been so lost in my thoughts I hadn't seen her come back in.

"I'm sorry, Momma," she said. "I just needed to tell you all that. I really am proud of you for doing this and I don't want to make this any harder on you. I just really, really miss you."

"Aw, Sweets, you don't ever have to be sorry for how you feel. You can always tell me anything. And I really, really miss you, too! It's the hardest part of being out here."

This time it was her hands reaching out across the table for mine. I smiled at the sweet gesture and she smiled back, giving my hands a squeeze just as I had hers. "What can we do to make this not so tough?" I asked her after the waiter set our plates down in front of us.

"Maybe you could call a little more often?" she suggested. "And maybe we could plan out the next time we can see each other way ahead of time so we can have it to look forward to?"

"Absolutely, those are great ideas. And maybe we could Facetime more often, too?" I added. With both of us feeling better by that point, we took our time finishing up lunch and then joined back up with the others.

Day 70: July 4, 2021

We feasted on the 4th in true holiday fashion. And then later in the evening, intrigued by my lack of experience regarding the popular pastime of smoking pot, the tramily made it their mission for the night to get me properly high. Being game to try, I gave it my best shot. Unfortunately, somewhere in between a light buzz from the beer I drank with dinner and the small dose of edibles after, that first joint a few hours later, which did so little for me we'd actually done an internet search to see if being immune to the effects of marijuana was a thing, and then a second joint (far too soon, apparently, after the first), I went from feeling absolutely fine, one minute, to spending the rest of the night sick in bed, vowing, wholeheartedly, "Never again!"

Day 71: July 5, 2021

With a newfound understanding for the term, "greening out," I woke up the next morning with a serious case of mom guilt over the fact that Hailey had been there to witness the whole thing. Worried I may have scarred her for life, it wasn't until she woke up around noon and assured me I hadn't, that I was able to stop feeling so bad. I apologized to her for my lack of adulting wisely, and then we had a good laugh over it, and she filled me in on all the fun she'd had with the others, playing games and watching a movie, while I'd been out of it.

Hoops was the first to head out, along with his new four-legged hiking partner. His brother-in-law had driven his dog down to him from Portland over the weekend. A big, sweet natured, cream colored poodle that, having recently worn out its welcome with his mom, who had been taking care of it, Hoops was now planning to hike the remainder of the trail with.

Knux and Prime were the next to leave. Some of Knux's relatives, who were also in town for the holiday weekend, had arranged to pick her up so she could spend a couple of days with them. And with rumors about her and Prime having struck up a trail romance being happily verified over the weekend, he was tagging along with her. After seeing them off, Hailey kindly volunteered to trail angel Soda Pop and Matt back to the trailhead.

With another whole day still before we had to be out of the Airbnb and say our good-bye's to Hailey, she and Santa and I decided to drive into Tahoe. After a fun leisurely lunch we got ice cream at one of the outdoor vendors and then walked down to the lake. Between the usual summer crowds and those still in town from the holiday weekend, the entire length of the beach was lined with people. Staking a claim to the only empty spot we could find big enough for the three of us, we laid out a big picnic blanket Hailey had in her car, and spent the rest of the afternoon laying out in the sunshine and swimming.

As we hung out in the kitchen making dinner later that evening, with Hailey and Santa discussing yet another book they'd both recently read, I couldn't help marveling at how well the two of them had hit it off. Of course, it helped that they had so much in common, with her being an English major, and him an English professor. They were both voracious readers, had very similar personalities, and were big time movie connoisseurs. Between book titles and authors, plot twists and storylines, movies and actors, there had rarely been a lull in the ongoing conversation between them. It made me happy. She'd never taken so well to someone I'd dated before.

"I like him," she confided in me as I was checking in to make sure she was comfortable once she'd gone to bed. "I like how he treats you. And how you seem so comfortable being yourself around him. I can see he makes you happy."

"Happier than I ever thought I could be," I agreed, smiling. "He's a good man, Hail, and I love him. And I love you, too," I added, kissing her forehead, and drawing her blankets up over her shoulders. "Night, Sweets," I said, turning to head towards the stairs.

"Night, Momma," she said, opening back up the book she'd been reading as I'd come in.

Day 72: July 6, 2021

We packed up the next morning and drove out to the trailhead. I stood in the parking lot with Hailey, both of us blinking back tears, while Santa unloaded our packs from the car and topped our water bottles off at the drinking fountain.

"Drive safe, Hun, and message me as soon as you get home so I know you made it." She nodded in agreement and then gave me a big, long hug. Unable to delay the inevitable any further, we said, "Good-bye," and, "I love you." Then she gave Santa a hug, as well, and got back in her car. Already missing her so much it hurt, I blew one last kiss to her, and then stood waving as she made her way onto the interstate.

Back on the trail, I spent the rest of the day following behind Santa, fighting hard to stay above the waves of sadness and guilt brought on by thoughts of my girls, and how much of their lives I was missing out on by not being home.

Day 73: July 7, 2021

I set out alone the next morning, getting a head start on Santa. Within the first 20-30 minutes, I began to notice evidence of Hoops in the form of an occasional paw print among the various shoe tracks in the dirt at my feet. I also came across something I didn't recognize. Something I was quite certain, in fact, I'd not ever seen the likes of before. Lying perfectly still, right in the middle of the trail, and no bigger than my fist, was a cream colored object, shaped a bit like an apostrophe. I stood over it, staring. Unable for the life of me to make out what it was, I squatted down as best I could under the weight of my pack for a closer look. There appeared to be markings of some kind on it—thin, squiggly, red lines. And on either side of the thicker end of this "apostrophe," for lack of a better word, two little bumps were protruding. About six inches away from it, also lying in the middle of the trail, was an even smaller, clumped up pile of what looked like animal poop consisting mostly of hair, but I couldn't tell for sure. I stood back up, puzzled. I poked at it gently and hesitantly with the tip of my trekking pole. It was squishy, like a blob of putty a child would play with.

"Oh my god!" I gasped, as my mind suddenly made sense of what I was seeing. Instinctively backing away from it, I cupped one of my hands over my mouth in horror, accidentally smacking my chin with the handle of my pole as I did. *It's a fetus.* I could see it now. The little colored lines were actually veins. And the bumps on either side? It's would-be arms, too early in this stage of development for any distinguishable paws or digits to have formed yet. My only guess as to what kind of animal it could have come from was a bear. I took a picture of it with my phone in the hopes that someone else might be able to help me properly identify it later. Unsure what, if anything, I should do with it at that point, I left it alone, and kept going.

I spent the next half hour or so, so disturbed by the thought of there being a momma nearby who'd just lost her baby, I couldn't stop crying. *Was she in pain? Had she been attacked? Was she upset about it?* The possibility had never occurred to me before that wild animals could have miscarriages, too.

As soon as Santa caught up to me I told him all about it. He hadn't seen it. Which meant something, or someone, had moved it in some way from the trail. Try as I might, not even the 20 miles I was able to put between myself and what I'd seen was enough to shake the image from my mind by the end of the day. It was all I could think about as I fell asleep that night. *Poor momma bear.*

Day 74: July 8, 2021

With the prospect of a good size lake waiting for us at the end of our trek today, and in the hopes of being able to reach it while it was still warm enough out to enjoy it, we woke up early, and kept a steady pace.

As the terrain grew increasingly rocky I wondered how Hoops' dog was holding up. It was uncomfortable enough walking across such an unforgiving surface with shoes on, I couldn't imagine what it would feel like with bare paws.

By midmorning, the trail spit us out onto a two lane road leading into Sierra City. More of a quaint little ghost town than an actual city, per se, it was home to a few shops, had one historic museum-type hotel, and a population too small to warrant the need for even one traffic light. After hitching a ride, even though it was no more than a couple of miles up the road, we stopped in at The Country Store where my next resupply package was waiting for me. Santa roamed the aisles, doing his own resupply, while I signed for my package and ordered us an early lunch from the little deli. Then we sat outside on a big wooden porch in front of the store with a handful of other new-to-us hikers and ate a meal from the deli. As we all got to talking, it turns out one of them was from the same city in Idaho I was from. Having just finished section hiking, he was gearing up to drive home. After rearranging our packs to make room for our newly acquired stash of supplies, we took him up on his offer to drive us back up the road to the trailhead.

Later that afternoon, having successfully reached the lake in time to go for a swim before the sun went down, we set up camp and did just that. Knux and Prime showed up shortly after—an unexpected, pleasant surprise. Stopping to rest with us for a bit, they filtered some water from the lake and filled us in on how their visit with her family had gone. Not unexpectedly, it wasn't long before their "short rest" turned into a decision to stay put for the night, and the four of us were sitting in the dirt together getting started on dinner.

Seeing as how Santa had recently replaced the pot I lost with an ultralight frying pan, we'd since upped our dinner game. And by upped I mean *way* upped. Rather than the typical, dehydrated, just-add-boiling-water meals we'd been used to, he'd started cooking us grilled cheese sandwiches with salami and pesto. As the smell alone was enough to cause anyone within a half mile radius out here to start salivating, he had mercy on Knux and Prime by making an extra one for them to sample.

The lake was calm and smooth when we woke up the next morning. A soft, tranquil mist rising up from its surface. Several other hikers had crashed our site during the night, and we all took our time enjoying the warmth of the sunrise before packing up and heading out.

After hitting the 1,200 mile mark we stopped to eat lunch along a ridge near the top of a mountain where we had good enough cell service, I was able to Facetime my girls. A message from Hoops came through as well. He'd sent it as a group text, letting us all know he'd decided to pull the plug on finishing the trail and was on his way home. His dog had injured its paw, and despite his best efforts to patch it up, unfortunately, it wasn't healing. And that he loved us all, and wished us the best.

Saddened by the news, Santa and I walked on from there recounting all the other hikers we'd met so far who, for various reasons, had chosen to end their hike early, as well as those who were still out here, and what our best guesses were as to the likelihood of each of them finishing.

We stopped for the day at the top of a mountain along the edge of a small, flat ridge. Nestled safely behind a short wall of rocks, and overlooking a stretch of wilderness so vast and so beautiful, before even taking my shoes off, which was normally the first thing I did once I was done for the day, I just stood there for several minutes, staring, as I took it all in.

Opting to cowboy camp, I laid out our sleeping bags, side by side, in the dirt. Not only was the weather perfect for it, but with such a clear view of the sky from this vantage point, and considering how removed we were from any man made lights this far out, these were prime stargazing conditions.

By midnight, having already woken up once to pee and twice as night hikers had passed by with headlamps, I'd seen numerous shooting stars, an assortment of constellations, and even the Milky Way. As I lay there waiting to fall back asleep each time, staring up at it all, I couldn't help smiling. Such a perfectly woven blanket of stars, so plentiful, and so bright against the darkness—it felt as if I were witnessing something magical.

Day 76: July 10, 2021

We woke the next morning to find a thin layer of haze blanketing the entire horizon to the east of us. Apparently, whatever fire had been responsible for the large plume of smoke we'd seen building off in the distance in that same direction yesterday had spread quite a bit during the night. As we made our way down the mountain, we began to smell it as well—the alarming scent of a forest in flames that every hiker out here dreaded. In addition to obviously posing a threat to our safety, wildfires were notorious for causing trail closures. Trail closures meant having to skip sections, which then meant the added stress of arranging detours. Detours meant delays, and delays invariably meant having to readjust your whole timeline. None of which was desirable.

Anxious to get a read on the situation, newswise, we stopped after a couple of hours, as soon as Santa saw he had service. With me being a Verizon customer, and there being no cell towers of theirs in the area, I was shit out of luck—until I got back within range of one again, that is. One of the perks for Santa, though, of being from Canada, was that since his service provider wasn't available here in the US, his phone would always just automatically connect to whichever signal nearby was the strongest, regardless of whether that company was AT&T, Sprint, T-Mobile, or Verizon. Resting for a few minutes while I ate a granola bar, I then kept going while he stayed put to finish checking in on things on his phone.

Before he had a chance to catch up to me, I passed another hiker heading southbound. Stopping the man, as he got to me, I asked if he'd heard any news of recent trail closures or fire warnings. He told me a section of the trail about a quarter of a mile ahead of me had just reopened after having been closed for several hours this morning while fire crews had been working to put out a fire there. I typed out a message to let the girls and my parents know we might be detoured soon. With my finger hovering over the, "send," button, I debated for several seconds as to whether or not to push it. The last thing I wanted was to cause anyone at home to be worrying needlessly. Hitting the back button instead, I erased what I'd just written, and slid my phone back into my pocket. Glancing behind me as I walked on, there was still no sign of Santa.

Half a mile later, as I got to where the closure had been, patches of ground were still smoldering. There were charred tree trunks, as well, and bits of ash floating through the air. And spots where the dirt had recently been dug up. And patches, here and there, on both the trees and the ground, coated with brightly colored fire retardant. It was eerily quiet, too—no birds chirping or leaves rustling in the breeze. And it smelled so strongly of smoke that I kept feeling the need to hold my breath.

Shortly after the burn zone, Santa caught up with me. Every few miles or so, from that point on, we seemed to spot another, new fire burning off in the distance. So many, in fact, that stopping to point them out to each other soon turned into a game of, "Who can find the next one first?" With the situation escalating from bad to worse the further north we traveled, by the time we reached what was to be the last reliable water source for the day, the whole sky was an unnatural looking, pale grayish-tan color, and teaming with fire crew helicopters. The constant, nauseating smell of smoke was inescapable, and we were seriously starting to worry there might be evacuation warnings soon. The water source, marked as a creek on Guthooks, was a 5-10 minute walk from the trail, along a two lane road we'd just intersected with. Leaving Santa to rest in the shade, as it was my turn to do the fetching this time, I took off to find it.

A good half hour later, cradling so many freshly filled water bottles in my arms they were beginning to burn, I made my way back up the hill towards Santa. "Quincy 22 miles," a sign on the shoulder read as I got near the top.

Unsure at this point as to what our next move was, I set the bottles down next to Santa, and rubbing my biceps, asked him, "So, what'd you decide? Are we gonna keep going, or hitch down into Quincy?"

His beloved England was playing again tomorrow, this time against Italy, in the final match of the Euros, something that had never happened before. Not wanting to miss it, he'd laid out his options for me as either a) finding a spot on the trail with good enough service to listen to it, or b) getting into Quincy where he could watch it on TV. I'd left the choice up to him, as I was fine to keep going but also wasn't opposed to a hot meal or a shower.

"Let's hitch into town," he announced. "With service being as spotty as it has been out here, I don't wanna risk not even being able to listen to it. Plus, we can get a hot meal," he added, smiling, "and get out of the smoke for a bit, and sleep tonight on a mattress."

"With pillows." I said, smiling. "I'm all for it, Santa. No need to convince me."

For the next two hours we sat by the side of the road in the hopes of flagging someone down for a ride. Two cars passed by in that time, neither of which even slowed down. Hungry, tired, and more than anything, disappointed, we gave up for the night. Pitching our tent in one of the designated spots back up the trail a little ways, the only other person camped there was a woman whose trail name was Pinata. After introducing ourselves and chatting with her for a while, we made dinner. Then as soon as the sun set we both went to bed.

Day 77: July 11, 2021

Hoping we'd have better luck this morning, as far as getting a hitch, we woke as soon as the sun rose and packed up in a hurry. Then we crossed over to a dirt parking area on the other side of the road where it was safer and easier to watch for traffic. Not that there really was any "traffic" out here. And then we just waited. And waited. And waited, watching and listening for the sound of a car coming. Pinata passed by after a while, as did a few other hikers. No vehicles, though, other than a couple of forest service trucks and one little sportscar—all of which were heading in the opposite direction of where we wanted to go.

An hour passed. And then two, at which point another hiker, looking to hitch into town, as well, stopped to join us. Desperately in need of a new pair of shoes, as the ones he had on were more duct tape than anything, he didn't want to risk trying to get any farther in them. As the three of us passed the time chatting about where we were from, I plugged my phone into my new solar charger (a gift my friend, Scott, from back home had recently shipped to me) and set it out on a rock in the sunlight. With the game starting soon, and our back up plan being to instead just keep going if we couldn't make it in time, I figured I should charge it now, just in case, as it was harder to do while we were walking.

Just as we were debating whether or not to head back down to the creek for more water, someone finally pulled over, and stopped. Agreeing to let us pay her for a ride, the three of us piled inside the backseat of her car. Drooling happily while he kept a friendly, yet watchful, eye on us, a very big, very old, yellow labrador sat across from her in the front seat as we wound our way down the mountain. Thirty to forty minutes later, after sharing a bit of the area's history with us and catching us up on the most recent wildfire news, she dropped us off in Quincy in the parking lot of a little strip mall. As our new friend made a beeline for the sporting goods store, I reached into my pocket for my phone to message the girls that we'd made it into town. It was empty. *That's odd. Where's my phone?* I looked around in the hip pockets of my pack where I sometimes put it. Just my knife and my chapstick, a mint, my prescription bottle, and a few empty wrappers. No phone. "Oh shit!" I said, turning to Santa, nauseated by the realization of what I'd just done. "I left my phone up there, charging. On that rock."

After trying his best to reassure me we'd find a way to get it back, he ducked into the grocery store to use the restroom. As I sat on the edge of the sidewalk, waiting for him, I grew more and more upset with myself. *What a stupid mistake.* I could see my phone now, sitting right where I'd left it. We'd been so excited about finally getting a hitch, we'd grabbed our packs in such a hurry I hadn't even looked back. *Why didn't you look back?...scan the area…make sure you hadn't forgotten anything? It would have taken you all of two seconds to pick it up. And now? Those two seconds are gonna cost you big time. No phone out here means no way to keep in touch with your girls. And no access to Guthooks. And no way to take pictures. And no keeping track of your mileage. And no way to contact Santa if the two of you get separated.*

Close to tears by the time Santa came back out, "What if my girls have been trying to get a hold of me?" I asked him. "And they think

I'm ignoring them because I haven't gotten back to them, Santa?" Handing me his phone, he calmly suggested I send them each a message, letting them know what happened and to use his number for now to get ahold of me. Once I did that, we posted a message on Guthooks as well, explaining right where I'd left it, and how to reach us in case anyone found it.

With that done, we walked through town until we found one of the few motels with a room still available. Given the recent surge in wildfires in the area, a good number of out-of-town fire crews were already occupying most of them. We dropped our packs off and cleaned ourselves up a bit, and then took off for the pub to watch the game. The place was packed. A couple of beers and a huge lunch later, much to Santa's disappointment, England lost to Italy on penalties.

With the start of a heat wave now in effect and the smoke continuing to worsen by the hour, we spent what was left of the day in the comfort of our air conditioned motel room.

Day 78: July 12, 2021

By morning, things had gotten so bad the National Weather Service issued a warning advising people to, "refrain from engaging in outdoor activities." And not only that, the Forest Service had chimed in as well, asking people not to endanger themselves (or fire crews for that matter) by going anywhere near active burn zones, now apparently including the one we'd just hiked out of.

"Great," I said, complaining to Santa as soon as we found all this out. "There goes our chances of hitching back up there today to look for my phone." No one in their right mind would be heading in that direction now. And that's assuming my phone was even still up there. With no response yet to the message we'd posted on Guthooks, there was no way of knowing for sure.

"Hey, what if we rent a car for the day and drive up there ourselves?" suggested Santa.

"Yeah," I nodded, smiling. *Why didn't I think of that?*

After 15 minutes of calling around, though, that option was off the table, as well. Not a single car anywhere in the area was available. Then Santa saw something on Facebook someone from one of the PCT groups he followed had posted about the wildfire situation being so bad in these parts, even the police were being recruited to help manage the scene. Which gave me an idea—a long shot, but worth a try. We walked down to the police station where, in a desperate attempt to get my phone back, I boldly asked the clerk behind the front desk if there was any chance someone from the station might be out patrolling by where I'd left it. And if so, if they'd be willing to stop and have a quick look. After pointing out where it was for her on a map, she disappeared into one of the back rooms. Returning a few minutes later, she apologized, telling me that with the current upswing in wildfire activity, there wasn't anyone available to do that.

Feeling discouraged, I sat down on the steps outside the station. Out of ideas as to what to try next, Santa checked Guthooks again to see if anyone had responded. This time someone had, not only to say my phone was still there, but, funnily enough, that it was done charging. Relieved to know it was still there, Santa then came up with perhaps his most unconventional idea as of yet. Willing to at least try it, we walked back down the road to the UHaul store we'd passed on our way to the police station. Half an hour later, he was dangling a set of keys to one of their moving vans in front of me, smiling triumphantly. "I'll drive up right now and get it for you," he said, kissing my forehead.

"Not all heroes wear capes." I said playfully, stretching up onto my tiptoes to give him a kiss this time.

"They sure don't," he said, laughing. "Good one, Bammer." Back outside by this point, we found the van we'd been assigned to.

Standing next to him as he unlocked it, my tone, serious now, rather than playful, "Thank you, Santa, for doing this," I said. "I love you."

"I love you, too, Girl." He gave me a hug and then got in the van and started the engine. Then, closing the door, he rolled the window down, and cranked up the radio—pretending to rock out, headbanging style, to whatever heavy metal 80's song the station it was set to was playing, before turning it back down.

Waving good-bye, he turned out of the parking lot and onto the main road. I stood, staring after him, as the van got smaller and smaller, in awe of his willingness to go so far out of his way to help me. *He really does love me.*

Returning to my senses, and having brought our dirty laundry along with me in a stuff sack, minus what we were wearing, of course, I set off to the laundromat. Passing a thrift store along the way, I popped in and bought a sundress. Dark blue with little white flowers, it was cotton and sleeveless, with a row of buttons running all the way down the front. It fit me perfectly, and the best part, aside from only costing five bucks, was that now I didn't have to sit around in my itchy, non-breathable, rain gear, sweating up a storm in the laundromat. Using the store dressing room to change into it, I stuffed what I'd just taken off into our sack of dirty clothes.

With the wash started, I walked over to a little retro looking drive-in with a walk up counter and treated myself to a jumbo size, soft serve ice cream cone. Trying my best to eat it faster than it was melting, once I finished it I got out of the heat by heading into the grocery store. I grabbed a cart and did some resupply shopping while enjoying the air conditioning, and then went back to the laundromat.

Santa pulled into the parking lot just as I was finishing up. Booty was with him as well. He'd been at the trailhead trying to hitch into town when Santa had shown up. Happy to see them both, and thrilled to now have my phone back, Santa handed me a handwritten note on a small piece of paper he'd found lying next to it. Addressed to "NOBO Hikers," it first relayed the information Santa had posted on Guthooks about me losing my phone, along with how to reach us. Then it asked for anyone planning to head into Quincy to please help by trying to get it to us.

Signed by someone by the trail name of Southern Hospitality, it ended by saying, "Keep trail magic & hospitality alive!!" It warmed my heart—the thought of a total stranger looking out for a fellow thru-hiker in this way. And it made me feel proud to know these were the kinds of people I was traveling this trail with.

The three of us caught up for a bit back at the motel before returning the UHaul. Then Santa and I spent one more night in town, watching movies, checking in with our families, enjoying the jetted tub in our room, and planning out our mileage for the next stretch.

Day 79: July 13, 2021

Between the current wildfire situation surrounding us, the record breaking high temperatures we were facing, and the air quality having now dropped into the "dangerously poor" zone, it was neither safe nor smart at this point to get back on the trail where we were. And as if all that weren't bad enough, the next stretch had completely burned up a few years prior, which meant not only no relief from the sun in the form of shade, but limited water sources as well. The only logical choice being to skip ahead, the question was, how far?

We spent most of the morning weighing our options, deciding in the end to get back on the trail near the next little town of Belden. We had to stop there anyway. It's where I had Hailey ship my next resupply package. Borrowing a marker from the front office of the motel, I spelled out, "Belden—PCT Hikers," in big block letters on a piece of cardboard. Then I held it up along the side of the road while we waited for someone to stop. Thankfully, we had a much easier time hitching out of Quincy than we had getting into it.

Once we made it to Belden, we stopped in at the little store (which also served as the post office) to pick up my package. Then we sat outside at one of the picnic tables as I dug through it. In addition to the things I'd put in there myself—a new pair of trail runners to replace my boots, a few days worth of food, and a fresh supply of electrolyte tables—Hailey had also thrown in my earbuds, a few letters, and a gift from Santa. The earbuds, because I'd asked her to. Having not been in the habit of hiking with them at home (more for safety reasons than anything, like being able to hear someone approaching) I'd started the trail without any. Since Santa had been sharing his with me, though, I'd warmed up to the idea of carrying my own. It was a nice form of distraction out here, being able to listen to music, especially during the ups when I was struggling to keep a good pace. I read each of the letters twice—one from Hailey, one from Madie, and one from my mom—before tucking them into my pack for safekeeping. And the gift from Santa? That was a surprise. After secretly getting in touch with Hailey to find out my size, and in the hopes of replacing my current pair, which had been quite literally falling apart, he'd ordered a new pair of hiking pants for me. Then he'd shipped them to Hailey, who'd agreed to add them to my resupply box. All without my knowing. I was touched that the two of them had worked together and gone to such lengths to surprise me. Using the bathroom behind the store to change into them, I happily tossed my old pair in the trash can. Other than being a bit long in the leg, they fit perfectly. Doing the same with my shoes, I double knotted the laces on my new pair of trail runners, and tossed my boots in the trash can, as well. Staring at them for a minute there on top of my pants, I felt a bit sad. They'd been the first pair of actual hiking boots I'd ever owned. Abandoning them here like this after relegating them to the garbage bin was no way to part with them. "You served me well," I said, twirling one of the laces between my thumb and my fingers before walking away.

With an entire week's worth of food now in our packs, plus, at least another five pounds of water, we walked along the side of the road from there until we got to the trailhead, at which point we then had a steep 6,500 foot climb in store. Dreading the ups, as Santa had looked ahead on the map and forewarned me, I had cued up a selection of energetic, fast past songs on my phone in the hopes that it would help. I put my earbuds in, hit "play," and fell in line behind Santa. Fully into my music by song number two, I found myself on his heels and itching to pass him—his slow and steady pace being no match at the moment for the rhythm I was feeling. Tapping his elbow with the side of my trekking pole to get his attention, as he had his earbuds in, too, I motioned with my hand for him to move to the side, stuck my tongue out at him, playfully, and like a show off, blew past him. Over my shoulder I vaguely heard something like, "You might wanna pace yourself," but I couldn't be sure, and the song playing was so good I didn't want to stop it to check. I just looked back, smiled and waved, and kept going.

The heat was relentless, as was the smoke, and the higher we climbed the more I started to feel it. Just here and there, at first, waves of nausea and dizziness. I took my earbuds out and slowed down. *Santa was right. I do need to pace myself.* After an hour or two, the passing waves became spells, lasting longer and longer. And then, it all took a turn for the worse. I was on a rocky ledge when it happened, and having long since caught up with me, Santa had passed me, rounded a corner, and was now out of sight. Feeling a strong urge to throw up, I sat down right where I was, on the trail. *Maybe it'll pass if I just rest here for a minute.* It didn't, though. And worse, my whole body suddenly felt weak. Too weak to keep going. So weak, in fact, that even the thought of standing back up felt impossible. I unbuckled my chest and hip straps and slid my pack off my shoulders. Then, using it as a pillow, I laid down. I'd never experienced heat exhaustion before, but having read enough about it to be concerned that might be just what was happening, a rush of panic set in. *This isn't smart. The last thing you should be doing right now is laying here, baking in the sun. What you need to do is catch up to Santa—to let him know you're not okay.*

My body just wasn't having it, though.

I heard the faint sound of voices. Growing louder as the minutes passed, I propped myself up on my elbows to have a look around. A few switchbacks below me, I saw a small group of hikers making their way up the mountain. Stopping once they reached me to ask if I was okay, I told them—as if trying to convince myself as well as them that I was strong enough to handle this—that I was fine. That I was just feeling the heat a bit. And that I wasn't alone—that my partner was just up ahead. Although they seemed reluctant to leave me there, they eventually continued on.

Once they'd gone far enough I could no longer see or hear them, I talked myself into trying to stand up. Peering out over the ledge as I slowly got to my feet, I couldn't help noticing what a long drop down to the bottom it was from this height. Feeling a rush of lightheadedness as soon as I was upright, my peripheral vision went dark, and then started closing in—the same god awful way it always does right before I pass out. Much like the curtains on either side of a stage being drawn shut at the end of a performance. Taking a few slow, deep breaths in an effort not to lose consciousness, I laid back down in the dirt with my head on my pack, and drew my knees into my chest. *You're okay. You just need a minute.*

The next thing I remember, Santa was standing above me. "Bammer, you can't stop here," he said, looking me over.

"I don't feel well, Santa," I said, hoping that would be enough to explain the situation. He knelt down beside me and put his hand on my forehead.

"You're too hot," he said. "We gotta find you some shade."

"I can't, Santa," I said, weakly. "I really don't feel well."

"I know," he said, sympathetically. "But you can't stay here in the sun like this. It's making things worse."

"But, I don't wanna move," I whined. He pulled a water bottle from my pack, had me take a few small sips, and then put it back.

"Come on," he said, lifting me to my feet. "I'll help you."

Once again standing, I felt a little more steady now that Santa was with me. Still a bit dizzy, although not as bad as before, and still nauseous, although the urge to actually puke had eased up, but my vision, at least, was back to normal, so that was a plus. Looking down at my pack, the task of picking it up, let alone carrying it right now, felt like entirely too much. As if reading my mind, Santa told me not to bother with it.

"Just leave it there for now," he said, leading me by my arm as we slowly started walking. "I'll come back for it once we find you some shade."

We made our way around the next couple of corners before finding what appeared to be the only shrub within a two mile radius big enough to produce a patch of shade I could actually fit under. Santa dropped an electrolyte tablet into one of his water bottles and then, handing it to me, told me to drink it while he went back for my pack.

Joining me on the ground once he got back, I asked him how he'd known to come looking for me. After handing me a protein bar and insisting I try and eat it, he went on to explain how he'd stopped to wait for me. How, once the group of hikers who had passed me caught up with him, he'd asked if they'd seen me. As soon as they told him they had and that I was stopped and wasn't looking well, he'd come to find me.

Scooching closer to him, I reached for his hand so I could hold it. "Thank you, Santa," I said, smiling at him. "I'm not–" I started to say. Turning my attention towards the ground by my feet, I took a deep breath. "I really don't–" *Oh, good lord—just spit it out.* "It's just that–" *It's just that, apparently, I have no idea whether to shut the fuck up or say what I need to to help you understand where I'm coming from.* Swapping his hand for a small twig lying by my shoe, I started drawing lines in the dirt with it. *Just tell him. He's not gonna make you feel weak for it—he doesn't do that.* "It's just that, I'm not used to letting people help me." Still staring at the twig in my hand, I snapped it in half between my fingers and let it fall to the ground. "And I'm sorry you had to. But I sure do appreciate it." Daring to glance back up from the ground, I looked up at him. "I'm glad you're here," I confessed.

"You have no reason to be sorry," he said, leaning in for a kiss. "And I'm happy that I'm here to help you."

"Not all heroes wear capes," I said, elbowing him playfully, trying to lighten the mood.

Feeling much better, although still not 100 percent, he then insisted on transferring a few things from my pack into his, to help lighten my load.

As we slowly continued climbing, the more evident it became that one of the larger wildfires burning just to the south of us was heading our way, and fast. By midafternoon we could actually see the flames—deep orange with violent looking puffs of black smoke rising out of them. It began raining ash down on us as well, although it took us a few minutes to figure out that's what it was—these multitudes of powder soft, grayish-white flecks floating around us. Before long the ground was coated with it, looking much like a light dusting of winter snow had just fallen. And, of course, the smoke just kept worsening. It grew so thick we tied bandanas over our mouths and noses to keep from breathing too much of it in. And the sky itself was nothing more than a hazy, dirty looking off-white color—blotting out the sun so completely there weren't even shadows on the ground.

Second guessing our decision to get back on where we had, we debated whether we should backtrack to the trailhead and skip further ahead, or keep going in the hopes of outrunning this. After confirming no new closures had been reported by the Forest Service as of yet, we decided to keep going.

Feeling utterly depleted by the time we stopped to make dinner, we set up camp and went straight to sleep as soon as we finished eating.

The next morning, with big plans to log a decent number of miles before the heat of the day hit, we woke up early. Trudging, once again, through thick smoke and falling ash, we neared and then passed the 1,300 mile marker, eventually covering 23 miles by the end of the day.

Day 81: July 15, 2021

Thankfully, by the next morning, although the smoke was still bad, we'd managed to get far enough away from the fires we no longer had the ash to contend with. A small win, but a victory, nonetheless.

Another, even larger, victory in store for us today, was the half-way point of the trail. A monument marking the spot lay waiting for us just a handful of miles ahead. After waking up early again, I got a head start on Santa. Far too excited to pace myself properly, the closer I got, the quicker I moved.

I had the place to myself when I reached it—a small stone pillar to the side of the trail. "Canada, 1323.2" was inscribed on one side of it, "Mexico, 1323.2" on the other, and "PCT Midpoint" down the front. A log had been laid down and secured in place behind it to be used as a bench. And resting on top of that was a small hiker box with a few trinkets, a notebook, and a pencil inside.

At first glance, this spot was no different from any other so far. Pine trees of various heights lining either side of a dirt path. The familiar rustling of a small bird or chipmunk, foraging around in the bushes. Rays of sunlight streaming down through gaps in the branches, illuminating an otherwise invisible sea of tiny particles floating around in the air.

It wasn't the same, though. This place, as I stood here, felt sacred. And not just because of the two and a half months it had taken to get here, but because not everyone who started out on this journey ever would. The fact that I was even standing here meant something.

I took my pack off, then knelt down next to the monument to take a few selfies. All smiles initially—the steady stream of conflicting emotions I'd spent the past several miles trying to sort through finally getting the best of me—by picture number three, I was crying.

Not wanting to go any further until Santa caught up with me, I sat down on the bench and tried to think of how to put my tears into words. Maybe I was just relieved at finally making it halfway? Or, discouraged that I still had halfway to go? Perhaps I was proud of the fact that for all this time now, in spite of how hard and scary some things had been, I'd beaten the odds so far—I was still out here, and still at it, and still just as determined to finish? I was missing my girls, too, of course, that could be part of it, now more than ever in the midst of such a big milestone. I was hungry, as well—that didn't help. And worn out. And tired of being dirty. Perhaps it was all of these things, all at once.

I brushed away my tears as another hiker approached. I didn't recognize him. Stepping aside from the monument so he could now have his turn with it, I did my best to act like I hadn't just been on the brink of having a meltdown.

Checking my phone to see if I had cell service, I walked a little ways back up the trail, and then dialed my brother's number.

"Hello," he said, answering. My eyes, again, filled with tears, now, from the sound of his voice.

"Hey, Eddie—it's me!" I said, relieved that he'd answered, as the buzzing and pounding I could hear in the background no doubt meant that he was busy running one of his construction sites.

"Hey! How's it going?" he asked. "Where you at?"

"I'm standing at the halfway point along the trail right now," I said, proudly. "That's where I'm calling you from."

"You're only halfway?" he said, sounding surprised. "I thought you passed that point a while back?"

Oh my god, are you serious right now? No one on the planet has a knack quite like you do for keeping me humble.

"No," I laughed, trying to sound like I wasn't offended. "I got elevation sickness awhile back, and that slowed me down a bit."

"Oh," he said. "Well, good job. I'm proud of you, Sis." I could tell by his voice that he meant it. *I guess that makes up for the "only halfway" comment.*

"You stay safe," he added, "and be careful out there."

"I will," I assured him, "and thanks."

"I love you, Sis."

"I love you, too," I said, smiling. I tapped the "end call" button, and then stood there, staring at my phone. *Thank you, God, for technology. And cell service. And my brother—how his no nonsense approach to life always has a way of making me feel better.*

Santa caught up a few minutes later. We sat and rested while we ate a snack. Then we took a few pictures together by the monument. Then, flipping through the notebook in the hiker box together, we took turns reading aloud through several pages of what those who'd come before us had felt compelled to record in it. Along with trail names and hometowns and the dates of when they'd passed through, a few had written out poems or left quotes or random tidbits of wisdom they'd gained since being out here. Anytime we saw a name of someone we knew, we'd stop for a minute and guess how far ahead they might be based on the date by their name. Then, with all the fascination and delight of a schoolgirl whose initials were being carved into a tree by her crush, I watched as Santa flipped to the most recent entry, and just underneath it, added, "BAMTA." This being the first time I'd actually seen our joint-couple trail name in writing, I couldn't help staring at it even after he'd finished. How five little letters could be arranged in such a way as to breathe life into this sense of togetherness and affection Santa and I had managed to find was beyond me. All I knew was that I liked it—so much, I made Santa walk in front of me as we started out again so he wouldn't see the goofy looking perma-grin plastered across my face.

Making our way from there, we started listing off all the people whose names we hadn't seen in the notebook, speculating as to whether each of them was still on the trail or not, and if so, how far back they might be. Having already said good-bye to what felt like far too many of the people we'd come to know and care about out here, the prospect of anyone else choosing not to push on towards the finish line was disheartening.

With everyone accounted for, we continued on in silence. Not the uncomfortable kind you feel the need to remedy by saying anything, really, just for the sake of talking, but rather, the kind where it's perfectly fine to get lost in your own thoughts for a while. I liked that about us—how we didn't always feel the need to fill the space between us. That sometimes, it was enough just to be near each other, walking along the same path, heading in the same direction.

Feeling the need to mentally check out for a bit after all the build up and excitement of reaching the midway point, I focused, absent-mindedly, on Santa's feet as I followed behind him. Watching as he swung, first one leg and then the other, always the same distance forward before planting his foot down again. And again. And again. Until the steady rhythm of his stride turned into a singsong chant-like series of repeating syllables in my mind.

Right-left. Right-left. Right-left.

Which made me think of the game, Twister. Right foot, green. Left hand, red. Which made me think of traffic lights. Which made me think of directions. Which made me think of North, which, of course, was where we were heading. And had been ever since way back in April. May. June. July, which was now. And the 15th, which was today. Which meant this month was already halfway over. Just like the trail. The entire first half of it, now officially behind us.

Half-way. Half-way. Half-way.

Which meant I still had the entire second half to go. And only a month and a half now until the end of August. Which is when I had to be done by. A month and a half. To walk as far as I just had—again—which had taken me nearly three months. Could I do it? If I really hustled? Could I make it all the way to the finish line in time?

Finish-line. Finish-line. Finish-line.

Which made me think of running. Which made me think of racing bibs, and water stations, and the boom of a gun going off at the starting line. Which made me think of my first half-marathon. How I'd gotten an email from the race coordinators the week afterward, apologizing for the fact that the course had been mismarked, adding on an extra three-quarters of a mile. Which made me think of how three-quarters of a mile was the equivalent to three laps around a high school football track. And how four laps is a mile. Which made me think of how Santa, in an attempt to help me better understand kilometers, which, not only Canada, but pretty much the entire rest of the world uses to measure distance it turns out, had told me two and a half laps around a track is one kilometer. Which meant five laps would be two. Ten laps would be four. And 20 laps would be eight. Kilometers, that is. In miles, 20 laps would be five. Which made me wonder how far, in whatever kind of measurement, it was until the next water source.

I dug my phone out of my pocket and opened the Guthooks app. Glancing at the ground every few steps to keep from tripping, I scanned the map until I found the nearest upcoming little water droplet icon. Tapping on it to pull up more details—precise location, how it ranks on a scale from being "surprisingly refreshing" to "you're gonna want to filter the shit out of this before drinking it," whether or not it's dried up by this point—a big, knotty root I failed to notice sent me stumbling.

Santa, who had, unfortunately, already witnessed this very scenario play out on numerous occasions since the two of us started hiking together, turned around just in time to watch the tail end of me not so gracefully avoid falling. "BAM," he scolded playfully, pointing to my phone, still in my hand. "That's as dangerous out here for you as driving drunk."

Smiling sheepishly, as I knew full well—*goddamnit*—he was right, I held my phone up all melodramatic-like, turned it off, slid it back into my pocket, and patted it a few times for safe keeping. Apparently satisfied, he turned back around, and we both continued walking. Paying close attention, as I took my first few steps, for any sign of pain indicating I may have perhaps rolled an ankle, I was relieved nothing hurt. A close call—too close for comfort as it, just as easily, could have ended my trip. Which made me think back to my first couple of weeks out here when, on two separate occasions, hikers had been airlifted out, both of them because of ankle injuries. And how, from that point on, the sound of a helicopter approaching automatically carried with it a sense of dread, that someone else's hike was now over as well. For the umpteenth time, I offered up a silent prayer that my own journey wouldn't have to end before I had a chance to make it to the finish line. Which made me imagine myself, smiling and filthy, standing next to the PCT monument at the Canadian border that I'd seen so many pictures of. Posing for my final, finish line picture—ecstatic, exhausted, successful. Which brought me all the way back to my original question of whether or not I thought I could make it there in time. Which made me wonder how I'd handle it if I didn't. And what would that say about me? And how, then, would I be able to face anyone back home? Which made me think of home. And going back there. And then what?

Then-what? Then-what? Then-what? Played out in time with my steps.

I'd done a great job planning for the PCT, but a lousy one concerning anything after that. Hell, I hadn't even figured out how I was getting home yet once I finished.

Of course, at least initially, I'd just pick up where I left off. Back in Idaho, with my girls, waitressing to pay the bills. But for how long? And then what? What did I want the rest of my life to look like?

And there it was. The same damn question I had been avoiding ever since my marriage had ended, taking the future I'd spent my whole lifetime mapping out for myself with it. And by avoiding, I mean as if I were allergic to it. And not mildly, like a slight rash or a six in a row kind of sneezing fit, but deathly, like how penicillin sends me straight into anaphylactic shock and I end up in the emergency room. Too afraid of the possibility of ever suffering that same degree of disappointment again to even contemplate answering it at that time, the PCT had been as far down the line as I'd been willing to commit.

This had actually served me quite well up to this point. Having the trail to plan for and look forward to these past several years had not only helped ease me back into the practice of setting at least some short-medium term goals for myself, it had served as a buffer between day-to-day life in the present tense and the eventual inevitability of one day having to come up with a new long term plan for my life.

Now, though, with the end of this trail being as far into my future as I'd dared yet to plan, I was right back where I'd started. Facing the same damn question, and feeling just as incapable of answering it.

Now what? Now what? Now what?

Although I guess I wasn't all the way back to where I started, entirely. Some things had changed. My girls were both grown now, for one thing. Which meant my options were a bit more open. Which made me think about how I'd always loved traveling. Which made me think of the Workaway program I recently looked into, where you sign up for anywhere from a few weeks to several months at a time to go and work somewhere else. With locations all over the world to choose from, it could potentially be a good way to experience some places I wouldn't otherwise be able to afford to travel to? Or maybe find work on a cruise ship? Or become a flight attendant? Which made me think of going back to school. Which made me think of Santa and him being a professor. I tried to imagine him, teaching a class. Which made me realize I'd never actually seen him dressed in anything other than hiking clothes. Which made me think of the closetful of clothes I had waiting for me back home—all clean and smelling of dryer sheets. I called to mind specific outfits. Trying to decide which one I'd pick if Santa and I were to ever go out on a back-in-the-real-world style date, like out to a show or a fancy restaurant or something. Which made me think about how everyday out here had a "being out on a date" like feel to it now, thanks to Santa. All the picnic lunches and cool swimming spots, cozy campfires under starry night skies. All the quiet sunrises and picture perfect sunsets. The excursions into town, hiding away in our tent together, and, of course, hiking.

Which made me wonder, once this whole, big, long, trail-style "date" of ours ended, where would that leave us? At the tail end of a summer fling, heading our separate ways? Or, would we end up staying together as a couple? If we did, how would that even work? We lived in two different countries.

As the questions kept coming, an unsettling sense of urgency began to take hold of me. Surprisingly intense, and getting worse by the minute, it soon felt as if a pair of hands were inside my rib cage, squeezing my lungs, making it hard to breathe. Unable at this point to keep up with Santa, after watching him disappear around the next corner, I stopped in the middle of the trail, and lifting my arms up, rested my hands on top of my head. This made me think of Jodie, my very first running partner back when I was brand new at it. How she'd shown me how to do this to help open my airways when I was feeling winded. I closed my eyes and focused on nothing but inhaling and exhaling. *Just breathe. It's okay that you don't have it all figured out yet. Just let yourself enjoy being out here. Let that be enough for now. Whatever comes next will work itself out in time. It always does.*

A few minutes and a couple of sips of water later I caught back up to Santa, who, thanks to having his earbuds in, hadn't even noticed I'd fallen behind. Tuning in, once again, to the rhythm of his stride, I wondered how many more miles the pair of shoes he was wearing would end up lasting him.

Last-ing. Last-ing. Last-ing.

Which made me think about how, these days, things weren't made to last nearly as long as they used to be. Especially appliances. Toasters. Blenders. Hair dryers. Which made me think of shampoo. And steamy bathroom mirrors. And the luxury of warm running water. Knowing damn well we were still too many days away from being near enough to a town to start indulging in those kinds of thoughts, made me think to ask Santa if he wouldn't mind sharing one of his ear buds so I could listen in on his podcast. I clearly needed to get out of my own head for a while.

Day 82: July 16, 2021

Whereas we'd willingly covered 30 miles yesterday, we actually *had* to do 30 today, thanks to some pretty hefty restrictions in Lassen Volcanic National Park, which we were about to pass through. No overnight camping was allowed without a bear canister. Seeing as how this was the only stretch, other than the Sierra Nevada Mountains requiring one, most of us had shipped ours home. Our only option once we entered the park was to keep going, all the way through.

Stopping to rest for a bit after our first 20 miles, we sat in the sand along the shore of a good size lake, while we ate a snack and took turns filtering water. Feeling sluggish, as by now it was late afternoon, a dangerously tempting thought came to mind regarding what a nice place to stop and camp this would be. Knowing the emotional risks involved with entertaining such thoughts, I dismissed it immediately. A little too late, though, apparently, because, thanks to my next thought—*Yeah, guess who won't be lounging lazily here on this beach for the rest of the evening?*—now I was cranky. And not only that, but resentful—of the next 10 fucking miles we still had to get through.

I was practically pouting as we packed up to keep going. Santa offered me one of his earbuds, in what I gathered by the look on his face was a hopeful attempt to distract me out of the foul mood I'd just fallen into. After several minutes of trying to decide what to listen to, we agreed on the audiobook, *Sapiens*, by Yuval Noah Harari.

Just past the lake, as we began the first chapter, we entered an old burn zone. Barren and bleak looking, the evening sun cast long sideways shadows off the charred, branchless remnants of whatever forest had been here before the fire had swept through.

Several hours, one colorful sunset, and two or three chapters later, we found ourselves in front of a forest service sign marking the northernmost boundary of the park. Finally free now to set up camp, we began to search in the dark, by the light of our headlamps, for a spot big enough for the tent. Unfortunately, there was none. Too many other hikers, in exactly our same predicament, had beaten us there. With no choice but to press on further, it was another 10-15 minutes before we eventually found a spot.

With the tent up and dinner finished, I watched as Santa took, first his shoes, and then his socks off. Not that me watching him do this was in any way whatsoever a normal part of our nightly routine, but as someone who wasn't prone to complaining, the fact that earlier in the day he'd mentioned his foot had started hurting, I was curious what might be wrong.

"Oh shit!" he said, staring down at his feet.

"What is it?" I asked, clicking my headlamp on to its brightest setting, and leaning over his lap so I could get a good look. "Oh my god, Santa!" I gasped. Both fascinated and horrified, I sat motionless, staring at it. "Does it hurt?"

"Yeah!" he said, laughing, as if that much, at least, should be obvious just by looking at it. "Like a son of a bitch," he added.

Not at all the bruise or blister I'd been imagining—there, along the outside edge on the top of his left foot, a little nearer his toes than his heel, was a huge, bulging cyst. Like a golf ball poking up from under his skin, which was red, as if hot to the touch, and stretched so tight it looked almost shiny. Having never seen anything like it, I was surprised, and quite honestly, a little impressed, something this severe looking hadn't slowed him down. I, for one, would have been planning the quickest route to get medical attention hours ago. Santa, being Santa, though, in sticking with his more "let's just keep an eye on it" approach to such things, popped a couple of ibuprofen, put his sock back on, and got a good, full night's sleep.

With it neither looking, nor feeling, any better the next morning, we slowed our pace a bit and took a few more breaks than normal. Stopping for the day at the end of 20 miles, along a wide open ridge, we took in a beautiful sunset as we ate our dinner, and then cowboy camped under the stars.

PART FIVE

The Big Shift

"All the art of living
lies in a fine mingling
of letting go and holding on."

–Havelock Ellis

Day 84: July 18, 2021

The upside to not sleeping in a tent is the time and trouble it spares you, not having to put it up or take it down. The downside? You're fair game to all the things outside, whether crawling, slithering, flying, hopping, buzzing, biting, or what have you. As a not so friendly reminder of this fact, we woke the next morning to find the back of Santa's T-shirt covered in tiny bite-size holes. Having used it during the night as a pillow, some critter, most likely attracted to the salty scent of Santa's sweat, had at some point snatched it right out from under him.

"At least it didn't run off with it," Santa said, after examining it. Then he slipped it back on and twirled around a few times, modeling his new "holes and all" look for me.

As we made our way through yet another long, hot day, the pain in Santa's foot progressively worsened from the dull throbbing sensation he'd begun to feel yesterday to a sharp pain now shooting up his leg with each step. I found myself beginning to worry, wondering how much longer this could keep up before it became serious enough that he might need to consider leaving the trail. The possibility of him not being out here with me anymore was too sad to fathom.

Having many of the same thoughts, apparently, Santa was the first to speak up. Halfway through the day by this point, we sat beside each other, resting, on a giant, old, ant infested log. Flicking them off, one at a time, as they neared me, I listened quietly as he told me he'd been thinking about what it might mean for the two of us if he ended up having to quit.

We'd had quite a few conversations over the past couple of months about our reasons for being out here and what the trail meant to each of us. He knew how hard I'd worked and how long I'd been waiting for my shot to be able to do this, and that nothing short of me sustaining a serious injury, or something terrible happening to one of my girls would send me home. That it wasn't just that I wanted to finish, but that I needed to. After first reminding me of all this, he then went on to say that he and

I were different in that regard. That if I had to quit for some reason, he wouldn't choose, or even want, to go any further without me. And that, not that I didn't care about him just as much as he cared about me, but if he had to leave, he knew I wanted this bad enough to still keep going on my own.

All of which was true.

Or, at least, it had been. Now, though, as I was hearing him say all this, I knew something had shifted. That how I'd come to feel about Santa had in turn changed how I felt about the trail.

Hopping down off the log, I stood in front of him with my hands on his knees so we were eye level with each other. "If you end up having to leave the trail, Santa–" I paused, sensing the gravity of what I was about to say next, and wanting to be sure I had his full attention. "Then I'm leaving with you."

He looked surprised. I was, too, in all honesty—those weren't words I ever imagined myself saying. But I meant it. And what's more, it felt right. Just as it had had a definite starting point, the trail would eventually end. Santa and I didn't necessarily have to, though. Which meant, crossing the finish line, although it was something I still very much wanted, was no longer as important to me than being with him was.

He smiled and reached for my hands. As he held them in his, his voice was firm. "You're not leaving the trail, BAM. Even if that means I come out and trail angel you every chance I get. And check in with you on your inReach. And cheer you on from afar. You're finishing this—one way or another."

"I mean it, Santa," I said. "You've come to mean that much to me."

"I'm flattered," he said, lifting one of his hands to my cheek and stroking it gently with his thumb. "I am. But you're not leaving the trail," he said, shaking his head, side to side.

With neither of us budging, in the end we agreed to take it one step at a time. The first of those being to get him to a doctor. At least then we'd have a better idea of what it was we were dealing with.

Knowing the town of Burney was just ahead which, although quite small, did have a medical clinic, Santa pushed on through the pain. We passed the 1,400 mile marker as evening approached. I was a little taken aback to see this one. Unlike any before, it was made out of animal bones. From the size of them, most likely, a fox or coyote. After a grand total for the day of 31 miles, we got as close to the main road into town as we could before we stopped for the night.

Day 85: July 19, 2021

As we neared the road the next morning I walked behind Santa, smiling to myself as our conversation from yesterday replayed in my mind. Surprised that I still felt okay about the possibility of choosing not to finish the trail, "Hike your own hike," came to mind—a common saying among thru-hikers meaning anything from "to each their own," to "mind your own business." Although I hadn't been familiar with the term before starting the PCT, I'd since heard others say it and voiced it myself, many times. And the more familiar I became with it the more fully I began to comprehend the deeper meaning behind it. So much more than a simple catchphrase, it's a mindset—one that encourages autonomy, honors uniqueness, and fosters personal growth—a blatant rejection of any "one size fits all" mentality in relation to pace, gear, techniques, goals, and values. *Hike your own hike—that's what's happening here. You're doing just that. In fact, you have been, all along, more and more, the longer you've been out here. Giving yourself permission to do things your way, even if that means going against what everyone else (including you yourself at the start of this trail) would do.*

We stood on the side of the road with our thumbs out just in time to hit the morning rush of commuters. As luck would have it, the first car to drive past pulled over and offered us a ride. Luckier still, the driver just so happened to be a nurse practitioner on her way into the clinic where she worked. Upon finding that out, Santa explained the trouble he was having with his foot to her, and asked if she had any suggestions. She offered to take a look at it if he stopped in during her shift. Then she pointed out where her clinic was as she was dropping us off.

First things first, we headed straight for the diner, where Knux and Prime, who'd beaten us into town by a day, joined us for breakfast. Then Santa walked over to the medical clinic to wait his turn to be seen, and I walked over to the laundromat where I changed into my rain gear while everything else was washing.

Meeting up again, shortly thereafter, Santa was very excited and extremely relieved as he told me all about the, "medical miracle," he'd just experienced. About how our driver-turned-physician had first sterilized and then completely drained the cyst on his foot. And then bandaged it up, giving him a syringe of his own, even, along with some extra bandages so he could do it himself if it filled back up again out on the trail. The best part, though, was that his foot now felt totally fine. Which meant no more having to worry about anyone leaving the trail.

With that taken care of, we checked into a motel where we quite happily spent the rest of the day holed up in our room, out of the heat and away from the smoke, which had only been getting worse now that a brand new batch of wildfires had broken out to the north of us, up in Oregon, as well.

Venturing out for a quick resupply towards the end of the day, we also met up for dinner with Knux and Prime, and Chaparral, which was a nice surprise, as I hadn't seen her in ages.

Day 86: July 20, 2021

Knowing that once we made it back to the trail it was only half a day's walk until our next stop, and being in no rush whatsoever to escape the cool comfort of our air conditioned motel room, we slept in until check out time.

Relieved that Santa was finally able to walk again without his foot hurting, we pushed on towards our next stop, Burney Falls. A state park nestled in the forest with a campground, a few hiking trails, a little store, and, as the name suggests, an impressive waterfall. Unlike any of the other attractions along the PCT, this one I was familiar with. My ex and/or our girls and I had stopped there on several different occasions over the years along road trips back to Idaho while we'd been living in California. Having made plans to meet up again with Knux and Prime there later that afternoon, I was excited for the chance, not only to see it again for myself, but to do so with tramily.

Thirteen dusty and hot miles later, soaked with sweat and happy to be done for the day, we made a beeline for the store near the entrance of the park. Weaving our way through swarms of tourists, we bought some cold drinks and ice cream. Then, we found the hike-and-bike section of the campground, as well as Knux and Prime who were already there, dropped our packs off, and wandered over, the four of us, to check out the falls.

Chaparral caught up shortly after. Joining us just in time for a special delivery of trail magic right to our campsite, courtesy of a friend of mine, Donny. Living relatively close to this stretch, and being familiar with the PCT himself, not only had he been cheering me on from afar since I started, but he'd kindly offered to drive out and spoil us. And spoil us, he did—with a cooler full of cold beer and sodas and an impressive spread of goodies. After not having seen him in three to four years it was fun to finally catch up in person again, and to be able to introduce him to everyone.

The next day we covered 21 miles.

And 27 the day after that. A mama bear with two little cubs staring us down as we made our way past her, the highlight of this one.

And then 12.

And then just over 23. All the while winding through a lush stretch of forest—the air so thick, with not only smoke, but memories, I was practically choking on it. Nevermind that it had been five years since I'd lived here, in this part of California—it was where my marriage had ended. And being back now was starting to mess with my head.

> iPhone note July 23, 2021 at 8:45 am:
>
> *I had a bone to pick, heading out here, with life. The unfairness. The betrayal. The darkness of it all, that seemed unsurpassable. I needed more than anything to get out from under what was causing me to feel less than…and some of that shit runs years deep.*
>
> *I'm out here because I needed to step away from everyday life long enough to be able to deal with my shit...like thinking I don't measure up/am not good enough.*
>
> *I've heard it said, "Never be with someone who thinks you're hard to love." But what the hell am I supposed to do with that if I'm that someone? I'm the one who thinks I'm hard to love. How am I supposed to get away from that?*

The downside of having all the time in the world to think about things is that your mind can very quickly take you down some very deep rabbit holes—much like this one. On the plus side, though, you also have time enough to try and dig yourself out of them. Not that it's easy, especially when it involves untangling thought knots like these regarding such deep seated feelings of unworthiness and self-loathing. Unfortunately, these were knots that had been tripping me up now for as long as I could remember. Sparked initially by the traumatic events during my growing up years, only to be fueled by self-sabotaging behaviors, the end result had been a harsh and twisted mindset in regards to myself which, looking back now, I could see had cost me dearly over the years—holding me back from things like asking for promotions, speaking up for myself, and believing I could do things.

Thankfully, having been hellbent on acquiring a healthier, more loving approach to how I viewed myself after my divorce, I'd made a lot of progress in this regard over the past several years. I'd gone to personal growth workshops and read a whole slew of self-help books. I'd joined a support group, and worked one-on-one with two different therapists. I'd learned about boundaries and how to set them, and what my strengths were and how to use them. All of this had helped, exponentially, to improve not only how I talked to and treated myself, but how I interacted with my friends and family. Even things at work got better. In fact, the only area of my life it hadn't helped, from what I could tell, was in regards to my romantic endeavors. Or, perhaps more accurately, my approach to them. Without fail, I repeatedly either choose to date people who were no good for me, or, if they were, I behaved in ways that kept them at a distance—calling the whole thing off entirely at the first sign of anything serious.

The bottom line was, for all the progress I'd made as far as learning to love myself, I still remained unconvinced that anyone else could. Despite successfully untangling all the other, outer strings of this thought knot, that for so many years had prevented me from feeling worthy or deserving of anything, really, this one last piece at the very center I couldn't seem to undo. At least, not alone. And for the life of me, I kept refusing to let anyone help.

Until now that is—until I'd found myself out here on the trail with Santa.

The difference was, for one thing, in dating-type situations back in the real world, whenever something came up or got a little too real for my liking, I had the option of leaving, which I usually did. Out here, though, with there being nowhere to go, my only options were to either deal with things head on as they arose, or pretend, in the hopes that Santa would neither notice nor call me out on my bullshit, that I wasn't having an issue with something in the first place. And while the first option was hard to fathom—the idea of showcasing my flaws and insecurities being one of, if not the most, nauseating thoughts I could imagine—the second meant closing myself off to the possibility of allowing him the opportunity to better understand how and why certain things were affecting me. And I already knew, all too well, where taking that route would get me. The same place it always had—nowhere.

The other biggest contributing factor in this equation was Santa himself. He was the real deal—the kind of man whose words matched his actions. He didn't just tell me he had my back, he demonstrated it, time and again. Nor did he simply tell me he loved me—he was loving towards me in everything he said and did. He was honest with me, too. Not once had he given me reason to doubt him. Because of all this, I had grown to trust him—first as a friend, and then as a partner.

And all these factors combined had created precisely the set of circumstances I'd needed in order to feel safe enough to finally allow someone an honest shot at winning me over. Which is why, that night back at Chicken Spring Lake, just before our first kiss, when I'd agreed to give us a try, I hadn't just been agreeing to date him. I was agreeing to give us a fair shot—which meant choosing to be honest and upfront with him as we moved forward together. And that's what I'd been doing. Every time. Every time my fear of commitment reared its ugly head. Every time an old insecurity caused by some other man's bad behavior during a much different time in my life popped up. Every time I was afraid that sharing my true feelings might cause him to think I was too much to handle, I mustered up the courage to do it anyway. And as I did, as I questioned and explained and even cried my way through it at times, he was there. Loving me, to my surprise, all the more for it.

Day 91: July 25, 2021

By midmorning, after making our way to a spot along one of the main roads where my friend, Donny, who'd trail angel-ed us back at Burney Falls, had agreed to pick us up, we piled into his truck and took off towards Mt. Shasta. And a nice, leisurely, diner-style breakfast. And a cozy little motel room. And a long, hot, soapy shower. And a laundromat packed with thru-hikers. And then, as a special treat that evening, an outdoor concert in the park that Donny had offered to take us to. I invited a woman named Pauline, who was staying in the room next to us to come along, too. Having traveled all the way from Mexico in the hopes of climbing Mt. Shasta, we'd met out in front of our motel that afternoon while a bunch of us had been waiting to check in. Curious to hear all about thru-hiking after noticing our packs, I'd filled her in on the gist of the PCT. Then she'd given me the lowdown on how her climb had gone. We'd hit it off instantly, so well, in fact, that after 30 minutes of chatting we were following each other on Instagram and promising to stay in touch.

Day 92: July 26, 2021

The next morning, after taking one last shower for no reason other than because I still could, we checked out of the motel and walked over to the main part of town. With our resupply out of the way, as Donny had been kind enough to run us by a grocery store after the concert last night, all we needed to do now was find a ride back to the trail.

Typically, under normal circumstances, this wouldn't be too hard to manage. Because of the huge number of hikers, though, who had skipped up to this point within the past day or two (some of them, hundreds of miles), we were finding it difficult. Of course, it made sense why they were doing it. With the whole wildfire situation to the south of us having only grown worse and more dangerous by the day since we were down there, they were trying to get ahead of the smoke. Crazily enough, in talking with some of them outside one of the coffee shops, we found out that the Forest Service had officially closed the trail where we'd gotten back on in Belden, after Quincy, the very next day after we'd passed through it.

The biggest downside to this new development, though, at least from a thru-hiking perspective, was the negative effect such a sudden influx of hikers was bound to have in regards to the amount of resources available, especially in smaller towns like this where they were limited to begin with. They simply weren't equipped to be able to handle too many of us at one time. And there were definitely too many of us here, now. Everywhere you looked, every restaurant and store, every street corner and public bench, was swarming with hikers. It was no wonder we were having trouble finding a ride with this much competition.

Of course, eventually, we did, although it took us half the day, and we had to pay handsomely for it.

All that aside, once we got back on the trail, Castle Crags State Park was up next. Nestled away in the Shasta-Trinity National Forest, this, too, like Burney Falls, was another one of the few places along the trail I'd previously been to. Only once though. Nearly 10 years ago. With my ex.

We'd been brand new to California at the time, having recently transferred there from Idaho for his job. Madie was in her first year of high school, and Hailey had just started middle school. The two of us, as something to do together on our days off while the girls were in school, had taken up hiking.

On this particular occasion, after dropping the girls off for school in the morning and driving out to Castle Crags, we mistakenly ended up starting out at the wrong trailhead. Checking the map as soon as we realized what we'd done, the good news was that if we just kept going, the trail we were on would eventually connect us to the one we were looking for. The bad news was, how far away that still was now put us in a bit of a time crunch. With just enough time left by this point to still try and do the hike we'd intended before we were due back to pick up the girls, we decided to go for it.

And that's when I remember it starting. A feeling, really, more so than anything—strangely unfamiliar and surprisingly intense—like I was experiencing some sort of next level sense of intuneness with my surroundings. Far more aware of things now as a result, I had to keep stopping, just to take it all in. The dull hammering of a woodpecker hard at work. The string-like veins along the surface of a leaf, slightly raised and clearly visible when lit from behind by the sun. The strong, fresh scent of pine. The high-pitched melody of a songbird. The soft and steady sway of the wind blowing through the trees. An impressively intricate spider web suspended between several bare branches, complete with a meal or two writhing futilely in protest. Last season's previously discarded collection of pine needles and leaves lying, bone dry and brittle, every which way on the ground. Sword-like rays of sunshine streaming boldly through holes in the forest's ceiling.

It was nature at its finest, in these, its simplest forms. And yet, an air of significance and mystery, even, seemed at work here as well. It reminded me of some far off land from the pages of a storybook from my childhood where I couldn't help feeling, at any moment, that anything at all might be possible.

Feeling both soothed and awakened by the whole experience, as we finally reached the point where the trail we were on met up with the one we'd been looking for, I noticed the letters, "P, C, T," spelled out across the top of the trail marker. "Pacific Crest Trail," I read out loud, leaning in close enough to make out the smaller print. Having unknowingly been traversing along a stretch of the PCT, and with no knowledge of what that even was, I can still recall standing there, thinking– *If the "Pacific Crest Trail" is what we just passed through, I want more of it.*

In the end, we did manage to complete the hike we'd been looking for. Although we weren't quite as successful in picking the girls up from school on time. As soon as we all got home afterward, I started researching. Quickly discovering there was far more to the PCT than I could possibly have imagined, the more I learned about it, the more I fell in love with the idea of someday doing the whole thing. Knowing at the time that if that "someday" ever were to actually happen it would be no time soon, we added it to our wish list of things to do once the girls were grown.

Of course, our marriage hadn't survived the passing of that time, which meant neither had any of the big "someday" plans we'd made together. At least not the "together" part of those plans—my desire to do the PCT had never wavered. I had just needed a little time to adjust to the idea of doing it alone.

Not that I was alone now. The irony of which was not lost on me, as here I was all these years later, walking the same exact stretch of this trail, now with Santa.

Day 93: July 27, 2021

We pressed on the next morning with a view of Castle Crags now behind us—tall, jagged peaks silhouetted against a gray sky. A storm was heading our way. I kept my jacket on for the downhill and flat sections as there was a slight chill in the air, tying it around my waist on the ups as I got too hot for it.

By midafternoon the skies finally let loose, and for the next several hours it rained hard, without ceasing. Surprisingly, my rain jacket eventually soaked through. Feeling miserably cold at that point, I talked Santa into stopping so we could set the tent up and try and dry off so I could warm up. Shivering by the time we set it up and got in, we combined both our sleeping bags into one big one, and then peeled all our wet clothes off. Laying naked next to Santa as he held me to help me absorb some of his body heat, we both dozed off at some point. By the time we woke up, the rain had eased to a drizzle. And while it felt gross putting all my wet things back on, with quite a few miles left to cover before we met our goal for the day, we packed up and kept going.

It did make for an especially beautiful sunset that evening, though, in the way only a storm passing through ever can. Shades of pinks, reds and oranges, purples, blues and yellows, all bleeding together, blanketing the horizon, shooting out from behind clouds. And the whole scene, changing, from minute to minute. Still walking by this point, I kept stopping every 20-30 steps to take yet another picture of it—certain it had changed just enough again to have gotten even prettier.

Finally stopping for the night after a long, wet 21 miles, the next day we managed an impressive 38.

Then 22 more, the day after that, landing us deep within the Trinity Alps Wilderness by this point, with a whole new set of stunning views, alpine lakes, and varieties of wildflowers.

Day 96: July 30, 2021

Needing to resupply and eager for a zero day, we caught a ride into Etna first thing in the morning. Once again we were met with a huge surplus of hikers. This time, though, it was far more of an issue than it had been in Mt. Shasta. Even the room we were lucky enough to end up getting, which the motel manager made it sound like was the very last room available anywhere in town that night, had been double booked. The only reason we got it, in fact, was because we were the first of the two parties who had booked it to show up. The stores, though, were where you really saw it. With too many of us buying up all the same items, certain shelves were totally bare. And not just in one or two stores, but in all of them. No more protein or granola bars. No more single serving pouches of instant mashed potatoes or tuna fish or chicken salad. No more trail mix or ramen or jerky. No more little travel size pouches of baby wipes or bottles of hand sanitizer. Considering how little that left you with, you either got creative, or did without.

There was one face, though, in this massive bubble of mostly new-to-us hikers I was especially happy to see—Chaparral. After telling us back when we'd run into her at Burney Falls about a job offer she got that had been way too good to pass up, and how she'd be getting off trail soon, I hadn't known whether I'd ever see her again. Grateful she'd decided to take a second zero day, as she'd gotten into Etna a full day before we had, we met up with her for breakfast as soon as we got there, and then again later that evening for a few beers. After which, we said yet another hard, sad good-bye to one more member of our tramily.

Day 97: July 31, 2021

Back on the trail after once again competing with the masses for a ride, we hit the 1,600 mile marker. Sixteen. Hundred. Miles. Of which, we had just walked every single one. Of course, we also still had over 1,000 left to go. I couldn't decide which one of these two facts sounded more insane than the other.

Towards the end of the day, after filling up at what was meant to be the last reliable water source for a while, we stopped, and set up camp. It was a few miles short of our goal for the day, but with another big summer storm about to rumble and flash its way right over the top of us, the vote to sit this one out from the comfort of our tent was unanimous.

Logging another 22 miles the next day, we then camped on top of an impressive cave type structure overlooking a beautiful valley. Aside from PrimeTime, who we'd met recently and since ran into a few times, who was camped right next to us in the only other site up there, we only saw two or three other hikers the whole day. Most people had opted to skip ahead from Etna past this whole section because of another new round of wildfires that had broken out in the area. As no official closures were in effect yet, we'd chosen not to, but with the air quality being as bad as it was, I sure didn't blame them.

Day 99: August 2, 2021

Wanting to get as many miles in as we could before it got hot, we woke up in time to see the sun rise. Greeted, as usual, by both the sight and smell of smoke as soon as we did, it was a less than reassuring sign that the rainy spell we'd just come through had done much of anything in the way of helping to subdue the wildfires.

Santa made coffee as I packed up the tent. Then we both choked down a protein bar—more because we didn't want to have to carry them any longer than because they sounded at all appetizing at this point—and started out. All morning long we walked our way across mountainsides, each one dotted with lakes and covered in tall, bright pink wildflowers.

The beauty of it all was almost enough to divert our attention away from how much closer and more intense the smoke was now getting.

Hour by hour, it continued to worsen until, eventually, we found ourselves standing at the top of a peak with a 360 degree view of what could easily have been a scene straight out of an Armageddon style, science fiction movie. An eerie mix of pale orange, dusty brown, and dark gray swirled above us in a cloud cover of smoke so thick it was blocking the sun—causing it to feel less like the middle of the day, which it was, and more like evening. Flecks of ash, too, were falling like snowflakes. We'd seen this back near Belden, only this time it was much worse—collecting on the tops of our packs, sticking to our eyelashes, blanketing the ground. Plumes of smoke rose up from multiple spots out across the horizon—new wildfires, most likely from lightning.

After taking a few minutes to absorb the shock of what we were seeing, we found a spot to sit down and rest and had our first real conversation about whether it was time for us, too, at this point to consider skipping ahead a bit. Aside from how bad this was, the fact that we'd been exposing ourselves to this kind of sub-optimal air quality for so many weeks now meant we'd both begun to notice some ill effects recently. A low grade sense of fogginess for one thing, making it a little bit harder to remember things, a dry, itchy throat, headaches, and a little less stamina in the lung capacity department, which, at least for me, was the most concerning.

Reluctant to have to skip any miles, though, and seeing how the forest service hadn't deemed this area dangerous enough yet to have closed it, we decided in the end, at least for the time being, to stay the course.

Day 100: August 3, 2021

Despite having covered a whopping 31 miles the day before, I woke up feeling energized and excited. For one thing, today was my 100th day of being out here on the trail. And for another, Seiad Valley was just ahead. This meant the promise of a hot breakfast in our very near future, along with my next resupply package, which, as an added bonus, meant notes from my girls.

Making ourselves comfortable once we got there in a cozy little outdoor eating area attached to the town's only restaurant–grocery store, we chatted over breakfast with a big group of mostly new-to-us hikers. The majority of them, having reached their limits in regards to dealing with so much smoke, were skipping ahead from this point into Oregon, if not quitting entirely.

Once again, checking in to see if there'd been any new, additional trail closures, and once again discovering there hadn't been, for the second time in as many days now, we made the decision to keep going. I picked up my resupply package and sorted through it, while Santa got what he needed from the grocery store. Then we packed up, wished everyone there that we knew we wouldn't be seeing again the best of luck, and got back to walking.

The first quarter mile or so of the road leading back up to the trail was lined with blackberry bushes that just so happened to be covered in perfectly ripe, warmed by the sun, bursting with flavor berries. Eating them as I walked, savoring them, one at a time, I stopped to pick, "just one more," small handful each time I ran out. By the time I'd had my fill, my palms and fingertips were stained a dark, juicy purple color.

That wasn't the final special touch the trail had in store for me in celebration of this being my 100th day, though. Once we got to the end of the road, just before reaching the trailhead, a young couple, who it turns out had just finished a several day section of the trail to the south of us, were providing trail magic in the form of homemade fruit pies and ice cream. It was a sweet and unexpected treat of which we gratefully partook, along with several other hikers who'd been lounging around in the shade there before getting started.

From there, we entered into another recently charred burn zone, resting often and doing our best to stay hydrated, as we pushed on through the heat and the smoke.

Day 101: August 4, 2021

After spending what would be our final night on California soil, we woke up early and set out eagerly for the California-Oregon border. Feeling a tad bit giddy once we got there, we were met by a handful of other hikers we'd been leapfrogging all morning. Joining them in the dirt, on the Oregon side, obviously, we basked in our accomplishment of finally being done with California as we sat and ate lunch. Then we all took turns taking pictures of each other next to the trail sign. "California/Oregon Border," it read. "Mexico 1694, Canada 958."

Once again marveling at how far we'd come, while simultaneously trying to wrap our heads around how far we still had to go, it wasn't long before we reached our next big milestone. The 1,700 mile mark, made out of branches rather than rocks this time, and lying on top of the grass, under a giant, old tree.

By the end of the day we were 30 miles closer to Canada.

Then another 25 by the end of the next.

And then, the day after that—having made plans with Hailey, first to meet up in Ashland, and then to drive up to Portland for a little tramily reunion—we got off trail and hitched a ride into town. After beating her there, we cleaned up in our hotel room and got our laundry done while we were waiting. Happy, as always, to see her again once she got there, we spent the rest of the day catching up as we walked around Ashland, exploring—in normal clothes, no less, that she'd brought from home for me to wear over the next few days (a pair of jeans, Converse shoes, and a favorite old T-shirt).

The next morning, after breakfast, we loaded our packs into Hailey's car and took off for Walkie Talkie and Lemonade's house in Portland. Music Box, who'd been a few days ahead of us on the trail, was already there, and Hoops, who also lived in Portland, was planning to meet up with us as well.

We spent the next couple of days seeing the sights, sharing meals, and relaxing outside together on Walkie Talkie and Lemonade's backyard patio. Hailey and I treated ourselves to a trip to the hair salon at one point, which, after three plus months of not having my split ends trimmed or my gray roots dyed, felt amazing.

Santa and I also, of course, had the business of resupplying to tend to, although, on a much larger scale than usual this time. For the remainder of the trail, any more resupply boxes we wanted to ship ourselves, we needed to send off from here. The trickiest part of that was that in stark contrast from California, the farther north we traveled from here, the fewer our options would be. There just weren't nearly as many places close enough to the trail to be able to ship things. We also had the issue of time to consider. Less than a month, in fact, was all either one of us had left before bills that would need paying and paychecks that would need earning would send us home. With so many miles still left to cover, and so few days left to do it in, we threw the maximum amount of miles the two of us could average on a daily basis into the mix, and did the math.

The numbers, unfortunately, didn't add up. There was simply no way the two of us could finish in time, at least, not together. The only way it could work would be if we split up. If Santa went on without me, he could walk a lot faster. So much faster, in fact, he could still potentially reach the border in time to meet his back-to-work deadline. I, unlike him, had an extra week or two of wiggle room to play with, which, at this point, at my pace, if I put in really long days like I used to, would give me just enough time to be able to finish.

Neither of us wanted to split up, though, even if that did mean we wouldn't be able to do the whole thing. This sad new development brought us to the point of now needing to figure out which part(s) of the trail we were willing to skip.

With several different factors to consider, namely, a) how bad the wildfires in Oregon were starting to get, b) the already huge and still growing bubble of hikers we'd been competing with lately, and c) a fairly extensive, already existing trail closure we'd soon be needing to get around anyway, we decided our best bet would be to skip up to the Washington border.

Day 107: August 10, 2021

Too quickly the weekend was over, and with the remainder of our resupply packages all boxed up and freshly dropped off at the post office, Santa, Hailey, Music Box, and I drove out to the trailhead near Cascade Locks.

It broke my heart, as always, to say yet another goodbye to Hailey. After one last, "just one last," hug this time, though, as I stood watching and waving as she drove away, knowing I'd be home in less than a month now made the sadness a little easier to bear.

Back on the trail, the three of us made our way across the Bridge of the Gods and then took turns posing for pictures in front of a big, green, "Welcome to Washington," sign. Then Music Box, being faster than, not only us, but pretty well everyone really, took off ahead on his own. It was a rough first day back after zeroing for so many days in a row, but, slowly managing to find our groove, we logged a solid 16 miles by the end of it.

After upping that number to 26 the next day, we felt perfectly comfortable confirming all the rumors we'd heard about the Washington section of the trail being utterly gorgeous to be true. Every minute of every mile so far was nothing but an endless array of lush, green, woods—thick with ferns and shrubs, streams and rivers, as well as an impressive assortment of uniquely colored wild mushrooms. All of which I kept stopping, quite often, to take pictures of. And the upside of having skipped as far ahead of the smoke and the fires as we had was how completely uncrowded it was here. We had the whole place to ourselves as we set up camp that night. We found a peaceful, sandy spot right on the edge of a fairly good sized river, just in time to enjoy a quick swim as the sun was setting.

The following day was pretty well the same, although we also passed the 2,200 mile marker. Arranged out of twigs this time, laying in the dirt off to the side of the trail, it felt a little weird seeing such a big jump in the numbers now that we'd skipped up into Washington. Once again we had the whole place where we chose to camp to ourselves that night. And we once again enjoyed an end of the day swim, this time in a lake.

Day 110: August 13, 2021

The next morning, thanks to a bet we'd made over dinner the night before, I got a head start on Santa. By 20 minutes, in fact, as that was the number we'd agreed on. The idea behind it was to test out a theory he'd come up with about how we might be able to shave some time off our average pace by tapping into a) my competitive "tendencies" (for lack of a better, less on the verge of needing a diagnosis sounding word) and b) the fact that I, for some reason, seemed to walk faster when he was chasing me. Not literally chasing, of course, just heading my way from far enough behind me that, not only could I not see him, but I had no way of knowing at what point he might catch up. The bet itself, though, was that if he was able to catch up to me in less than 40 minutes (my 20 minute head start, times two), then he won. If, on the other hand, it took him any longer than 40 minutes, I won. The winner would receive one point. Plus, one additional point for every 5 minute increment either over or under that 40 minute cutoff it took him.

The whole points thing was something we'd come up with a few weeks back as a fun way of raising the stakes a bit—mostly when trying to settle which of us happened to be right about something. Like who a particular actor was from a movie we'd been talking about. Or the name of a certain plant or type of insect or cloud formation we'd just come across. Or who the original artist was for a song one of us couldn't stop humming.

With Santa currently beating me 8-2, the stakes for me at this point had never been higher. Which wasn't to say, in all this time we'd been playing, that I'd only ever earned two points. You could also lose points, which I had, by betting them. Like, for instance, "I'll bet you three of my points,

–insert whatever–." Lose that bet, and not only do you lose those points, but the other person gets them.

In a hearty attempt to try and even out the score a bit, and fueled by nothing more than a protein bar and my ridiculously competitive spirit, I stopped only twice over the next 13 miles—once to take a selfie next to the Indian Heaven Wilderness sign as I passed it, and once to pee.

Apparently, Santa's theory had been right. Between the excitement of seeing him again once he caught up, the suspense of having no idea when that might be, and a potentially game-changing number of points on the line, I'd kept moving the whole time much quicker than usual. So quick, in fact, that by the time I got to the end of those 13 miles—which was as far as we planned on going today as we'd arranged for a ride from that point into Trout Lake for the night—I was nearly two hours ahead of schedule. With Santa still nowhere in sight, I took a big, grinning selfie with the road I'd just reached in the background, as proof of my win. Making note of what time it was, for the sake of bonus points now, I then sat, picking and eating huckleberries from the surplus of bushes around me, while I waited for Santa.

Unfortunately for him, once he finally caught up, "I beat you!" was, more or less, pretty much all he heard from me for the rest of the day. Whereas I'm not a sore loser (this, he already knew), I am a terrible winner (as he was now finding out).

With Trout Lake being more of a dot on the map than an actual town, the only place we could find to stay for the night was a popup style camper tent someone had set up in their front yard and listed on Guthooks as a room for rent. Thankfully, use of the bathroom and the washing machine inside the house were included.

Finding it hard to fall asleep that night—which, between the muggy heat and Santa's snoring, wasn't all that surprising—I thought back over the day. About how, when I'd first woken up, I hadn't been particularly stoked about the idea of spending yet another day walking. In fact, I was actually kinda dreading it. Not that I didn't still enjoy being out here. There were just times, every now and then, when the rhythm of it all felt a bit too monotonous. And then I thought about our bet. How that one little thing had helped make the miles feel more like play and less like a chore today. Now that I thought about it, this was the case with nearly everything when it came to Santa. In the past couple of months of us spending all day, every day together, everything had become either more manageable, more meaningful, more memorable, or more fun, thanks to him.

Day 111: August 14, 2021

With the forecast calling for yet another day of uncomfortably hot temperatures, we got an early start heading back to the trail the next morning. As early as we could, anyway. A place of this size meant there were far fewer trail angels offering rides, and by the time we'd signed up for one, the first couple of carfuls out to the trailhead that morning were already booked up.

After making good time once we finally got started, halfway through the day, as quickly as a set change between scenes during a stage performance, the landscape shifted. The dense woods we'd been walking through, pretty much nonstop since stepping foot into Washington, were now replaced by a wide open, picture perfect, grassy meadow—with streams lined with river rocks and wildflowers running through it, views of far off mountain ranges, little clusters of trees here and there, and a whole assortment of dirt paths. Only one, of course, was the PCT. All of the others were shorter and fairly easy to access from here, apparently acting as magnets for backpackers of the 3-5-day-trip variety.

We'd been running into them all day. Hearing wild tales, in fact, from nearly all of them who happened to be coming from the direction in which we were heading, about a dangerous river crossing coming up. One woman, still visibly shaken by it, described the "whole experience" as having been scary enough to have brought her to tears.

The more stories we heard, the more curious I became. And the closer we got to it, as someone who generally finds river crossings more thrilling than intimidating, the more my excitement grew, as well.

Unable towards the end to keep myself from rushing ahead, I stood alone on the sandy riverbank once I reached it, scoping things out as I waited for Santa to catch up. It was definitely bigger than any of the other rivers we'd crossed so far without the aid of a bridge of some sort. The water raged loudly—churning with such force it was murky and brown from all the dirt in it. Most notable, though, was an almost dam-like pile up of debris stretching all the way across, from one side to the other, in one spot. Granted, it was no more than a mess of logs, leaves, and branches wedged precariously between various rocks, it was, by the looks of it, apparently, the only way to get across. Having arrived just in time to watch a couple of hikers as they were finishing up, I did so intently—feeling oddly nervous for them, and hoping, with each step they took, their footing held and no one fell in and got swept away. Failing to notice I'd been holding my breath, I exhaled deeply once they both reached the shore. After congratulating them both on a job well done, they passed along the specifics of the strategy they'd chosen. Breaking it down into three different sections for me, they pointed out which logs to maneuver my way across and which ones to avoid, warning me which way the current would be pulling in a couple of the more treacherous spots, just in case I fell in.

On the one hand, I felt super appreciative for such a detailed blow-by-blow of what to expect. On the other hand now, though, because of how technical it all sounded, I also felt nauseous. Plus my palms were starting to sweat. And my mouth had gone dry. And my heart was racing. Knowing it would only get worse the longer I stood around waiting, as soon as Santa caught up and I had a chance to fill him in, we got busy making our way across. With Santa in the lead, he waited for me to catch up at the end of each section before attempting the next one.

Safely on the other side, and proud of ourselves for barely even getting our shoes wet, we sat and rested while we filtered some water which, even after filtering, still looked more dirty than drinkable.

As we were packing up, another hiker reached the spot we'd just crossed over from. I recognized him, as we'd chatted in passing several times throughout the course of the day. He was an older man on his own, and by the looks of it, a little unsure as to what his best option for crossing might be. Happy to help guide him—although with the water being too loud to yell over, it was more like a game of charades, than anything—I was just as proud of him as I had been of us once he made it across.

Day 112: August 15, 2021

We spent the whole next day trekking across the sides of mountains, crossing back and forth over trickling streams, climbing up and over peaks, splashing cool water from little pools at the base of waterfalls on our faces, weaving our way through valleys, and best of all, passing through fields covered in wispy, little, pale yellow, flowering plants that were so fun and different looking, like something straight out of a Dr. Seuss book.

There was no denying it was the peak of summer now in the mountains. The proof was in everything, all around us.

I walked the last few miles of the day alone. Being mostly uphill, I had wanted to take my time rather than struggle to try and keep up with Santa. He, on the other hand, had wanted to waste no time in finding us a campsite before all the good ones filled up. As was always his style, he did. This one, though, high up, right along the edge of a rocky ridge overlooking the valley we'd just climbed up out of, was a doozy, even by his standards. I made it there just in time to watch the sunset with him. Then we ate and cleaned up and, after the solid 30 miles we'd just covered, fell fast asleep.

As was more often the case than not, I woke up having to pee in the middle of the night. Slipping first my jacket and then my headlamp on,

I climbed over Santa as quietly as I could on my way out of the tent. I cringed a bit as I slid my still-warm-from-my-sleeping-bag bare feet into my still-damp-with-sweat shoes. *Ew!* Then, looking up as I reached to click my headlamp on, I froze, awestruck by the multitude of stars and the flurry of activity above me. So much was happening—twinkling, darting, glowing, pulsing—it felt otherworldly, magical, alive. After debating for several seconds whether or not to wake Santa up so he could witness this, too, I remembered why I'd come out. I found a spot to pee. After that, I found a rock big enough to sit down on, and with my head tilted back and my face to the sky, I admired the view until my neck started to hurt.

Day 113: August 16, 2021

We woke up early enough the next morning to set off just as the sun was rising. Soon finding ourselves face to face with a giant snow filled crevice, the fact that this mountain was named Old Snowy now made absolute sense. A bit taken aback at the sight of this much snow this late in the summer, we stood speechless, staring. Granted, we were pretty high in elevation, which meant it was cooler up here. Plus, we were along the backside now, which meant it saw more shade than sun—it still just felt out of place, though.

With no apparent way around it, a narrow pathway of footprints running straight through the snow, seemed like as good of an invitation to cross as any. Thankfully, the surface was more cold and crusty than melting and mushy, which, for us, meant the difference between being able to walk quite easily right over the top of it, rather than having to posthole our way through it. With the still rising sun hitting the last little patch of snow as we neared it, it looked as if a carpet of tiny, rainbow colored, twinkling lights had just been rolled out for us.

Shortly past that point the trail intersected with an alternate stock route. Our options now were to either continue along the trail as usual, or veer away from it along the alternate for about half a mile before rejoining it. Considering the advice we'd read last night on Guthooks about the pros and cons of both options, we opted for the latter. The views were meant to be better, for one thing. For another, the amount of snow still on the main path sounded less than fun to try and navigate considering how steep of a fall you'd be in for if anything went pear shaped.

After that, having joined back up with the main trail, we then made our final ascent up and over the pass. Unable to hear each other over the wind, as there was nothing up there to shelter us from it, we used hand motions more than anything as a way of communicating. Not that we really had much we needed to say. The view was so incredible, it was more a matter of pointing at different things we wanted each other to see—Mount Rainier being one of them. Noticeably higher than anything else around it, capped with snow, and—apparently capable of producing its own storm system—a dark, swirling mass of cloud hovering in place over the top of it. A sea of other mountains, as well, one entire range after another, stretched out all around us in every direction. Above us, pockets of powdery blue peeked out from behind billowy clouds, as the final rays of the sunrise were beginning to fade. Best of all, though, directly in front of us, was what's known as the Knife's Edge. A long, narrow, jagged looking strip running along the topmost edge of what appeared to be the length of a whole range of mountains. It was a bit intimidating, to say the least, as the trail continued right over the top of it. The good news for us, though, was that there wasn't any snow on it—that being one complication that, without the proper equipment, could potentially render this section impassable. As we got to it, we stood beside one another, checking it out for a minute. Wondering if this, quite possibly, could be what standing at the top of the world felt like, I looked over at Santa, studying his expression to see if he was as taken with all of this as I was. The fact that he seemed to be made me love him all the more. For all the differences between us—where we came from, how we'd been raised, the paths our lives had taken—as well as the many things about each other we were still learning, this was one thing that would never need explaining. Our shared ability to not only be impressed by nature, but deeply moved by it.

Turning towards me once he noticed I was looking at him, the change in his expression as our eyes met caught me by surprise. As if, what he saw when he looked at me was even more beautiful and more pleasing to him than all of this was. How a single look could make me feel so special was beyond me. But it did. As well as making my head spin and my heart melt and giving me goosebumps and wanting to kiss him—all at once. *How'd I get so lucky to have found this guy?*

Embarrassed by the fact that I was, by now, most likely blushing, I pulled my phone out of my pocket and started taking a bunch of pictures. Following suit, Santa took his phone out, too, and took some pictures, as well. And then, alternating every so often which of us was in the lead, we made our way out across the Knife's Edge. Slowly at first, as, unlike any other surface we'd encountered along the trail so far, this had us walking over loose slabs of shale. Each one a different shape and size, clanking noisily as it shifted beneath us under the weight of our carefully placed footsteps. It was so uneven, in fact, that in my best attempt to avoid rolling an ankle I made a deal with myself that if I wanted to have a good look around, I had to stop first and stand still. As the sun's warm glow stretched out over more of the landscape the higher it rose, I did so quite often, taking one picture after another, confident of the fact that, one day, when I found myself looking back on the PCT as a whole, this right here would be one of, if not the, most impressive parts of it.

Later that afternoon, and 20 miles closer to Canada, we made it to White Pass where we splurged on hot pizza, cold beer, and a room for the night.

Day 114: August 17, 2021

It was cold and rainy the next morning. Not that the temperatures hadn't been cooler in general up here in Washington. Most days I'd been starting out wearing more layers, in fact—at least until the afternoon sun got around to warming things up a bit. This was the first time I'd felt the need to start out with my gloves on, though.

It was a 10 minute walk up the highway to get back to the trail from the place where we stayed. By the time we got there, the rain had died down to a light drizzle. Continuing on, we spent the better part of the morning passing by a series of ponds and lakes, each with a misty fog rising off of them. We also hit the 2,300 mile marker—light gray stones in the shape of each number atop the rain soaked dirt.

The rest of the day, aside from an occasional lull in the rain, was pretty much just more of the same—soggy, stormy, and cold.

At the end of 22 miles, we set up camp on top of a summit in a little wooded area, hoping it might help block the wind. Having cell service for the first time in a while, although it was spotty, I made a little video to serve as proof to the world I was still alive and doing well and, after several tries, was finally able to post it on Facebook and Instagram.

Day 115: August 18, 2021

The next morning was even colder. So much so, as we went about our regular routine of me packing the tent up while Santa read aloud what the day had in store for us according to Guthooks, I was actually glad when he announced we'd be starting off with some ups. The chance to climb meant the chance to get warm.

Of course, as soon as we did, the usual shedding of layers began. First my coat which I would tie around my waist. Then my beanie which I'd swap out for my ball cap. Then my gloves which I would shove into the hip pouches of my pack. Until we reached the top of the next windy summit, that is, or started heading down the shady backside of a mountain, and I, once again, grew cold enough to have to put it all back on again. Not that it took even that much at times. Not since I'd turned the big 4-5 a year ago. The best part of this (and by best, I mean worst) had been the perimenopausal hijacking of my internal thermostat, rendering my body practically incapable of regulating itself normally now—external variables such as actual temperatures or the weather be damned. Seeming to wax and wane a bit for months at a time as far as severity, thankfully, I'd been more in the waning stage since I'd been out on the trail. Until just recently, that is. Washington, unfortunately, was beginning to feel more like a never ending cycle of being either too hot or too cold which, of course, as anyone who knows anyone who's ever been through perimenopause can tell you, is just the proverbial tip of this sadly under-discussed (considering half the population will experience it) iceberg. Not to mention the whole mood altering aspect brought on by all the hormonal chaos.

That being said, while my emotions felt more like light background music normally, in my waxing phase they felt like someone turned the volume up past "base-thumping" all the way to "so loud the neighbors would be justified in calling the cops to complain about it" and then broken the dial so I had no control over it—which is right about where I was now, unfortunately.

Where I also was now, was still 300 miles away from the finish line, with just a little over two weeks to get there. After doing the math again last night, this meant we needed to be logging some pretty major miles every day now in order to make that happen. Today included, which, thanks to my cranked up emotions tuning into the "Tired Turned Pissy" station right around the 20 mile mark of our 30 mile goal we'd set for the day, not only was I ready to call it quits, I was actually pouting so hard I was annoying myself. Purposefully lagging far enough behind Santa at this point so as not to risk annoying him, too, I had my earbuds in and was listening to music when, stepping forward with my right foot, the front of my shoe snagged on something, causing me to fall to the ground. Hard enough, in fact, to not only knock the wind out of me, but one of my earbuds, which went flying as well. Stunned, initially, and then embarrassed, I took a quick *god, I hope nobody saw me do that* look around. Relieved to discover I, indeed, was alone, I turned to my now throbbing foot. *What the fuck?* Still wedged under the gnarled tree root I had apparently caught it on, between the tip of my shoe and just below where my laces started, not only was the entire width of my shoe split open, but my toes were all sticking out. Tucking them back in, I pried myself loose from the root, and then fished around on my hands and knees in the grass for my missing earbud, until I eventually found it. Tempted to cry, but too tired to actually do so, and grateful, at least, I hadn't rolled an ankle, I laughed it off as I stood back up, brushing away the dirt from my hands. And my pants. And my elbows. And the one side of my face I'd landed on. *Stupid root.*

I didn't catch up with Santa until I got to the next water source, where he'd been sitting for who knows how long, waiting for me. After recounting my whole "foot versus root" incident for him, I did my best to repair my shoe with what little duct tape I had with me. Not that it stuck for long. Within half a mile it had worn loose enough to be more of a nuisance than anything—flapping around, collecting dirt and pebbles and bits of twigs and dried leaves. Eventually I just peeled it off and stuck it inside my hip pouch .

It was a few hours later by the time we finally made it to the end of our 30 miles. I got there first, just as the sun was setting, and set the tent up next to the only other hikers we had seen throughout the day. They were a young couple, recently engaged. Spending a week together out here on her first ever, apparently, backpacking trip, he was happily showing her the ropes.

Santa, having developed a stomach ache that, unfortunately, had him on the lookout for a place to dig himself a toilet, had insisted a mile or two back that I go on without him. Looking quite pale and haggard by the time he finally showed up, he dropped his pack outside the tent, and clutching his stomach, climbed straight in and laid down. Refusing to eat dinner at this point for fear it would just go straight through him, it was all I could do to get a couple of Pepto Bismol tablets and a few sips of water with electrolytes in him. Feeling bad for him and not knowing what else to do, I sat outside the tent, watching the stars emerge, while he fell asleep.

Day 116: August 19, 2021

Thankfully, by the next morning, although he was nowhere near better yet, he was at least feeling well enough to keep walking. Slowing our pace a little, and stopping a bit more frequently to rest, we spent the majority of the day playing leapfrog with the young couple we'd camped by. With the two of us passing them at one water source or resting point, and the two of them catching up and passing us at the next. The most impressive of these spots was a big log cabin a group of local snowmobilers apparently built as a storm shelter, and then generously decided to allow the public to enjoy as well. With a woodburning stove and enough room to sleep at least a dozen people, it was a magnet for thru-hikers.

One of them, by the name of Sebastian, was on the front porch enjoying a late breakfast when we showed up. We'd met him once before, a few days prior. An attractive 20-something from Sweden with longish, unruly looking hair, a thick accent, and a fun, energetic sort of surfer-meets-hippy vibe. Having slept there overnight, he gave us a tour of the cabin, which, of course, didn't take long. Then we sat outside on the front porch with him, along with our new leapfrogging friends, who'd just caught up again, listening as he read us a poem by Rudyard Kipling that someone named Nemo had recorded in the hikers' logbook he'd found inside.

> "Children of the Camp are we,
> Serving each in his degree;
> Children of the yoke and goad,
> Pack and harness, pad and load.
> See our line across the plain,
> Like a heel-rope bent again,
> Reaching, writhing, rolling far,
> Sweeping all away to war!
> While the men that walk beside,
> Dusty, silent, heavy-eyed,
> Cannot tell why we or they
> March and suffer day by day."

Managing an impressive (considering one of us still wasn't feeling great) 28 miles by the end of the day, we once again set up camp by the same young couple. This being the last night of their trip, they planned on getting off the trail the following morning. As we chatted with them one last time, the woman mentioned her disappointment at not having been out here long enough to have earned herself a trail name. Remembering how eager I was to get mine when I'd first started, I dubbed her Bright Eyes, in lieu of her big blue eyes, and for her gentle spirit like the character in the children's book, *Watership Down*. Delighted, although unfamiliar with either the book or the movie, she promised to check it out once she got home.

Day 117: August 20, 2021

For the second day in a row now, Santa woke up feeling sick to his stomach. We ruled out anything food related as the possible cause of it, as I was fine and we'd both been eating the same things. Our best guess at this point was that it was either the flu, or he drank some bad water. Considering his opinion in regards to the importance of first filtering everything before consuming it out here—as in he oftentimes thought it completely unnecessary—it was likely the latter.

Knowing, for his sake, that the sooner we could get to the next town, the better, we pressed on through the first half of the day until we got to a forest service road where, thankfully, we were able to hitch a ride with a day hiker and his dog who'd just finished their hike, into Snoqualmie. We got a room. And some NyQuil, which Santa took a dose of and then went straight to bed, where he remained for the next day and a half while I tended to him. Between running out for food periodically, worrying about how I wouldn't be of much help to him if he got sick like this out on the trail, and studying the map for ways to make up for the miles we weren't doing—it was a stressful couple of days.

Day 119: August 22, 2021

With a concentrated dose of rest seeming to have done the trick, he finally woke up after our second night there, feeling well enough to get back to the trail. Deciding our best option would be to skip up to the next town of Skykomish, we made arrangements for a ride with an old family friend of mine, who not only lived in the area but was familiar with the PCT. Having done some smaller sections of it herself, previously, she'd messaged me, way back before I'd even started, offering to help out if I needed anything once I reached Washington. Happy for the chance to introduce her to Santa, we filled her in on the whole story of how we'd met and become BAMTA, and then, having not seen her in years, she and I spent the rest of the drive catching up.

Back on the trail, we soon entered the beautifully lush Wenatchee National Forest. Not that we got too far after getting a late start, but we did manage to get several hours of hiking in. We stopped near a lake just as the sky, which had been taunting us all day with the possibility of rain, finally made good on its threat. We rushed to set up the tent. Then, climbing inside to stay dry, we cooked our dinner under the shelter of the rainfly. Off and on, all through the night, the rain continued. Waking periodically, I would lie in the dark, listening to it hitting the top of the tent, until I finally dozed off again.

Day 120: August 23, 2021

The next morning was the coldest it had been so far. Whereas every other time I'd gone to bed wearing a beanie, I'd always warmed up enough at some point during the night to take it off, I woke up still wearing it this time.

Reluctant to leave the warmth of my sleeping bag, I lingered lazily for several minutes, until ignoring my body's urge to pee was no longer an option. I dug around for my hiking pants and my bra—having flung them both carelessly towards the foot of the tent last night after changing into my base layer. Then, shoving them into my bag with me, as they were far too cold to put on without warming them up first, I fished around in my pack for a clean pair of underwear and a, at least less dirty than yesterday's, pair of socks.

Finally dressed and with an uncomfortably full bladder now, I emerged from the tent and set out to relieve myself. Unlike on most occasions, though, where, after finding a spot you then had to squat, this time there was an actual toilet in the woods nearby. A rare luxury, no doubt—the proof being that even Guthooks had it marked as a point of interest. Following Santa's directions, as he'd just returned from paying it a visit himself, I made my way along a windy side trail until—there it was. In plain sight amid the pine trees, stood a large, somewhat rudimentary looking, box-shaped, pit toilet (not that I hadn't seen a pit toilet before, just never right out in the open like this). Made entirely out of wood, complete with a hinged lid, it was perched atop a small platform, and positioned in such a way as to offer a full view of the lake below to whomever had the pleasure of doing their business while sitting on it. *A view while you poo*—I couldn't help from thinking as I, quite bravely by my standards, tried it out—*what a concept*.

With that out of the way, we ate breakfast and checked Guthooks to see how far away the next water source was so we'd know how much we needed to carry with us from here. Then Santa went down to the lake to fetch it, as it was his turn, while I deflated the air mattresses, and packed up. Shaking the moisture from the tent, I draped it over my pack. In part so as to not get anything inside my pack wet, but also in the hopes that the breeze would help dry it out as we walked. Crawling into a still wet tent after already walking through cold, rainy weather was just about the worst kind of way to end a day out here. And by the looks of the sky this morning, there was no telling how much longer this storm system we were in was bound to keep up.

Having camped at the base of a valley in a thick forested area, we climbed steadily up and out of it for the first couple of miles. The dirt beneath us, being damp, was a darker-than-unusual brown, and as we brushed past the shrubs lining the trail, pools of rain water on the leaves began to soak through our gloves and the front of our pants. Before long, my right sock was soaked through, as well—my latest strategy for patching up the slit across the top of my shoe, having failed. Since duct tape hadn't worked, when we were back in Snoqualmie, I'd wrapped strips of KT tape all the way around the top of my shoe several times. Having already worn away along the edges of the sole yesterday, now that it was wet, the rest had also come loose. It not only felt uncomfortable having a wet foot, but every time I took a step now it made an annoyingly loud *squish*.

By midafternoon, to our surprise and delight, the clouds had cleared almost completely, giving way to blue skies and much warmer temperatures. This meant the only thing still under the weather now, unfortunately, was Santa's poor stomach. Not that it had gotten any worse, it just still wasn't entirely better.

Partly as a way of distracting himself from not feeling well, and partly just him being next-level crazy about football, we started listening to FPL (Fantasy Premier League[29]) podcasts together. Pausing it now and then so I could ask a question or he could elaborate on something, I did my best to keep up. Not that a sports podcast would ever be something I'd listen to on my own, but how excited he was to be sharing it with me made the whole thing kind of fun. As an added bonus, it made the miles pass a little quicker as well—all 25 of them, in fact, by the time we were done for the day.

Day 121: August 24, 2021

While it was more the norm than not for me to get a headstart first thing in the morning, doing so today quickly turned into a full blown worrying session. For one thing, Santa had woken up with his stomach feeling noticeably worse. For another, it was taking him much longer than usual to catch up. My imagination, running wild with all sorts of worse case scenarios, soon had me convinced that he was anywhere

---

[29] Equivalent (at least to my understanding) to fantasy football in the US, only "football" as in soccer, and rather than choosing players from NFL teams each week, they're from the English Premier League.

other than a short ways behind me, about to catch up. Like, maybe on his hands and knees, puking his guts out in some meadow—all alone, except for a giant, hungry Grizzly who was sneaking up from behind him to tear him limb from limb and then eat him. Or, a dizzy spell had caused him to trip, sending him over the edge of a steep rocky cliff, where he was now lying, all crumpled up with a bunch of broken bones, with no way to call for help because his SOS device broke loose from his pack along the way down, and was now crushed to bits, lying 50 feet away from him, even. Or, maybe he'd just gotten tired, and laid down to rest his eyes for a bit, and fallen asleep, and then a poisonous snake had bitten him, and now he'd never wake up again.

Reaching the next water source, with a stomach ache of my own by now, I thought it best—on the off chance he might still be alive—that I stop here and wait for him. Thankfully, completely unscathed, he eventually arrived. Grateful and relieved that we were, in fact, still in this together, I made him take the lead from there. And for the rest of the morning, that's how it went, with Santa getting a little ways ahead of me on the ups, and me catching back up with him on the downs.

Getting hungry for lunch, we picked a spot ahead on the map near a pond to stop for a picnic. With one more gradual, although fairly long hill to climb before getting there, knowing he could make better time than me, which meant he'd have more time to rest, and finally feeling okay enough to let him out of my sight again, we agreed I'd hang back at my own pace and meet him there.

Ten minutes or so into walking alone I was deep in thought, staring mindlessly at the ground a few steps in front of me, when something slammed into my forehead—so hard I saw stars as it sent me stumbling backwards. That "something" being a tree which, inexplicably, happened to be suspended, horizontally, across the trail, at precisely the height of my forehead. And not just a branch but a full on tree, which made the fact that I hadn't seen it more surprising than it being there in the first place. Although the reason for that, embarrassingly enough, was no mystery—having recently started tilting the bill of my ball cap further down to shade more of my face from the sun, I was in turn obstructing what would otherwise be in my eye level field of vision. Obviously.

Smacking straight into it, from practically a full throttle, speed-walking pace, after stumbling backwards, I stood, hunching forward slightly, with my hands cupped over my nose, which was throbbing. My eyes watered. And a helicopter-like, whooshing sound pulsed in my ears.

Examining the scene once I was able to stand up straight, it appeared that this tree, having fallen over at some point (most likely during a storm), had wedged itself as it landed, just so within the limbs of a few other trees, to now be running parallel to the ground—five feet up in the air, no less. Mortified that I was even capable of such an outlandish act of clumsiness, my only consolation was that no one had witnessed it.

The initial impact, having first jammed my sunglasses into the bridge of my nose (hence the throbbing), had then flung them off, onto the ground. Bending down slowly, as I reached my hand out to pick them up, I saw blood—all over my fingers. Confused by the fact that I hadn't injured my fingers— *My face! Oh. My. God.* I dug my phone out of my pocket and held up the camera so I could see myself. The inside of my nose was where the blood was dripping from. And I had a big, red, already-swelling welt in the middle of my forehead. The worst part, though, was a new little chip in one of my top two front teeth—my good one, no less. *Ugh.* I'd already knocked the other one out back in high school, whitewater rafting at summer camp when some kid named Ian's big, fat, wooden oar wasn't anywhere near where it was supposed to be during one of the gnarlier sets of rapids. As in, it wasn't supposed to be smacking me in the face, knocking my goddamn tooth out! Granted that was more than 30 years ago now, and I'd since had some pretty realistic looking crowns installed in its place. Even so, to this day, I still suffered the occasional post-tooth-trauma type nightmare—like I go to bite into something and, instead, all my teeth fall out.

More annoyed now than anything, I gently ran the tip of my tongue back and forth along the edge of my tooth where the chip was as I stared at myself in my phone screen. Eventually, having seen enough, I took my pack off and sat on the ground with my head in my hands, fighting the urge to cry while I waited for the whooshing in my ears to stop. Once it finally did, I dug two ibuprofen out of my pack, swallowed them down with a sip of water, and then slowly stood up. Slightly nauseous and a tad bit woozy, I tucked my sunglasses away in my hip pouch—my nose far too tender to wear them now. Then I flipped my ball cap around so the bill was now facing behind me. *Fucking hat.* And then, ducking well below the tree this time as I made my way past it, I kept on, albeit slowly, towards where Santa was most likely, by now, already waiting for me.

Nervous I may have knocked my tooth loose, in addition to chipping it, every so often I kept reaching up to give it a little wiggle.

Joining him, once I reached him, in a patch of grass where he was resting, I wasted no time in telling him all about my literal run in with the tree. He listened, sympathetically. Then, once I'd finished, he pulled his bandana off his head, revealing a big bloody gash along the top of his scalp.

"Oh my god, Santa!" I said, leaning in towards him for a closer look.

"Same tree," he said matter of factly, pointing to his wound.

"No kidding?" I said, shocked by this.

"Yep," he said, nodding. "It looks as if that damn tree had it out for us both!" Laughing by this point, he ran his fingers gingerly over the top of it. Surprised he hadn't said something sooner, I started digging through my pack for my first aid kit. Pulling practically everything else out in the process, as the less frequently I had use for something, the further towards the bottom it usually was. Recounting his own man-versus-tree ordeal as I cleaned him up, I then secured a strip of gauze over the worst of it with some bits of KT tape.

After a second dose of ibuprofen a few hours later, my nose finally stopped hurting. I also seemed to be in the clear in regards to my tooth now, as well—it didn't appear to be loose. And better still, at least for the time being, Santa's stomach wasn't giving him trouble.

With our final few miles for the day, downhill for the most part, we enjoyed the sunshine and the smoke-free Washington skies and a comfortable pace. Feeling relaxed and content as we did so, I found myself beginning to mourn the fact that our time out here was nearing an end.

From there, as I began to imagine myself on the other side of this finish line, I was surprised to find, for the first time, that not only was I comfortable with it, but a little excited, even. I spent the rest of the time it took us to get to our campsite daydreaming about what life with Santa, back in the real world, might look like. I pictured us hiking together in the fall with the leaves changing and us both wearing sweaters. And meeting his friends up in Canada that he's told me so much about that I already felt like I knew them. And sitting next to him in a movie theater with a tub of popcorn between us and one drink with two straws. And dressing up and going out to dinner. And introducing him to Madie, as she hadn't met him yet.

And then, 24 miles closer to the border, we pitched our tent for the night.

Day 122: August 25, 2021

The next day we upped our mileage by 12 for an impressive grand total of 36. Or, as Santa would put it, an even more impressive sounding, nearly 58 kilometers. Winding through thick patches of forest, crossing over mossy-edged streams, making our way along rocky ridges, we summited one spectacular view-offering mountaintop after another. One of which, after discovering one too many hidden lakes to resist, we stopped to have lunch on. The crystal blue water was so undisturbed that a full color mirror image of the tip of the mountain behind it and a few white puffy clouds above reflected off the surface. I filtered some water while Santa set the food out. Our latest attempt at mixing things up had us experimenting with wraps. As far as tortillas, having tried all the flavors, the spinach and herb were our favorite. We'd layer them, first, with little carry-out style packets of mayo and/or mustard. Then, either pouches of tuna fish or chicken, or slices of salami with ham or turkey. Then, whatever kind of cheese we were carrying, which ranged from cheese sticks, to little Babybels, to actual packets of the pre-sliced stuff. And then, for a bit of a crunch, we'd top it off with a handful of corn chips. In addition to that, we usually had some kind of chocolate covered nuts or a candy bar for dessert. The idea was, the more calories the better. As a 5'4" female who'd never in her life had any trouble putting or keeping weight on, this had been a bit of a mind fuck in the beginning—requiring a fair bit of mental rewiring as, for the first time ever, I was scanning nutrition labels in search of the highest amount of calories instead of the lowest. With a full day of thru-hiking burning an average of 5,000-6,000 calories, there was no getting around it, though—food was fuel.

Another thing there was no getting around was the short supply of campsites we encountered that evening. After showing up to the spot we'd planned on stopping to find it jam packed with already sleeping hikers, we searched as quietly as we could by the light of our headlamps in a desperate attempt to find a free, flat enough patch of ground that was big enough to pitch our tent. With no luck, we'd had no choice but to keep going—for another two miles, according to where Guthooks was saying the next place with any spots flat enough to be able to camp would be. It might as well have been 20, though, considering it was already after 11:00 pm and we'd been walking since 7:00 that morning. We were both nearing the point of exhaustion.

Pouting (quite heavily), I lagged behind a bit once we got back on the trail. After about 10 minutes of fighting as best I could against the bitter disappointment of not being able to just lay down and sleep already, I gave up. Calling out to Santa that I needed to rest for a minute, I sat down in the dirt right there in the middle of the trail. Backtracking to where I was, he seemed confused. "You okay, Bammer?" he asked, kneeling down next to me, the stream of light from his headlamp shining straight into my eyes. I raised one of my hands to shield them.

"I can't do it, Santa," I said, shaking my head. "I'm too tired. And it's too much. And I just–" Choking back tears, I wiggled my arms out of my pack and, leaning into it like a giant pillow, laid my head down. "I just can't, Santa. I'm sorry."

Stroking my cheek with the back of his hand, he let out a long sigh and then slowly stood back up. "You rest," he said, setting his pack down beside me and pulling an empty bottle and the water filter out of his pack. "I'm gonna walk back to the stream we just passed and filter us some more water."

Feeling just better enough by the time he returned to give the whole two more mile thing one more shot, step by step, together, alternately climbing over and shimmying under what felt like an infinite number of damp downed trees, we covered the distance we needed to. Not that the next site wasn't crowded, as well, once we got to it but, thankfully, squeezing one more tent in there wasn't a problem. I set it up while Santa cooked us a super late dinner. After which, having fallen asleep with our forks practically still in our mouths, we were both out for the night.

Day 123: August 26, 2021

By the time we climbed out of our tent the next morning, the campsite was pretty well empty. Not that we were even expecting to, really, but of the few stragglers still there, we didn't recognize anyone. With Music Box most likely at least a few days ahead, and the only other remaining members of our tramily now quite a ways behind us, it was a rarity anymore to see someone we knew.

On my own for the first part of the morning, as I got a head start, I found myself daydreaming, this time about reaching the northern terminus. Once Santa caught up we spent the next little while brainstorming—trying to come up with a plan as far as what to do once we finished. Of course, the main thing at the top of that list was to get him checked out by a doctor as soon as possible. While he still had an appetite and no trouble eating, he'd reached the point now where everything he put in his body was running right through him, causing him to drop so much weight he was beginning to look almost skeletal. Quite honestly, it was a mystery to me how he still had it in him to keep on at the pace we'd been going. It was hard enough on me, and I wasn't ill. Nonetheless, with zero quit in him this close to the border, it wasn't even something he talked about.

It was chilly enough that I kept my jacket on throughout most of the day. And overcast, too, although, thankfully, it didn't actually rain. We passed through fields full of rocks and boulders, which led us into forests, which opened up into meadows. We climbed over (mostly Santa) and shimmed under (mostly me) countless fallen trees. We crossed big rivers and small streams. Once again, still walking, in the dark with our headlamps on by the end—now 28 miles closer.

We dialed things down a bit the following day. Hiking only as far as we had to in order to catch a shuttle into Stehekin, we then treated ourselves to a much needed break. Checking into a room once we got there, we ate, napped, showered, did laundry, and drank some.

Feeling refreshed the next morning, we grabbed some goodies for the road at their, if not world-famous, then at least trail-famous bakery, and got back to the trail.

Logging 18 miles by the end of that day, we then did 23 the next.

Day 127: August 30, 2021

And then, much to our delight, we found ourselves at the ranger station in the Harts Pass campground—with nothing left now between us and the border but the next 30 miles!

We dropped our packs and each took a turn in the outhouse. Then we sorted through the hiker box, which was disappointingly empty. And then added our signature, "BAMTA," to the trail register, smiling as we saw where Music Box had written his name. The date next to it, suggesting he was most likely already home by now, meant he'd been the first in our tramily to actually finish.

Normally, from this point, once you got to the border, you'd just continue on into Canada for another eight miles or so into Manning Park in British Columbia—which was large enough it was fairly easy to get from there to an airport. Either that, or, if home happened to be someplace you could get to by car (like in Santa's case as he lived just a few hours away), arrange for whoever would be picking you up to meet you there.

Thanks to all the travel restrictions still in place because of Covid, though, crossing the border wasn't an option for any of us doing the PCT this year. For one thing, the extra permits required to do so weren't being issued. And even if they were, you'd still have to show proof of testing negative for Covid within the past 48 hours. Considering how far away the nearest testing site was, even if you could get right in for an appointment, by the time you got there, and back, and then up to the border, your results would no longer be valid.

That being the case, and this being the last place you could access by road between here and the border, unfortunately, after touching the finish line, we all had to turn around and come all the way back here—as in the whole 30 miles and multiple mountain passes—just to get off the trail. And even here we were still in the middle of nowhere. Thoroughly disappointed, although not surprised—we'd all known this could be the case, assuming travel restrictions didn't ease up—we sat and had lunch while we came up with a plan.

Aiming, in the end, to be back here by the day after tomorrow, we broke up the 60 mile (roundtrip) total we had left, accordingly. We'd do 13 more miles today. Then set up camp for the night and sleep. Then wake up super early and, leaving our tent (along with the majority of our gear) where it was, slackpack[30] the final 17 miles to the finish line. Then turn around and do another 17, for a total of 34 for the day, getting us back

---

[30] When a backpacker hikes without carrying the full weight of their gear.

to the tent where we would once again sleep. Then wake up the next morning and do the final 13, putting us right back here.

Full from lunch, and excited about finally being in the home stretch, we pressed on, putting the first phase of our plan into motion.

Unfortunately, we didn't quite get there. Stopping after eight miles, rather than 13, which, falling short of our plan by five and then doubling that (there and back), meant we'd now be tacking an extra 10 miles on to tomorrow's grand total.

Day 128: August 31, 2021

It was still dark when our alarm went off the next morning. And cold. Santa made us coffee while I got dressed inside the tent. Then, grabbing a few things from my pack I didn't want to leave behind—chapstick, the water filter, my rain jacket, bug spray, my inReach, sunglasses, my ball cap, and the first aid supplies—I left everything else where it was and climbed out. Zipping the tent flap behind me, I felt a slight wave of panic at the sight of our sleeping bags and air mattresses still laid out. I knew not carrying the extra weight would allow us to move faster, but leaving behind our only means of shelter felt a bit reckless.

This was our plan, though. And while the whole slackpacking part of it, being Santa's idea, had required a good deal of convincing to get me on board with it, the bottom line was that I trusted him. Not that it was something I would ever do alone, but he knew our limits just as well as I did, and if he didn't think it was a good idea he wouldn't be pushing for it.

Taking a seat next to Santa on the log where he'd been drinking his coffee, we dumped out what little we had left in our food bags onto the ground in front of us. Then we took turns picking out what to bring with us, none of which could require cooking, as the stove itself wasn't coming. Shoving a protein bar in one of my pockets and a water bottle, as best I could, in the other, I added the rest of the essentials I'd grabbed to a small pile of things Santa planned on carrying in his otherwise empty pack. Eager to get started, I chugged the rest of my coffee and gave him a kiss. Cutting through the campsite, I took off towards the trail by the light of my headlamp. "See ya in five minutes," I called out over my shoulder.

"Five minutes," he called back.

Making my way through a dense fog-like mist once the sun began rising, I was so overcome by the enormity of what today had in store, I found myself crying. After so many days. And nights. And weeks. And months. After all the time I spent missing my girls. And craving things I couldn't have. And being dirty. And feeling tired. And doubting whether I even had what it took to be doing this. All of it now was about to come to an end. And for the first time, I felt ready for it.

It was an hour or so before Santa caught up, just in time for us to begin our first ascent of the day together. The steeper we climbed, the more the temperature dropped, giving the pine trees around us a frosted sort of snow-capped look at a certain point. We kept our pace steady and our breaks to a minimum, as neither one of us had any doubts about how long of a day this was going to be.

As the morning wore on we began to see other hikers, all of whom were heading in the opposite direction, back towards Harts Pass. All of whom looked utterly exhausted. And all of whom saw fit to offer us an enthusiastic, "You're almost there!" as they passed. To which we responded with some form of, "Thank you," and, "Congratulations." Out loud, at least, anyways. Sick with envy and by no means being my best self, what I was honestly thinking was *Oh, fuck off. You're done. And good job. Or whatever. But stop rubbing it in.*

It started raining around noon. We stopped for a quick bite to eat, and I got my rain jacket out of Santa's pack and put it on over my puffy. I was soon soaked through, regardless, as the brush lining the trail along the final stretch nearing the border was so overgrown, the amount of moisture I absorbed as I pushed my way through it was no match for my rain jacket.

And then, at half past two (which I only know because I'd been taking my phone out every 30 seconds for the past 20 minutes to take another *Are we there yet?* look at the map), we stepped out of the woods into a narrow clearing, and there she was—the monument marking the trail's northern terminus. The past four and a half, strenuously long, and yet, gloriously satisfying months having all led to this—a cluster of five wooden pillars, each a different height, with a PCT trail marker staring back at us from the front of the tallest one, a small US flag pegged to one side, and a Canadian one on the other. Knowing full well this was my first time laying eyes on it, I was taken aback by how familiar it seemed. From pictures, of course. Similar to what I imagine standing face to face with a famous actor you've seen time and again on the big screen would feel like.

Still overcast, yet no longer raining, it was quiet, aside from a few songbirds. Taking it all in, I could see now the narrow clearing we were standing on was itself the actual border. A stark contrast from the giant wall hovering between the U.S. and Mexico back at the start—this was more of a void. A bare strip of land where the trees had been cleared, running in a straight line for as far as you could see. Thick forest on either side of it.

With our backs leaned up against the trunk of an old pine tree, we sat next to each other in the dirt, facing the monument, and had something to eat. Another hiker, a man a little older than us, showed up a few minutes later. After congratulating him, he sat down and joined us in a sad discussion about how, if it weren't for Covid, we'd only be eight miles away from the parking lot inside Manning Park right now, rather than 30 something back to Harts Pass. Then we all took turns signing our names in the trail register and posing for pictures in front of the monument. And then, with over 20 miles to cover to get back to our tent, we turned around, got back on the trail, and, once again, started walking. Right back into the same thick, wet stretch of overgrown brush. Up and over all the same passes. Crossing all the same streams, passing all the same lakes, rounding all the same bends. Through all the same meadows, patches of forest, and rocky terrain. All of it requiring the same amount of effort and energy that getting there had—minus the excitement of reaching the border to fuel us, it now felt like torture.

The sun set, eventually, and while we hadn't planned on still being at it this late, we soon found ourselves night hiking.

With one final climb left before reaching our tent we stopped to rest to try and gather our strength. I sat down in the dirt, so exhausted by this point, holding my head up was work. Noticing a flat patch of ground next to me—*If I lay there, I could sleep*—I thought, staring at it. So tempted by the idea I could feel myself smiling, Santa's voice startled me.

"Come on, BAM," he said, standing in front of me. "Final push." He reached down for my hand, "Then we sleep," he added, pulling me up. "You got this," he called out over his shoulder, leading the way. I followed behind him, staggering, slowly, as the light from his headlamp bobbed over obstacles, shone back towards me now and then, and disappeared around corners.

Roughly nine hours after leaving the border, for a grand total of nearly 44 miles that day, we finally made it. Relieved to see that the tent was still standing and, not only that, but that everything inside of it was just as we'd left it, I crawled into my sleeping bag—knowing this would be the last time for a long time I'd be doing so—and fell asleep.

Day 129: September 1, 2021

I woke the next morning to the familiar sound of Santa making coffee just outside the tent. My entire body felt stiff and achy as I sat up in my sleeping bag. I took a couple of ibuprofen, and then laid my clothes out in front of me. The same ones I'd worn yesterday, and the day before, and the day before, and the day before that. They weren't just dirty, they stunk—bad. And worse, they were still slightly damp from yesterday's rain and sweat. Staring at them, miserably, tears blurred my vision. I didn't want to put them on. Not again. Not now. Not after we'd already technically finished the trail. I wanted clean clothes. I wanted a long, hot shower. I wanted to lay back down. And sleep. For a whole day. On a mattress, though, with clean sheets. I was done—with every fiber of my body, every ounce of *I can do this* had been drained from me. I didn't want to walk any further. Not this morning. And certainly not the entire eight miles it was going to take us to get back to Harts Pass.

Eight miles. That was all that now stood between me and being done. Between me and being home with my girls. Between me and the life I'd worked so hard to make for myself before I'd started this journey, and whatever came next.

Eight. More. Miles.

If only I were already done.

Exhausted, I hung my head and cried into my hands as quietly as I could, hoping Santa wouldn't hear me. If he did, he would ask what was wrong, and I didn't want to have to explain this. This lack of stamina or enthusiasm or whatever it was, fueling this desire in me to quit. It was too weak, too unflattering—I was too ashamed to admit I was feeling it. What I wanted, instead, with everything in me, was to finish this strong.

Wiping my face with the backs of my hands, I took a long, slow, deep breath. In my lap, tear stained spots of dark blue speckled my otherwise teal colored sleeping bag. Brushing lightly across them with the tips of my fingers, as if reading braille, I thought back to all the other tears I had cried on my way here. Tears of sadness, especially when I was missing my girls. Tears of laughter with tramily. Tears of pain and frustration, exhaustion and hunger. Tears of wonder and awe at the natural beauty around me. Tears of surrender, of triumph, and on occasion, revelation. All of them had helped me move forward, all the way to the finish line yesterday.

You did finish.

And you are strong.

And these tears on your sleeping bag don't negate that fact, they're proof of it.

Just eight more miles now. And all you have to do is the same thing you've been doing ever since you started—the next thing.

Which brought me back to the dirty clothes laying in front of me. I put them on.

And now, the next thing.

I deflated our air mattresses, rolling each of them up snuggly before stuffing them into their bags. Then I packed up our sleeping bags. And the tent.

And now, the next thing.

I tied my shoelaces. I put my pack on. I picked up my trekking poles. And then started walking. One by one, as the miles wore on, my spirits lifted. Until eventually, the only next thing left to do was to sit around with a handful of other hikers at Harts Pass and wait for a shuttle to come pick us up.

And make our way back to the real world.

And then, whatever comes next.

EPILOGUE

*"The highest reward for a person's toil
is not what they get for it,
but what they become by it."*

–John Ruskin

February 22, 2022

After nearly six months of visiting back and forth between the US and Canada, keeping in touch through texts and phone calls and Facetime, and missing each other so much it no longer felt bearable, Santa and I made BAMTA official by tying the knot—on a sandy beach along the coast in the Mayan Riviera, with seagulls screeching, ocean waves crashing, and Lemonade and Walkie Talkie as witnesses. Having stayed in touch with them after the trail, the vacation itself had originally been their plan. It just so happened to work out that we were able to join them. And what better place, we'd decided, to get married.

Lemonade kept me company while I got ready beforehand, then walked with me down to the beach where Santa, Walkie Talkie, and our officiant were waiting. Santa, having finally recovered after being so sick towards the end of the trail—which it turned out parasites from drinking unfiltered water had been the cause of—looked strikingly handsome in a pair of gray slacks and a white, button up, collared dress shirt. I wore a lacy white dress my girls helped pick out, and aside from not having them or the rest of our family there, the ceremony was perfect—with rose petals lining the "aisle," sheer flowy fabric draped over the canopy we exchanged our handwritten vows beneath, the smell of the ocean, our bare feet in the sand, a soft breeze, the sunshine, a beautiful bouquet of fresh flowers the resort had arranged for me, and the songs in the background, all from the "BAM's Jams" playlist Santa made for me during our time on the trail. And afterwards, a fun champagne toast, and dinner served right there on the beach for the four of us, and then fireworks, even.

My favorite part, though, was exchanging our vows—Santa's face as I read mine to him, how touched and happy he seemed, and how hearing his made my heart melt.

"Santa," I began first, "from the moment you walked into my life—drenched in sweat, smoking a cigarette, and happy as a clam in that damn desert heat—you've had a calming effect on me. That's one of my favorite things about you. Although the list is long…seeing as how you're everything I've ever wished for in a man. You're honest and kind. You're handsome and passionate and loyal. You're strong, you're smart, you're patient. You're attentive and respectful and generous and fun.

No one in my life has made me feel so well loved as you have. Thank you for seeing and accepting me as I am.

I never told you this before, because everyone knows you can't tell your wishes before they come true because then they might not. But after our time at Chicken Spring Lake, every star I wished upon along the rest of the trail…my wish was always the same—that you and I would end up together, forever.

You're my home, Santa. You're my future, and my heart. You're my wish come true, and I promise to spend the rest of my life doing everything in my power to make you happy, to be a wife you can be proud of, and a partner you can always count on. To walk alongside you through whatever life brings. And right behind you on the ups.

May you never doubt my love for you. And may the magic that is BAMTA never fade. I love you, Santa!

For always and forever, your BAM."

After I finished, we stood staring at each other with big, goofy grins.

Then, it was Santa's turn. "Bammer," he read from a page in a notebook, "from the moment I met you—when you "crashed my campsite"—I knew I'd never met anyone like you before. I've never known anyone who radiated warmth, and energy, and light like you do. I've never known anyone who was such an impossible combination of beauty and wildness, strength and tenderness, who seems so alive and open to the world, but also mysterious.

As we moved together through deserts and forests, the ups and the downs, over rivers and mountains, and we became friends, then tramily, then tentmates, and then BAMTA, a feeling grew until I knew in my bones that I'd never felt this way about anyone before, and never could again. Everything about you and I has always felt like a miracle or a dream to me—that I get to be lucky enough to bask in that light of yours forever, and that you would choose to spend this life with me.

You're amazing, and that's changed me forever, and I promise that I'll never take that knowledge, or you, for granted.

I promise that I'll try to live up to you, to be worthy of all the love and the beauty you share with me.

I promise that I'll take care of you and my stepdaughters forever, in every way I can.

And I promise to never forget what we learned in the wilderness together—that we should be adventurers in this short life, who burn for each other, and who are hungry for intensity, and joy and experience.

I promise to be the best possible character in the story of your life, and to be the husband, best friend, and partner you deserve.

I promise to love you always, with all of me, in sun and in shadow.

I promise BAMTA forever."

August 18, 2025

Looking back on my experience along the PCT I hardly recognize the woman I was when I started. I know she *wanted* to feel strong and capable. She didn't, though—not then. What she did do was meet me half way. I'm so proud of her for that! Because who I am now is strong as shit and capable of anything, and I have her to thank for it. For swallowing her pride, facing her fears, and allowing herself to be vulnerable. For letting the desert and the mountains, the forests and the flowers, the rivers and the birds, the sun and the moon and stars be the medicine that healed her. For starting something she wasn't sure she could finish. And for giving who she used to be permission to become who she was meant to be—BAM.

ACKNOWLEDGMENTS

My husband, Santa, for quite literally walking beside me through the biggest and most extreme emotional journey of my life. Whose unwavering love for me has helped heal me in ways I was incapable of achieving on my own. And whose relentless belief in my ability to transfer the contents of this book from the depths of my mind out onto the written page is why you're reading this now. You have my whole heart and my deepest gratitude—BAMTA forever.

My daughter, Hailey, who, had it not been for her coming out to visit me along the trail, I would have been far too homesick to keep going. For shipping all of my resupply packages. For keeping things afloat while I was away and for not burning the house down—you did good, Kid. For each of the notes and messages you gifted me with while I was out there. Rereading them when I was struggling or at times when I was missing you girls helped fuel me with the strength to keep going. Your love, your friendship, and your support were and remain among the things I treasure most in this world. Thank you for all of it, Sweets.

My daughter, Madison, for looking out for your sister for me while I was gone. The peace of mind that came from knowing the two of you were there for each other was priceless. For always answering my facetime calls when I was needing more than anything to see your face and hear your voice. And for all your sweet words of encouragement that helped carry me through—thank you, Love. You always have been and forever will be the very first of the very best things that have ever happened to me.

I know the thought of your mom wandering around alone in the wilderness scared the hell out of you girls. Thank you both for believing in me enough to see past your fears of all that could go wrong, and choosing instead to share in my excitement.

My good friend, Don, who not only shared my fascination for the PCT, but spent countless hours helping me plan out the logistics of making the whole thing possible. Thank you for your support and encouragement all throughout my journey.

My mom and dad—thank you both for all the life lessons you've taught me through the years, but perhaps most importantly for instilling me with a love for nature at such an early age and demonstrating so beautifully how to respect and appreciate all that goes along with that.

Each and every member of my beloved tramily: Lemonade, Walkie Talkie, Knux, Prime, Hoops, Chaparral, Matt, and Soda Pop. As well as extended tramily: Brightside, Booty, Lefty, Produce, Delayed, Itsy Bitsy, Pinata, Keebler, Paco, Big Red, Bluegrass, and Primetime. I was utterly unprepared for the sense of belonging you all showed me. Thank you for reminding me what a difference the power of friendship can make. The bond we formed along the trail is a gift I will treasure forever. I love you guys.

To the entire PCT Class of 2021, well done, my fellow thru-hikers—we fucking did it. And to Nivil, specifically, you, my fellow road walker, still owe me a milkshake.

To Cameron, for transforming my humble manuscript into an actual book. Your willingness and expertise are so greatly appreciated—not only by me, but everyone reading this.

And last, but not least, the PCTA, for their ongoing dedication to both physically maintaining the trail as well as preserving the integrity of the experience for all those choosing to hike it. The work you all do is so very much appreciated.

The top 10 questions I get asked about doing the trail:

Q: Did you do it alone?

A: I started out solo, yes.

Q: Were you scared?

A: At times, yes. But I'd promised myself years ago not to let fear stand in my way of doing things in life that make me feel most alive, and I had no intention of breaking that promise.

Q: Did you carry a gun?

A: I did not. I had purchased a .38 revolver specifically for this journey, but after researching all the different states' permit requirements it seemed like too much of a hassle to bother with, so I didn't take it.

Q: Did you lose a ton of weight?

A: No–damn it! My body did change though. I got stronger and all the various muscles in my legs got super defined. There's a saying along the trail that by the time you finish a thru-hike, the guys look like they've been starved, and the girls look like super models. Go figure.

Q: What was your favorite part?

A: Two sections in particular especially impressed me: the John Muir Pass in the Sierra Mountains, and the Knife's Edge which traversed along the top of Old Snowy Mountain in Washington. Aside from the scenery though, my favorite part of being out there was the bonds I came to form with my tramily members.

Q: What was your least favorite part?
A: The ups.

Q: How much did it cost?
A: About $5,000.

Q: What did you eat?
A: My two main staples were dehydrated backpacking meals and protein bars.

Q: Are you going for the Triple Crown next?
A: Hell, no.

Q: Was there anything you wished you'd done differently?
A: Yes, I would have taken a regular battery pack rather than solar chargers—they are *so* worth the extra weight! I also would have worn Injinji toe socks from the get go so as not to have been tortured by blisters.

www.ingramcontent.com/pod-product-compliance
Lightning Source LLC
Chambersburg PA
CBHW050857160426
43194CB00011B/2194